New Growth

For Rebecca + Stephen —
Kentucky writer & artist —
with joy in sharing lives!

Libby
25 August 2018
(see pp. 171-72)

New Growth
Recent Kentucky Writings

edited by

Charlie Sweet and Hal Blythe

Jesse Stuart Foundation
Ashland, Kentucky
2007

ISBN: 1-931672-43-1

Book Design by Brett Nance
Cover Art by vanAnnies

Published By:
Jesse Stuart Foundation
P.O. Box 669 • Ashland, KY 41105
(606) 326-1667 • JSFBOOKS.com

Contents

Introduction

This anthology grew from a column for the *JSF Magazine* called "In Jesse's Shoes," wherein each issue we introduced Kentuckians to the next generation of its writers. And what gave us that idea? Like the Good Book says, "For every thing there is a season...." That season was the post-winter thaw and we, mesmerized by the spectacle of spring bursting forth, were surrounded by lush green where months ago brown and gray layered the landscape. The early crocus and daffodils were being replaced with golden spirea, wine-red weigela, and brilliant white rhododendrons. Purple loosestrife streamed toward the skies, reminding us again that nature constantly replaces itself.

So it is with our native-grown literary talent. Suddenly Arnow, Warren, and Stuart blossom to be followed by McClanahan, Bingham, Mason, and Hall, then Walker, House, and Wilkinson. You'll recall how in early spring Wordsworth's heart leapt up when he first espied the daffodils. We're likewise excited by the first green nubs poking their heads through the earth because we realize with proper nurture they will explode, filling our dark and bloody ground with color, texture, and beauty.

Part of the mission of the Jesse Stuart Foundation is to recognize new talent, to give it the same kind of boost Jesse Stuart himself did when he served as a writer in residence at Eastern Kentucky University or visited various writing conferences. So we've asked three Kentucky writers who have established themselves as experts in their field to help us run a talent search for emerging writers in the Commonwealth. Silas House, who ten years ago was virtually unknown and now has become one of our nation's best novelists, selected the fiction herein. Frank X Walker, who has gained international fame as an Affrilachian (his term) poet, chose the poetry. And George Brosi, editor of *Appalachian Heritage*, was in charge of sifting through the creative non-fiction pieces. We publicly thank this all-star team for helping us recognize the next generation.

Plants grow best, as any gardener knows, when the soil is prepared. Today's Kentucky writers emerge from a literary soil well cultivated by those who have gone before. Literary anthologies are no exception. And now a confession. This anthology was begun well over two years ago, and we delayed its publication. Why? Just as many individual writers emerge, so, too, do collections of their works. In the last few years alone, two excellent anthologies have appeared, and we did not want to step on their toes; in fact, our purpose has been to supplement their fine work. In 2001 Morris Allen Grubbs, who admitted that his ana was descended from Hollis Summers' *Kentucky Story* (1954), published *Home & Beyond: An Anthology of Kentucky Short Stories* that, as he says, "reflect life in later-twentieth-century Kentucky and America" (xi). Grubbs broke his stories into three groups—1945-1960, 1960-1980, and 1980-2000—choosing his stories because "they are prime examples of the modern short story" and because "they form a cyclical quest for identity, meaning, and wholeness in a turbulent and mutable world" (xi). In 2005 old friend Wade Hall edited *The Kentucky Anthology*, recognizing 179 writers (including us) from John Filson in 1769 to contemporary Frederick Smock. Part of his purpose, Hall admitted, was "to tantalize you to read additional works by the writers in this book as well as other Kentucky writers who are worthy of your time and patronage"(6).

Consider us tantalized. *New Growth: Recent Kentucky Writings*, then, was created as a natural continuation and extension of this lineage. Since collections of prominent Kentucky writers from the Commonwealth's origins to the present already existed, the next step seemed to be to publicize those emerging writers who were more than buds in the soil. After all, as *Tobacco Road* novelist Erskine Caldwell once wrote, "Publication of early work is what a writer needs most of all in life." We are proud to offer these writers the opportunity to be heard; in fact, the original title for this anthology was Recent Kentucky Voices, but as we have just mentioned, we wished to stress the heritage aspect of this anthology.

Many anthologies center on themes, and, as Morris Grubbs discovered, Kentucky writers have been consciously or unconsciously preoccupied with home and beyond, "the mysterious pull of their homeland" (xi). Wade Hall, even in an historical collection, found the idea of identity prominent in Commonwealth writers, quoting Jesse

Stuart's *Kentucky Is My Land* as epitomizing this theme:

Kentucky is neither southern, northern, eastern, or western,
It is the core of America.
If these United States can be called a body,
Kentucky can be called its heart.

There was no pre-anthology agreement with the three writers making the selections for this collection on what themes, concerns, settings, characters, idiosyncrasies, etc. to look for when choosing writers. Nonetheless, you will note several concerns that weave their way throughout the stories, essays, and verse. Maybe Robert Frost, a non-Kentuckian who once ate at Boone Tavern in Berea, was right when he wrote:

The land was ours before we were the land's.
She was our land more than a hundred years
Before we were her people...

Writers have roots, some running quite deep into the land. Didn't a wag once define a Kentuckian as someone who died not more than 25 miles from where he was born? Tapped into common soil and nurtured in a similar environment, plants adapt to and reflect this micro-climate. In an acknowledgement of this phenomenon, we have placed questions at the end of each selection to tantalize your thoughts. We have included bios of the authors as well as short genesis pieces on their works to stimulate you into thinking about what you have read. And at the end of this anthology, you will find a series of questions designed to cut across the readings, to elicit your thoughts, and to provoke you into that highest order of thinking Benjamin Bloom's former students labeled synthesis. Jesse Stuart claimed that teaching was "the greatest profession on earth." We hope this collection both teaches and delights you.

At the outset we apologize to all the excellent writers we have omitted. We had only so much space for this project, we had a huge number of submissions, and we realize that there is no way to be completely objective in our selections. That's one reason we devised this project with three sub-editors; as the baseball umpires know, we want as many eyes on the ball as possible. Besides, the existence of an abundance of promising writers suggests the need for another *New Growth* collection down the road.

Admittedly, some writers contained herein are “newer” than others. Providing a definitive definition of what “new,” “recent,” and “emerging” meant proved too daunting for your editorial quintet, so don’t email and ask us. Maybe before the next collection we will have figured it out.

Another problem was representation. It was neither possible nor necessarily desirable to seek equal representation from all 120 counties (“How about we allot one work/county?” “But some counties haven’t produced recent writers.”). Yes, the Jesse Stuart Foundation is located in the far Eastern corner of the Commonwealth, but Silas lives in southeastern Kentucky, George in Berea, Frank currently in Cincinnati, and Hal and Charlie in Richmond. Should we have found geographically representative editors? Actually, the sub-editors had absolutely no restrictions placed on them, and the selections in their sections are theirs alone.

We would be remiss if we did not acknowledge the help we have had along the way. Jim Gifford, CEO of the Jesse Stuart Foundation, has encouraged us for years to work on this anthology. Chuck Campbell and Bryan Jackson, our editorial interns, performed tirelessly, making certain we had the works, bios, and genesis essays; in addition, they helped format the book and provided the end study questions. And, we can’t thank George, Frank, and Silas enough for providing an expertise we lacked. We also appreciate the many creative writing students we have taught over the past thirty-plus years who keep surprising us with the quality of their work. No doubt we could have compiled an anthology of their best stories and poems.

A word about our format. Years ago we came across a collection of Jesse Stuart stories wherein Jesse had provided some actual study questions. The paperback version of *Clay’s Quilt* comes with its own “A Reader’s Guide” that provides both an interview with Silas and group questions/topics for discussion. You will notice we borrowed those approaches for this anthology because one of the book’s values is its possible inclusion in the classroom, be it in secondary or higher education. We asked the writers to provide genesis essays as doorways into their works. Students should be able to see, for instance, the roots of poetry and use of similar approaches. This collection, then, is meant not only to recognize the upcoming generation of Kentucky writers, but to encourage the next by offering insights into the origin of a work as well as some techniques from what Stephen King calls the writer's "toolbox."

As teachers of English with a collective background of some 80 years, we have another confession to make, but don't tell our students. As hard as it was, we tried not to use our red pen. In *The Art of Fiction*, Henry James writes, "We must grant the artist his subject, his idea, his donnee." Part of that donnee is playing with literary and grammatical conventions. OK, we proofed the writers' bios and genesis essays, but their stories, poems, and creative non-fiction are presented to you the way we received them (OK, OK, we changed a few grammatical elements in their pieces because the elements were confusing, and if there is a rule in writing, it has to be, "Thou shall not confuse thy reader").

In the 19th century Kentucky was at the crossroads of western migration and expansion. We believe this collection will demonstrate, along with the earlier noted anthologies, that the Commonwealth is once again becoming the epicenter of literary output. Too often the media paint a picture of America as a bi-coastal country with little in between. One message from *New Growth* is that there are other, important voices that will be heard. Check out this collection and see if you don't agree.

* *An earlier version of this essay appeared in JSF Magazine, Vol. I (2005).*

Recent Kentucky

FICTION

with Introductory Comments by

Silas House

I hesitate to write an introduction to this fine collection of short stories because I believe the work speaks for itself. So I will be brief in telling you that the emerging writers herein are among the best the state has to offer. These stories will take you everywhere from the fantastical but beautifully acute world of Western Kentuckian Matt Jaeger's story "The 30th Annual Naming of Boy Howell" to the harsh reality of modern Eastern Kentucky found in "Rabbit Blood," a story by Mike Hampton. Aimee Zaring's "An Otherwise Flawless Canvas" takes us to the countryside outside of Louisville, and Jess Stanfill's "Creases" puts us in the kitchen of a young rural Kentucky woman trying to understand her mother while they wash dishes together. You will meet people like J.B. in Michael Croley's "A Place to Cross," a country boy who wants to better himself, and will be taken to Hampton's Cross, the town so vividly created in Bev Olert's "Tabernacle of Love" that you'll always swear you've been there once or twice. And there are many other memorable places to encounter, many other characters who seem to possess beating hearts in this collection that brings together some of our state's most promising fiction writers.

Kentucky has a long legacy of producing some of our nation's most talented and prized storytellers. Once you read the following stories, you'll be reassured that that heritage is alive and well.

An Otherwise Flawless Canvas

Aimee Zaring

Diana looked out an upstairs window of their new house and bristled when she saw the obnoxious swing set in the backyard. They had been in the house almost a month now, and Warner still hadn't dismantled it as promised. "I can't believe it bothers you so much," he would tease. The primary-colored eyesore looked like something straight out of a McDonald's playland, an anomaly against the pristine backdrop of rolling hills. Beside the swing was a small vegetable garden in which Diana was afraid even to tinker, certain her hand would ensure a quick end to any living seed.

She dropped the Venetian blind slat. Her first Mother's Day without a mother. Back in her counseling days she might've asked a grieving client, "How does that make you feel?" What a ridiculous question, she thought now, as if identifying feelings diluted the pain. That morning she had watched a TV special about Mother's Day. Anna Jarvis, the recognized foundress of Mother's Day, told a reporter before her death that she was sorry she ever started the national holiday, so disgusted had she become with its excessive commercialism. She died broke, nearly blind, childless.

Diana had talked to her mother only once about her decision to remain childless, about this time last year, after reading a newspaper article on infertile women fighting Mother's Day blues. "It makes me sick to think of all those wasted eggs," one of the interviewed women had said of her presumably fertile friend, who'd chosen childlessness. Diana had immediately called her mother to argue the defendant's case—to essentially pick a fight with a mother—but before she could even finish her feeble argument, her mother had calmly replied, "I've known women who've felt more alone in motherhood than in solitude. It's not for everyone."

The room in which Diana stood, evidently once a nursery, had initially been her least favorite. She disliked the lemon chiffon walls and the dragonfly and ladybug border that ran along the chair rail. The previous owners had left a shelf mounted on the wall, supported by two rusty scrolled brackets, like the remains of some lost civilization. In the center of the room was the rickety children's table and chair set her sister had given her years ago, should Diana's nieces and nephew visit. Facing the eastward window was her grandmother's old rocking chair. Except for a crib, the room was like a ready-mix—just add baby.

But the nursery had begun to grow on her. She liked watching the sun rise beyond the ridge while rocking in her grandmother's chair and the afternoon shade, perfect for taking naps. Warner had turned a bedroom down the hall into his study, but this was her room, to do with as she pleased.

She heard a low buzzing outside and sent the blinds up with a zip. The sun was painfully bright, casting its prismatic rays like a net. She opened the window, inhaling the smell of freshly-mown grass. In the field bordering their own, marked by bold, yellow KEEP OUT postings, the neighbor was riding a mower, shearing long, diagonal stripes. Diana began sneezing and shut the window. A wet spring so far, her allergies constantly flaring, and she'd ventured outside very little, her dreams of exploring the land foiled by nature herself.

Warner's hammering downstairs began wearing on her nerves. His weekend project: installing bookshelves in the living room. His level of efficiency never ceased to amaze her. He could achieve more in a few hours than she could in a week. Time—all she seemed to have these days, yet what did she have to show for her efforts? She hadn't even finished unpacking. "Di, we have our whole lives to get the house the way we want it," Warner once said. "What's the rush?" But lately he'd grown impatient with her. "You think too much," he'd say when she'd show him another design idea from a magazine. "Just try it and see." Warner wasn't afraid of failure; the greater threat was stagnancy.

Though smaller on the inside than it appeared on the out, the turn-of-the-century Colonial Revival seemed like a mansion compared to the tri-level she had grown up in and the small apartment she and Warner had occupied in Tennessee. She didn't know where to begin with the house; she only knew something had to be done. She spent her days pacing the floors, starting one project and skipping to another, just passing time until Warner returned home.

On the first day Warner had gone to work, her first day alone in the house, she felt like an employee playing hooky. She had never felt such freedom, this being the first time in her adulthood that she hadn't been in school or working. After the initial excitement wore off, however, she remembered she wasn't free at all, that on her shoulders now was the prodigious burden of grief. The empty house soon began haunting her with its phantom creaks and sour, old-person smell which greeted her on the second-floor landing every time she climbed the steps. In the upstairs hallway, large enough for an end table and two chairs, the floor was uneven, dipping in the center. Although the inspector had deemed the home structurally sound, it was here, in the hallway, where she found herself tiptoeing as if to make herself lighter, for at any moment she feared the floor might buckle and collapse.

The phone rang. When the hammering continued downstairs, she stomped to the hall, signaling to Warner that she was no closer to a phone than he.

"Brigette had the baby!" her mother-in-law chirped. "Lincoln Karl Lancaster. Born two oh-five. Nine pounds, two ounces, twenty inches."

Diana walked back to the nursery window. "Everyone okay?" she asked, watching one of the swing's black bucket seats sway eerily in the breeze.

"She arrived too late for the epidural," Erma said. "But she did it. She was my brave girl."

Diana lowered herself into her grandmother's rocker, a crust of dissatisfaction slowly encasing her. She tried to see beyond the swing set, to see the same breathtaking view she'd witnessed on that hopeful day in March, when they'd first found the house, but when she gazed out at the sweeping vistas now, all she felt was lost. Her mother's death had spoiled the landscape.

They had found the Colonial Revival under less than ideal circumstances. Warner's job offer with Health Network had come so quickly that he and Diana found themselves with virtually a week to find a home. They drove up from Tennessee in early March. Linda, the fast-talking, over-perfumed realtor, took them to one neighborhood after another, pointing out the family-friendly aspects of each house, despite the fact that they had informed the mother of three that they had no children. "Maybe not now," she had sing-songed.

They shuffled through the parade of homes, sluggish from the car ride, Warner checking water pressure and Diana inspecting laundry rooms for natural light. They wanted a fairly new, contemporary house requiring minimal maintenance, but all the homes fitting these parameters, and within the price range they could now afford, looked alike: large eat-in kitchens, impractical formal dining rooms, four and five bedrooms, and finished basements piled high with forgotten toys. The conformity of each house to its neighbor—a narrow vision passed down from developer, builder, landscaper, and finally owner—demoralized her.

On Sunday they grabbed a real estate listing from a convenience store and, with the cockiness of city slickers on their first camping trip, ventured beyond the city limits without map or guide.

They rode along the northeast fringes of the Louisville metro area, about thirty minutes from downtown, where Warner would be working and where he had grown up. The four-lane highway seamlessly converged into two lanes, the scents of fast food grease and exhaust fumes from the city slowly dissipating. Black fences ran parallel to white, separated by a gray ribbon of highway stretching up and down and side to side, yielding to the land's topography. They passed rundown cottages, sprawling ranches, and half million dollar-plus homes, but the land seemed to equalize each dwelling, downplaying the extravagant and elevating the ordinary.

Beyond the wood-slatted fences, horses galloped, their sleek chestnut coats gleaming in the sunlight. Diana had seen this same scene on the cover of the brochure she'd picked up at the rest stop on the drive up. She had lived in Indiana and Tennessee, what she considered the North and South, but where did Kentucky fall geographically? The brochure described Kentucky as the most northern southern state and the most southern northern state. The description seemed to reflect her own state of mind. She was neither here nor there, just somewhere in the middle.

They turned onto a tree-lined lane, passing a handwritten sign: "Slow. Unsafe Curve." For miles they drove, toward the river, the road progressively tightening and curving. "Stop," Diana suddenly said. "I think that was it."

Warner checked the rearview mirror, reversed, and pulled into a paved driveway. Diana stepped out of the car. A crow, perched atop the house, squawked and flew off. The naked tree limbs overhead rubbed against each other in the wind, as if for warmth. Somewhere in the distance a weed whacker droned.

The house was on a grander scale than anything they had looked at so far, and much older. A Southern house, Diana decided—all pride and charm and perhaps a little shame, too, the REDUCED sign at the curbside jerking in the unpredictable wind. The house had black shutters, a white clapboard frame, and a long front porch supported by four columns. A neat procession of four windows downstairs, and five up, and two stone chimneys at either end of the house. But the most striking feature was the audacious, bright red door, flanked by two rockers, the color of blond brooms, on which she pictured Warner and herself sitting on lazy Sunday mornings, blowing on steaming cups of coffee.

When she was younger, her family had taken a trip to Colonial Williamsburg where she had watched period re-enactors spinning and weaving. She couldn't imagine growing up in that time, walking out the front door of a symmetrical home wearing a bonnet and carrying a bucket for fetching water at the well. A life of repetition, aching bones, early deaths. But there had been something about that life and place that had made Diana return to it again and again in her mind, something remotely appealing, a timeless dignity and simplicity behind the drudgery.

Warner jogged up to her, popping the real estate listing against his palm. Updated wiring, newly renovated kitchen, working fireplaces, nine and a half acres. "Either this place is a steal or a money pit." He inspected the porch and the front door's threshold. He disappeared around the side of the house.

She knew what he was probably thinking. This house would make an impression, would fit his new directorship. Company barbeque picnics down on the farm. Warner understood the challenges and demands of an older home, having grown up in one. And during a time when the stock market continued to plummet, the land would make a wise, safe investment. But the thought of filling a house so large, finding a function for each room, petrified Diana.

"Come here," Warner called. "You've got to see this."

She walked toward the backyard, her hair whirling around her face. The sun was warm, but the wind was a reminder that winter still owned the season.

As soon as she rounded the side of the house, the world suddenly opened up, acres and acres of undulating hills leading nowhere and everywhere at once. "Warner," she murmured, and they reached out for each other's hands, like two children who had stumbled upon something beyond their years.

Except for a farmhouse in the far right corner of her vision, Diana imagined that the land had remained unchanged since early settlers had discovered it. Clusters of old trees dotted the landscape as though added with a paintbrush for balance and interest. Was this what people meant by the phrase God's Country? The land seemed like a continuum on a great wave, as though God had snapped a picnic blanket and held it over the earth, letting it flutter and settle naturally in peaks and valleys, and then said, on this ripple called Goshen, "Here, feast!"

And then she saw it, the glaring blemish on the otherwise flawless canvas. "What is that?"

Warner turned. "What, that?" He smiled. "That's a swing set."

Of course she knew what it was, but what was it doing here? Maybe if it had been an old tire hanging by a rope from an oak tree.... But this swing belonged in a fenced backyard that overlooked another yard and another swing set just like it.

"Well, what do you think?" Warner asked. "Should we look inside?" He began reaching for his cell phone to call the realtor, but she touched his sleeve. She didn't want any outside party interfering. They had found this place on their own, together. She wanted to arrive at their decision the same way.

She felt the weight of the house behind her, the tug of tradition, history. But then she looked out at the land again. There was no horizon, only the suggestion of more hills, more trees, something still out there, beyond her field of vision.

She turned to him. "I know it's crazy, but let's just say yes. No matter what we find inside, I want this to be the view we wake up to every morning."

The swing set's wavy yellow slide, bright as a ripe banana peel, blazed in the sun. "On one condition," she added, nodding toward the swing. "That contraption has to go."

Warner smiled as though it were already done.

In the living room now, Warner stood shirtless, trying to hold a shelf in place while hammering a nail into the wall.

"What in the world?" she said. "This is a two-person job. Why didn't you call me?" Warner removed a nail from between his lips. "Shouldn't you be using screws?" she asked.

"Don't even start," he said. "This thing has been a royal pain. And what's up with the AC?" He wiped the sweat from his brow with his forearm. He stepped back and motioned to the set of shelves he'd already completed. "Well," he said dispiritedly. "What do you think?"

The shelves were slightly crooked, sloping downward. She remembered when she had painted the kitchen cabinets. Some of the paintbrush bristles had stuck to the paint, and when she tried to pick them off, they left behind hairline fractures. She and Warner were not handy people; they needed better tools. She lacked math skills, and Warner patience. Look at us, she thought tenderly—playing house.

She walked over to him. The sun-drenched wood floor felt warm against her bare feet. She put her arms around him and nuzzled her face against his reddish-blond chest hairs. This was the part of his body she knew best: the breastbone. The sweat on his skin, the grit on his body reminded her of the ocean. She stared at his arm and suddenly felt the urge to lick it, taste his salty sweetness on her tongue.

"I take it you like," he said.

She nodded, overcome with love for her husband, their new life in Goshen, financial woes behind them. She imagined languorous evening walks down country roads and endless weekend mornings, reading to each other amusing editorials from the newspaper. Who cared that it was five o'clock and she hadn't started dinner yet, or that she didn't even have any ingredients to fix it? Warner would be perfectly content eating cereal. How lucky she was to be married to a self-sufficient man whom she didn't have to coddle like an infant.

She felt toward her husband the way she expected most mothers felt toward their children—she'd rather die than live without him. She'd heard friends and colleagues say that if forced to choose, they'd sacrifice their husbands for their children any day. Such comments disheartened her, seemed testaments to how truly fragile marital relationships were.

Standing on her tiptoes, she kissed Warner's neck, chin, and lips, her hands rising to his face. She felt the hammer press against her spine. She slipped her tongue inside his mouth.

Warner suddenly broke the kiss and gathered her hands in his. "My Diana," he said, as if patronizing a child, as if guessing what she longed for this day wasn't him. Or more likely—he was already measuring for the next row of shelves—he simply wanted to finish his project.

"Who was on the phone?" he asked.

"Oh, yeah," she said blandly. "Your sister had the baby. They want us to come see."

When they arrived in the cramped hospital room on the "Mother-Baby" floor, Warner congratulated Mark and accepted a cheap cigar. Diana looked over Erma's shoulder at Brigette, who was nursing. "It's okay," Brigette said, waving Diana over.

Brigette had once been the only woman on Warner's side of the family to whom Diana could speak on subjects other than motherhood and children. But she could already feel the tenuous thread of in-law camaraderie fraying. It seemed all her friends were having babies, and now she was being cheated out of yet another friendship. She pictured future family gatherings: tedious conversations about weather and recipes, Brigette trying too hard not to talk about her child, and she trying doubly hard to show interest in him.

"That's it, a little lower; let him latch on," Erma instructed Brigette. To Diana, she whispered, "Having a little difficulty, but sometimes it takes a while. They'll find their rhythm."

Karl, Warner's father, stood next to Erma. He appeared shorter, thinner, and more tired than he probably was. Erma had that gift of distortion. The room was surprisingly cold, an organic scent, like dry cereal, circulating every time the air kicked on. The TV in the armoire was tuned to Jeopardy!

Diana couldn't imagine all that Brigette had gone through in the last twenty-four hours: contractions, rips, stitches, afterbirth. Once she'd watched a live birth on TV, the father sobbing as he cut the umbilical cord. "We did it!" the mother cried. "Look what we created!"

Brigette was explaining how she had to be carried from Labor and Delivery to her hospital room on a stretcher. "A stretcher!" she cried, laughing in a way that invited everyone to join in, but more from embarrassment than mutual gaiety. "The nurses have been great. They treat me like royalty." Diana imagined a harem surrounding Brigette, fanning her with palm branches, dangling grape clusters into her mouth.

"So, what do you think?" Brigette asked. Diana came around to the head of the bed. Lincoln was wearing a soft, blue cap, his face a healthy pink. His purplish nails looked buffed and polished. His little arms and legs squirmed beneath his blanket, and his puckered lips were shaped like a diamond.

She had to concede that for a newborn, Lincoln was exceptionally cute. She liked his name, too, its connotation of freedom. But Brigette would never know freedom again, at least not in the way she had once known it. Over the years, Diana had collected her own favorite baby names, solid and simple like Michael, Timothy, Elizabeth. She had never divulged these names to anyone, afraid someone else might use them, afraid to hear her own voice speak them. The names seemed sad to her now, like lightning bugs trapped in a jar.

"I think you need one of these," Brigette said to Diana.

"Oh, Brigette, leave her be," Erma said, reaching down to cup Lincoln's cone head, her eyes misting. "To each his own."

What a difference a baby made! Diana couldn't believe this was the same woman who had taken her aside at her wedding reception and said, breath smelling of dark ale, "It would be different if you and Warner couldn't. But if you can, if you're able…. One isn't the loneliest number. Two is. I promise you that."

Diana suddenly wished to please Erma, be the woman in the hospital bed who roused such tenderness and joy and peace. She pictured Erma stopping by the house with casseroles and outrageously expensive baby apparel, leaning over the counter at the bakery to show customers her only son's child. Look at the fine coloring, the noble jaw line.

Abigail, Warner's eldest sister, walked in with an It's a Boy! balloon. Diana had not only forgotten a present for baby but also a Mother's Day gift for Erma and Brigette. She thought of all the childless women (whether by choice or chance) who would never receive a card or bouquet of flowers or box of chocolates this holiday. And the millions who no longer had a mother to send these to.

The room had grown stuffy, more well-wishers filing in. Someone remarked that the baby had Brigette's nose. Another thought he had Mark's forehead. Definitely Mark's large feet. He would be tall for sure, a basketball player. Or a piano player, like Brigette. Look at the slender fingers. No, hell no, a basketball player.

Why couldn't the child this one day, his birthday, look like himself? Be his own little person? Was there no separating the creator from the created?

She felt sorry for Brigette, this gross intrusion on her privacy. But the new mother, already leaking breast milk on the front of her open-backed gown, seemed oblivious to the spectators, as though she had already been stripped of everything related to self. What more could anyone take?

But a mother's love had always seemed to Diana not entirely selfless, nor unconditional. How many times had she heard parents grousing about poor decisions their children had made, ones that defied their own expectations or agendas? Or the times when, watching parent and child interact in front of company, she had felt like she was watching a puppet show? Johnny, name all of the U.S. presidents and the years they served. Suzie, show Diana how you can put your legs behind your head. Look at the future senator and Olympic gymnast! It was one thing for parents to derive joy from their children, but another for them to use those children to make up for their failings or shortcomings, to fulfill their own dreams.

She remembered her own mother's imploring eyes. She'd always felt like she owed her mother something. Certainly gratitude and respect, for giving her life—if that could be considered a gift in such troubled times—but something else, something as elusive and indefinable as a mother's love. Diana had never questioned her mother's love for her. Only her devotion. She had always felt like she had torn her mother away from another calling.

As a child, Diana often found her mother behind closed doors, reading in her favorite dark turquoise armchair, whose worn seat offered little cushion between tailbone and wood frame. She remembered pushing the door open, her mother's head slowly turning, as though pulled by a string, and then that twitch of a smile, of indifferent acknowledgement, and her head lowering again, and then, if Diana had not yet pulled the door shut, the tentative lifting of her eyes, like a dog waiting for a scratch, or perhaps a kick.

"All I know is," Mark was saying, "I have a whole new respect for my wife. You couldn't pay me a million bucks to go through what she did today."

Warner was looking at his baby sister as if for the first time. Diana couldn't remember when he'd last looked at her that way—reverently—if he ever had.

Warner had always seemed proud of her work as an esthetician, although his eyes lit up when he informed others that she also had a master's in psychology, as if to say, This is what she does, but look what she is capable of!

At breakfast that morning, when she had complained that the house was driving her nuts, that she wasn't cut out to be a home-and-hearth gal, Warner suggested she consider going back to work. Before the move, they had agreed she could take her time finding a job, since Warner would be earning more income. She had intended to use this transitional period to fix up the house, take an art class, learn another language, perhaps even read the Bible, but she was beginning to feel that more was expected of her. Warner had been raised by a career-driven mother. Maybe it was ingrained in his mind that a wife should work outside the home. She couldn't help wondering now, as she watched Mark lean over to kiss Brigette's cheek, if Warner would have a deeper respect for her if they had a child.

"So, what's the word on you two?" Karl asked Warner, grinning mischievously. "You think you'll ever have one of these?"

But behind this question, Diana heard another: Who will carry on the Schlosser name?

Warner looked down at Lincoln, a pinched expression on his face. "Who knows?" he said. "Maybe."

Maybe? Warner wouldn't meet her eyes.

They had talked about it, of course, before marrying. "I guess I'm kind of selfish," he told her in their favorite Thai restaurant in Indianapolis. "I want to travel. I want to be able to enjoy what I work for. My parents spent all they earned on us. Never took a vacation. Drove the same crummy car and gave us the new ones. And for what? One time Brigette told Mom she hated her, hated the bakery, hated everything German. Mom just stood there and took it. I saw her in the kitchen later, crying into an oven mitt so no one would hear." The candle flame on the table stretched upward, then flattened. "Besides," he said, taking Diana's hand and kissing the back of it like an old-fashioned suitor. "I kind of like the idea of having my wife all to myself."

Months later, after their engagement, Diana had pictured a romantic future: jetting off to a Caribbean island at a last minute's notice, building Habitat for Humanity homes. Two happy, healthy, generous individuals professing their undying love till the bitter end, when they would die tragically and instantaneously in a car crash, but together. Always together. Party of two.

Brigette finished nursing and held the baby out for any takers. Warner, the closest, accepted the invitation. And how natural he looked with a baby in his arms, rocking and patting the little bundle. He walked over to the window and propped his nephew up in his arm, showing him the darkening world, the newly black-topped parking lot. Diana walked over and stood beside them, but when she looked out the window, all she saw was a homogeny of yellow stripes.

Abigail asked to hold Lincoln next, and soon the newborn was being passed around in a sea of germs and smothering love. Brigette looked anxious and kept fingering the identification tag around her wrist. Only when Lincoln was returned safely into her arms did she finally seem at peace. "I never knew," she murmured, her eyes glittering with tears of joy, new love. "No one ever told me."

Diana pictured the ivory porcelain statue of Madonna and child on her mother's dresser, the Blessed Mother leaning over the infant Jesus on her lap, her eyes pale, vacant, like a Greek statue's, and her son smiling, reaching up with both hands to touch her face. The statue now seemed to Diana a portal into the unknowable, the eternal. She wondered if there was a way to experience mother love, without having a baby.

As they were leaving, Erma wrapped Diana in a bountiful hug. "I know this must be a hard day for you," she said. She pulled back and smiled absently, consumed with her own contentment.

Back home, Diana headed straight for the nursery. She dug in the closet for her keepsake box and dumped its contents on the children's table. The box contained things a mother would show and eventually pass down to a child: a high school ring, the face of a penny she had sketched in surprising detail, a black-and-white photo of her mother in a baby carriage, and a pair of yellow baby booties her grandmother had knitted—for Diana's firstborn.

Why was she holding onto these things? Who would possibly be interested? Perhaps Warner. Maybe her sister or nieces. But only a child—one's own flesh and blood—would truly appreciate these keepsakes, consider them keys to a mother's soul. But there were no guarantees. She thought of all the people who had boxes stowed under their beds, on high shelves, in basements behind furnaces—poorly hidden, begging to be found.

Her mother used to take classes in candy decorating, macramé, cooking, flower arranging, landscape design, pottery. She made latch hook rugs, whittled wood, painted (oil and acrylic), and sketched bowls of fruit. But nothing satisfied. "I can't find the right medium," her mother would complain when Diana called from her dorm room. During semester breaks and holidays, Diana would search the house, wondering what her mother had been doing with her time. Where was proof of her art? She found it one day in a white wicker basket in the basement under the ping-pong table. How sad this extension of her mother's heart looked, like a pile of unchecked dirty laundry. What had her mother been trying to accomplish all those years? What unborn child was growing inside her, kicking and screaming, aching to come out? After her mother's death, she tried to find the white wicker basket, but never could.

Warner silently entered the room. "Who's this?" he asked, picking up the black-and-white baby photo.

"Mom."

He kissed her on the temple and they studied it for a few seconds. He set the photo down. "Is this a penny?"

"Oh, God, don't look at that."

"Did you draw this?"

"A long time ago. Now give it."

He held the drawing at arm's length. "This is really good. How old were you?"

"Ten, twelve. Something like that."

"We should frame this."

"Or," she said, snatching the drawing and returning it to the box, "we could put it back in the closet."

He stared at the drawing. "I had the weirdest dream last night," he said.

"What about?"

He looked at her. "I dreamt you were pregnant." He laughed self-consciously.

She laughed, too, though her stomach had knotted.

"It seemed so real," he said. "Even after I woke up, it took me a minute to realize you weren't."

"Maybe it was just a prediction about Lincoln's birth."

"Oh," he said, sounding a little disappointed. "I hadn't thought of that." She leaned over to pick up the box, but he turned her around by the shoulders and kissed her.

She smiled against his lips. "Oh, now you're in the mood."

He lowered her to the table. The overhead light stung her eyes, and the black window loomed large in her periphery. His eyes asked if she was sure, and she kissed him. She felt blood draining to her face. She stared past his shoulder at the light's frosted dome, the faint outline of the bulb underneath.

Her friend Lori had told Diana that she knew the exact burning moment when she had conceived, and would never forget the way she and her husband Sam had gazed into each other's eyes.

The miniature table rocked and staggered, a table on which no child of their own would ever roll out play dough or build a block house. She would never see her own smile or Warner's eyes lighting in another's face. Never witness Warner holding their child in his hands. Never hear the words, I love you, Mommy. She wished Warner would look at her, but his eyes were tightly closed, as if he were trying to envision the pregnant Diana of his dreams.

For a while she lay on the table, listening to Warner taking a shower down the hall. The overhead light was still on, and she imagined someone peeking in the window at her. She crawled across the floor and switched off the light. She groped for her clothes in the dark, unable to shake the feeling that had first crept up on her in the hospital—a sense of inevitability, impending doom. She tried to force the feeling down, like a piece of gristle, but it was too big.

Maybe, Warner had said. Was he posturing for his father? Stating the obvious—who indeed knew what the future held? Or was the comment intended for her, to hint at some growing ambivalence on his part?

And now a dream that she was pregnant? What if Warner had begun contemplating a family? She should have asked him pointblank. Since when had she not been able to talk to him about anything?

She and Warner had always seemed a page from the same book. The beauty of their marriage was that even though they might disagree on minor issues, they shared the same core beliefs. But ever since her mother's death, she sensed a watermark had developed, an unspoken tension, threatening to warp the smooth, even surface of their relationship. Hadn't there been fewer kisses hello at the door? More yes-no responses? A lack of physical contact up until tonight? But even tonight's closeness felt distant. The water stopped running, and she listened to the dying stream of water pinging against the faucet.

"What about you?" Warner had asked in that Thai restaurant years ago. "Why don't you want any?"

"I don't know," she said.

"Sure you do."

"It's not one big thing. More like a compilation of little things. Sometimes I wish I did want them. I think it would be easier."

"How?"

"You don't have to explain why you want to be a parent, but you do if you don't."

She now found her underpants under the table and worked them up over her hips. She stared at the yellow baby booties in the box on the floor.

She smiled, realizing what all this nonsense was about. It was about Lincoln, the miracle of new life; and death, too, for she couldn't seem to disentangle the two in her mind. How could one look at a new baby without being reminded of one's own mortality? Neither she nor Warner was getting any younger, and it was only natural, healthy even, to reevaluate their life choices from time to time.

Warner appeared at the door, a towel wrapped around his waist. He flipped the light switch. "Hey, I was just thinking—"

"You're dripping."

"Oh." He stepped off the hardwood floor and onto the area rug in the hallway, which she had purchased to conceal the dip. "I was just thinking, forget what I said this morning, about going back to work. I know you're busy with the house, and there has been so much you've wanted to do." He pointed to the box on the floor. "You could do anything. You could be an artist if you wanted."

She scoffed at this.

"I'm serious. This is your time. I'll support whatever you want to do."

How did he always know just the right thing to say, at just the right time? Her time.

"Hey, Warner?" He had already left, but came back to the doorway. "I read there is going to be a lunar eclipse this Thursday."

The first time a total lunar eclipse could be viewed in the Americas in more than three years. They had watched the previous one as newlyweds, huddled together in a wool blanket on their postage-stamp lot.

He turned the light off. "The solar eclipses are cooler."

She sat in her rocker and looked out the window. The moon was beginning its ascent. In a few days it would reach full term, and for a small window of time, in a phase called totality, the earth would block the sun's light from the moon, turning it copper, the mournful color of dried blood.

She looked at the dark yard below, moonlight glinting off the yellow slide. She wondered what tools she might need, if she had enough strength, to tear down the swing set herself.

Aimee Zaring

Aimee Zaring was born and raised in Kentucky. She is a graduate of Bellarmine University and holds an MFA in Writing from Spalding University. Her work has appeared in several literary journals, and she is the recipient of an artist enrichment grant from the Kentucky Foundation for Women. She has recently completed her first novel.

Genesis for *An Otherwise Flawless Canvas*

This story, which has now grown into a longer work, arose at a transitional time in my life. My husband and I had just moved back to Louisville, our hometown, after being away for many years. My husband settled into his new job, and I, in my early thirties, finally committed my days to the occupation of which I'd always dreamed: full-time writer.

It was during this time that I began to reevaluate my husband's and my decision not to have children. Maybe it was because so many of my good friends were starting their families. Or maybe I was still influenced by one of the tenets of my Catholic upbringing—that marriage and children went hand in hand. Or maybe I was simply restless and unsure of my vocation, lured by the promise I thought motherhood offered—purpose, direction, validation.

And there was the societal pressure to have children—from family members, friends, and sometimes even strangers. Though I kept reading about how deliberate childlessness had gained in popularity and was supposedly more socially acceptable, I still found myself having to defend my decision more times than I cared to count. Maybe in another geographical region, in a less traditional town, I wouldn't have felt like the odd woman out. (According to a U.S. Census Bureau report for 2003, sixty-seven percent of women in Kentucky, ages fifteen to forty-four, were mothers. This rate was among the highest in the nation. The national average was fifty-seven percent.)

I decided to write about some of the external and internal pressures a childfree woman (particularly of childbearing age) faces in today's society. I wanted to show that the decision to remain childless isn't always cut-and-dry, a matter of not liking children, or being selfish, or having an all-consuming career that prevents one from having the time or energy to raise a family. And it is a decision that isn't made once, but over and over again. I also wanted to center this story around a life and a death, because I think often times the impetus to have children stems from an innate human need for immortality, to leave something lasting behind.

A Place to Cross

Michael Croley

The ride down to the bar is short. Only fifteen minutes or so. The night is crisp with snippy breezes, and the clouds covering the moon and stars make it so dark I turn on my high beams as I drive. But really, I could drive this piece of road in my sleep.

My dashboard light reflects in my windshield and it reminds me of that old Meat Loaf song, and I sing it to myself in a whisper, as if someone might hear me if I'm too loud. I take a left on Fowler and see the shadowed outline of the bar and sit higher in my seat, readying for my approach to Chopper's.

My tires splash in the gravel parking lot, spreading it, and there is a yellow glow from the one streetlamp that rests on the side of the building, next to an old television antenna. I park near the front door, blocking in someone's LTD, and grab my cigarettes off the passenger seat.

Inside everything is broken down and except for a few neon beer signs hanging on the walls, it is brown everywhere. The windows are tinted and you can't see outside. Smoke hangs in the air and looks thick enough to gather and fold into sheets. Old electrical wire spools serve as tables and yellow foam is spilling out from rips in the vinyl-covered chairs between people's legs. The customers look up to me from their beers and then to Deb, knowing I've come for him.

At the end of the bar I see my brother, his head in his hands, shoulders leaned against a Michelob Light sign.

"Get up, Delbert!"

"I'm trying to," he says and makes an attempt to stand.

I go to him, but I'm careful not to put my arms on him just yet. I wait for him to reach for me.

He's falling all over the bar and the customers turn in their seats, hands still holding their beers to watch us.

"What are you looking at?" I shout. They keep staring, though.

He's so drunk he can only hold himself up by using the bar stool as a leaning post.

For a moment he rises to his full height and stands sober and I see my brother in a way I've always remembered him. Deb's wearing a plain red tee shirt tucked into a pair of faded blue jeans. His hair is dark black and long, parted down the middle, and there are some specks of gray in his goatee. He's powerful looking. His muscles rip out of his tee shirt and veins show through his tan skin. When he isn't drunk, my brother is a beautiful man. I grab Deb, putting his arm around me, and carry him to my car.

Everything's back to normal. People have turned back around in their seats and they don't pay me any attention when I approach Tommy, the bartender, to settle up Deb's bill.

"How much'd he have?" I ask.

"Enough," he says.

"How much is enough?"

"He went through about half a fifth of Turkey while he was here. Passed out a lot of shots to people, but he was already drunk when he come in."

"Then why'd you serve him?"

"Same reason I always serve him. It don't do no good to tell him no. You know how he gets. Wants to fight you, pissed off at everyone. I can't afford to have him tear up this place like the last time he threw a fit." He opens his arms up to show me the room. "Better off to just let him drink till he's finished and call you."

"Just the same, Tommy, you shouldn't have served him."

"Listen here, Ben, I ain't the one that's got the problem. Maybe if you'd quit feeding him money to live off of he wouldn't be able to afford to drink, or be in the kind of shape he's in." His eyes narrow as he says this to me.

"That's none of your business," I tell him and put the cigarette out on the bar. "How much does he owe?"

Tommy eyes the butt on the wood and takes a deep breath. Black and gray ash is smeared and smoke rises from where it lays.

"Fifteen dollars," he tells me.

I pull a twenty from my wallet and hand it to him before I walk outside. I look up for the moon, but it's still not come out. I kick at some gravel and listen to them spread and bounce across the lot.

Deb is passed out when I get to the car and stirs a little when I get in, mumbles that he's cold. I start the car and turn the heat on. The car jerks when it catches the pavement, and we take off down the road, headed for home.

In the rearview mirror I look and see bags under my eyes. I yawn and light another cigarette, and roll the window down to flick my ash. Air runs over my temples and through my hair. It calms me a little and I look at Deb, resting in a ball against the door, and I can see his eyes moving underneath his eyelids while he sleeps, and I wonder if he is dreaming about tomorrow or yesterday.

Sometimes, I think how Deb got started drinking like this isn't important. The circumstances that can drive a man to drink aren't nearly big enough as the reasons to quit. I try to think about what it was in our past that has decided to reveal itself now in my brother's behavior, but I can't see anything. I look hard, I try to look at Deb as if he were just another man coming to get a job in the warehouse whose past I only know by what's on their application and they tell me in an interview, but even then I can't understand it.

A possum is in the driveway when I pull in, and I honk the horn to get it to move out of the way. It turns its head and looks at me then scampers into the yard. I pull ahead into the garage. Deb is snoring; his head rests against the window. I leave him inside the car and go in the house. I sift through an old crate of books that belonged to our father. Nearly all of them are Louis L'Amour's. I pick one out—Last of the Breed—and start on it.

Our old man loved L'Amour. Read one of his books almost every weekend when we were growing up. In the summers, he'd prop himself up in a chair behind the house and get a beer and set it in between his legs while he read. I always liked watching him read those books. It was the only time he ever seemed to sit still or wasn't working down at the garage. Even though our mother wouldn't let us bother him, it felt reassuring to know he was there with us, and not bending underneath the hood of a car, scraping his knuckles on engine blocks.

When the sun rises over the mountain I put the book back in the crate among the stack and walk out to the car and ask Deb if he wants breakfast. He shakes his head no. I ask him if wants to get out of the car and go inside and he waves me off. Inside I put on a pot of coffee, and turn the television to Sunday Morning with Charles Kuralt. He's in California's wine country. I've never been any farther west than St. Louis and watching him walk in those vineyards, along the slopes of mountains tells me I could feel at home three thousand miles away from here.

Deb is rummaging through my cabinets and it wakes me up.

"Keep it down in there," I shout.

"Sorry," he hollers back. "You got any peanut butter?"

He's whistling to himself and I pull myself out of the recliner and yawn as I walk into the kitchen.

"I thought you were asleep," he says.

"I was."

"You want some food?" he asks.

"No," I tell him and walk over to the coffeepot and pour myself a fresh cup.

"How long you been asleep?" he asks.

"Not as long as you," I tell him.

The toaster pops. Deb grabs the slices, spreads peanut butter on them, and eats them slow, his elbows resting on the counter while he chews. He drinks a glass of milk and smiles at me.

"I'm going to take a shower," he says and walks down the hallway to the bathroom.

I put my cup in the microwave to warm it and sit at the kitchen table and watch the seconds tick away. Deb's in the bathroom singing to himself and I shake my head and laugh a little.

When we were kids, our father used to take us down to the garage with him. We were always begging him to go. Our mother would pack us a lunch and stand at the door as we climbed into the old Dodge pickup. I rode in the middle and had to lean way over on Deb so our father could shift the truck into second and fourth gear.

At the garage, I remember how the cars looked so big up on those hydraulic lifts, and the whirring sound of drills in our ears that caused the floor to vibrate as they pulled off lug nuts and removed the tires. We stayed out of the way and watched him from the back of the garage as he slid under cars, grabbed wrenches and screwdrivers from the large red toolbox. At lunchtime he would carry his lunchbox out behind the garage and we ate by a field that led to the train tracks. We were always there at the beginning of summer, before the wet heat hit, and a breeze made the tall grass in the field sway.

Deb looked at Dad one day and said, "When I grow up, can I work here with you?"

Our father put his sandwich down in the lunchbox and wiped his mouth. His fingernails were black with grease. He turned and looked back at the garage and then down at Deb. "You don't want to work in there, Son," he said. "You want to be an engineer or an architect. You don't want to be no mechanic. You're better than that."

Deb didn't say anything and I just sat there watching Dad take slow bites, and listened to the deep sighs of his breath through his nostrils.

My gaze is broken by the microwave beeping, and my eyes hurt when I turn away to look out the window above the sink. It's a cloudy day, and the rain has started to sprinkle. I watch the clouds as they move and shift, and the small drops of water crawl down the glass.

I decide to go sit on the back porch even though there is no cover over it and watch the rain. The rain picks up and brings with it a coolness that makes me shiver. The cup feels warm in my hand and I bring it close to my face so that it is touching my upper lip and the steam is warming my nose. I can hear the sounds of the forest and listen to the cracking and popping of animals running over dead leaves and through small trees.

"Don't you know it's raining out here, Brother?" Deb says and startles me. My coffee flies out of the cup and spills onto my legs. I fan away the heat and try to wipe the coffee off at the same time.

"You scared me," I say.

"What're you doing out here?"

"Just watching the rain."

"Looks more like you're in the rain," he says.

"Well, that too. Why don't you pull up a chair?"

"You think too hard, buddy," he says and walks back into the house.

I finish my coffee while the tops of my shoulders become soaked with rainwater. I can see the flicker of images through the window and Deb's body on the couch. His feet hang over the edge, and the remote control rests on his chest.

Six months ago everything was fine. Deb finally got a good job working for a local bottler in town and delivering Pepsi to vending machines and restaurants all over the county. His hours were good and he finally got some medical insurance. I thought life was looking up for him and the hard knocks he'd been taking were all going to smooth out.

Of the two of us, Deb has always been the smarter one. Nothing's ever been hard for him. The things I succeeded in, like playing sports and getting good grades in school, took a lot of time, effort I didn't want to spend, but for Deb, those things came as natural as walking. Growing up, it was always clear who the star in our house was. But Deb always had a temper, one he couldn't seem to control. Our mother said he got that from her side of the family, but I never saw her go on a tear like Deb and I never saw it in my grandparents either. Deb's temper always got him in trouble.

I come inside and see Deb rubbing one hand over the other like he's trying to warm them and I see they are cut and swollen.

"From last night?" I ask.

He holds them out into the light, and it reminds me of a woman looking at her freshly painted nails.

"Yeah. But you know what they say, you should see the other guy," he says.

"Why don't you put some ice on them? Maybe the swelling will go down."

"If you make the pain go away, you make the fight go away. I don't want to forget."

Deb rolls over onto his side and grabs a magazine off the coffee table in front of the couch. His back pops and he makes a strained, grunting noise as he lifts the magazine off the table.

"Who would want to forget that?" I say.

"Don't start, Ben."

"What?"

"I don't need your smart mouth. Mind your own business. I'm a grown man, little brother."

"Then act like one." My ears get hot and my shoulders hunch up.

"Just lay off, Ben!"

"How much longer are you going to live this way? When are you going to start doing something with your life?"

"Like you? That's some life you got. Cooped up in a warehouse all day, barking roughnecks from Jackson and Clay County around all day in a shirt and tie while they do all the work."

"It pays for you to get out of jail. Pays for you to eat and get drunk on. If I didn't have this life you wouldn't have much of one either."

Deb stands up. He's three inches taller than me and just as broad.

Three years ago, he nearly killed a man. It was a terrible sight. The man just wouldn't stay down. He'd gotten a good lick on Deb early in the fight, cutting open his eye. Blood ran down Deb's face into his goatee and he could only see out of his right eye, but the other man's face was just a mess. His nose looked shattered and was twisted to the left and his jaw was leaning to the right. He kept his fists in front of him but he didn't have the strength to hold them up. People were yelling at the man to stay down, but he kept getting up. Deb can be violent like that. He's not the kind of man you cross.

Deb was ready to pounce on him one more time, when I jumped through the air and tackled him. His body was covered in sweat and I could smell the salt and blood mixing on his skin. He cocked his fist back until he saw it was me, and then he put his hands up in the air, grabbed my shoulders and pulled me into him. I'm thinking about all this as we stare each other down, my breathing and pulse begin to race.

"You want me to leave?" Deb asks.

"I want you to act your age," I tell him.

"I'm going to do what I want. If I want to go out and get drunk then that's my business. Okay?"

"Well, start spending your own money then. I'm not your damn keeper."

I walk back outside where the rain has picked up a little. I pace my deck, listening to the hollow thumps of my steps on the boards, and then look back out to the forest and pat myself down for my cigarettes. I turn to go back inside and get them when Deb comes out carrying two coats and says, "Let's take a walk."

"It's raining," I say.

"I can see that. Come on, let's go."

"I'm not going out in the rain."

"You're standing out in it, you might as well walk a bit."

The rain is falling at a slant from the wind. We start walking down the steps off the porch toward the trail worn in the forest.

"How's work going?" Deb asks.

"Fine," I tell him. "Same old complaints."

"About what?"

"Usual stuff. Too many hours, not enough money. Our margins are falling short, sales are down, drivers are unhappy, and we might have to lay off some people."

"You in charge of all that?"

"Pretty much," I say. "I don't much want to talk about it."

"Well, you'll get things figured out. That's what the supervisor does, and that's what you've always done, figure things out," he says.

I look at him when he says this, but he's only looking at the ground, paying attention to where he walks.

I'm walking in front, pushing small limbs to the side of my face, and holding them for Deb to pass through. The air smells damp from the rain and wet, dead leaves. As I walk I can hear my footsteps snap small branches and shuffle the brush. Deb's walk is silent and careful. He's more in tune with nature than I am.

"You never were a good hunter," he says. "Too loud when you walk. Always scaring off the animals."

"Hunting was your thing, not mine," I tell him.

We go deeper into the woods and are in the thick of the trees where the rain can't reach us for the canopy. Deb and I pull off the hoods on our coats, and I hear Stone Creek rising fast to the left of me. It bubbles over rocks and sticks, running toward the Cumberland. Deb and I pause to listen to the forest and above the sound of water I hear a thrush rise out of a bush and take off to the south. Its wings make strong, hurried beats as it becomes a black dot on the horizon.

"Let's keep walking," Deb says and touches my elbow. "I'll lead for awhile."

Deb heads us toward the creek. There isn't a trail and we step over rotted out logs into ankle-deep leaves. We get to the creek and Deb wants to cross, though it has risen level with the bank.

"There ain't a good place to cross," I say. "I don't think I can jump it."

"We ain't old men yet. We can make it," he says.

"Why do you want to?"

"For the hell of it. Let's get to the other side."

"I don't want to get any more wet than I already am," I say.

"Then make sure you clear it on your jump."

Deb takes a couple of steps back and runs toward the bank and jumps across with ease. "Your turn," he says.

The creek is five-feet wide. Water is moving even faster than it sounds, and there are small funnels in pockets along some of the rocks down stream. I take a couple of steps back and get up a run and start to jump and stop.

"Come on, just jump."

"Shut up," I tell him.

I back up again and take off. On the last step my foot flies out from under me. I fall in the creek and water is at my waist. I hear Deb laughing.

"Good one, Brother. I thought you had it for sure." He is bent over with his hands on his knees, laughing.

I wade over to the other side of the bank. "Help me out of here," I say.

Deb reaches down his hand and I take hold of it. His grip is strong and sure and I come out of the water. My clothes are heavy and cling to me.

"You know the worst part about all this?" he asks.

I am shaking my arms out to my side, and pulling the fabric away from my skin. "What's that?"

"You have to jump back across to get home." His laugh echoes through the valley.

"Thanks for telling me," I say and begin to laugh myself.

We walk toward the pond and sit on the bank and skip sandstone into the water. Some of the pieces break before they reach the water and some don't even make one skip; they just fall apart against the surface. I pick at some grass between my legs and feel for rocks along the ground. Deb sits with his knees pulled to his chest and crosses his arms over them to rest his chin. Crow's feet are around the edges of his eyes and I want to be able to tell what it is he is looking at or thinking.

"Deb, your drinking has got to stop." I tell him and then regret it for picking back up the conversation at the house. We don't spend time like this anymore.

"I don't need a lecture from you, Ben."

"Just money," I say.

"I don't need your damn money, either."

"Jesus, Deb. I'm just trying to help you out— "

"Help? You call telling me how to live my life help? I don't need your charity. I don't need you bailing me out, picking me up. I don't need any of it."

He's up now, walking around in small circles, back and forth. I watch him pace. His forehead is wrinkled in pain and he rubs his hands.

"Then what do you need?"

"I don't know. I know I don't need you treating me like you're Daddy telling me what to do, acting like I've let you down."

"I'm not trying to be like Daddy, but don't you think it's about time you grew up a bit? Them bars and booze ain't taking you anywhere, Deb. Look at your hands for christsakes. If you'd just learn to control your damn temper every once in a while we wouldn't be having this conversation."

"Here we go," he says. He picks up a rock and throws it clear across the pond.

"What are you talking about?"

"You know exactly what I'm talking about."

"Well, I thought you would have learned your lesson three years ago."

"It always comes back to that, doesn't it?"

"You were in the wrong, Deb. You know you shouldn't have hit that boy in the restaurant. And you especially shouldn't have done it with your damn nametag still on."

"Don't tell me what is right and wrong, Ben. You didn't see him hit his son. You didn't see that little boy's body crumple against the garbage can."

"Fine," I say. "But was that worth losing your damn job over? Some jerk that hits his kid? Now, look at you, quitting one job after another, acting like we're still kids."

"Dad wouldn't have let it go. He wouldn't have let some guy hit his kid for no reason. You know that."

He looks at me and I can still see the anger in his face.

"It's not up to you to make everything right that's wrong."

"We weren't raised to let that kind of shit go on and you know it. I did what was right."

"You're not the only one who pays for your choices, Deb."

All he had to do was walk away. All he had to do was ignore it. Hell, if I'd just had him over to dinner that night rather than him going into the restaurant he wouldn't have seen that man, Burt Hamlin, smack his son just for pestering him about an ice cream cone. If he had just gone home and changed shirts, Lawson would have never known Deb worked at Pfizer and been able to find him the next day, following him after his last doctor's office visit to the bar where the fight started in the parking lot.

That's when Tommy called me and I came down there, a mob around the two of them. After that it was easy for Lawson. He filed a lawsuit against Deb and the company. They let him go, settled the suit. Deb's assault charge was dropped, but he was different after that, lost his ambition and started hopping jobs.

I get up from my spot and go to him. I want to speak, but I don't know what I can say that I haven't already. Our conversations, like his drinking, have become habit. They don't pull us closer and they don't lead to resolution. Instead, they increase our distance, making me see Deb only through my memory.

He is breathing fast. His chest rises in big heaves and I can see his breath fog as he exhales.

Thunderclaps shake the ground, opening up the sky for the rain to push down harder, rippling the water in the pond.

"You ready to go home?" Deb asks.

"Whenever you are," I say crumbling a piece of sandstone in two and watching the dust sprinkle the top of my shoe.

We walk back through the woods. We don't talk to one another. I don't bring up last night and I don't think about what will happen next Saturday or even what might happen before then. I pull the hood on my coat up and follow Deb's lead through the woods. We come to the creek again. He jumps across and holds out his hand for me to jump to. I jump and he grabs me to make sure I don't fall backwards. He leads us a different way home, away from the trail we walked when we were kids. He slows his pace so that I can keep up with him, and motions for me to walk without disrupting the natural sounds of the forest. I watch him make a way for us, stepping over rocks, ducking under branches. He turns and looks at me from time to time, checking to see he isn't too far ahead. Rain pounds its footsteps around us. Wind whistles through the trees, and I feel the cold in my jeans but we are almost home.

Michael Croley

Michael Croley grew up in Corbin. He holds a Master's in Creative Writing from Florida State University, and his work has been recognized with awards from the Kentucky Arts Council. He currently lives in Memphis, Tennessee.

Genesis for *A Place to Cross*

A Place to Cross came to me when I was still an undergraduate. The story since its inception has always had a very quiet feeling to it. There is, in some ways, little crisis to deal with, and the power of the breakdown between these two brothers has to be conveyed through the way Ben tells the story. I wanted to write a story about brothers where the older one, whom the younger has always looked up to, has made a mess of his life when he had so much promise. I did that, but then the story became about unconditional love. Love in that form is rarely, if ever, simple, and I wanted the story to push that to the surface, to show how Ben resolves this in his own mind at the story's final scene.

Her Leg

Jackie Rogers

Mother Grace only had one leg, but that never bothered me. No one else even mentioned it, so I sure wasn't going to make a big deal out of it. She was what my uncle called "estranged," but I couldn't tell that much about her from the picture. All I could tell was she had dark hair parted right down the middle, a long slender body, pierced ears with dangly earrings, a lacy white dress and both of her arms.

What I admired most was her balance. Having never met her, all I had to go on was the black and white 5x7 in a silver frame that sat on my dresser. Every time I went to get a pair of panties out of the top dresser drawer, there she stood, straight up, as pretty as you please on her left leg. Every morning I stood with my arms at my sides, and lifted my right leg. I tried to stand perfectly still and smile for an imaginary camera. My best time was 17 seconds. I figured I probably got balance from Mama and her sister, Mary Jean. They were all the time falling down and breaking stuff. Mostly they broke lamps and knick knacks, but one time Mama broke her little toe.

One night in April, right after I turned seven, Daddy shooed me out of the kitchen where he and Mama, Uncle Junis, Uncle Marvin and his wife, Aunt Gladys, were gathered up around the table talking. Uncle Junis didn't have his guitar so I wasn't too interested anyway.

I wandered off to go through Mama's jewelry box and her purse too if it was on her dresser. Instead, I found a half-smoked cigarette stubbed out in Daddy's ashtray on the bedside table. It smelled kind of like my hair when I caught it on fire with a candle last summer. I put it to my lips and drew a deep breath. Even unlit it stung. I held the butt at the very end of my fingers watching myself in the mirror as I ghost smoked. When I heard chairs scoot in the kitchen, I slid the cigarette back into the ashtray. At the top of the stairs I could see Uncle Marvin standing at the front door with his right hand on the doorknob, motioning for Gladys. "If you change your mind, let me know and I'll pay my fair share. As a matter of fact I'll pay for half of it and all you all got to come up with is the other half between you. Not a bad deal. Come on, Gladys." He waddled down the driveway and flumped down in his Cadillac before anyone else could say a word.

Mama just stood there twirling a curl with her index finger and tapping her foot. Daddy leaned on the back of the recliner. "He's just talking, Pete. He'll come around. Until then, what are we going to do?" Junis said.

"We're going to have to take turns," Daddy said. "That's the only way I know to do it."

Junis nodded and said, "Who's first?"

"I was thinking you could take her for the summer. You know that's my busy season. I've got two houses that need sheet rocking as we speak."

"I can appreciate that, Pete, but I've got my plans too. Everybody always thinks because I get the summer off I don't have anything to do. I'm taking a group of eighth graders to the Grand Canyon in July. What am I supposed to do about that?" Junis' voice got faster and higher.

"Then how do you suggest we do this?" Daddy asked.

"Paper, rock, scissors."

"Are you serious?" Daddy asked, but Junis already had his fist planted firmly on the palm of his left hand.

"Ready?" Junis was rocking back and forth like he was in tournament play. Mama snorted and went back in the kitchen for about ten seconds. They cracked their fists on their palms in unison twice and the third time they made their choice. They were both rocks. "Again." Slap, slap. Rocks. Automatically they went again. Daddy went with paper and Junis stuck with rock. As soon as he knew the results he said, "Best two out of three."

"That's not how it works, little brother." But Junis wouldn't hush, so Daddy gave in and the contest continued.

By round three, I was the cheerleader. I yelled out, "Rock," for Daddy to pick.

Junis said, "Quiet now, Chick. This is serious." On the last go I told him it was just a game like kickball and he picked rock and lost to Daddy's paper and said, "Do over."

"No matter what, this is the last one," Daddy said. Junis nodded and they began.

I yelled, "Scissors!" and Junis listened. After choosing paper, Daddy closed his eyes and let his head fall back.

"That does it then," Junis said. "You've got the first six months. I'll get the next."

"I think two months at a time would be more realistic," Daddy said. "Let's just see what happens. You'll help though, right?"

Junis tugged at the skin over his Adam's apple and said of course he would help, but not right now as he had plans.

"Help with what? I'll help."

Daddy finally smiled. "You sure will, big mouth. First you're going to have to help your mama fix up your playroom. You got to move all your toys and dolls and stuffed animals to the attic to make room. We're going to bc having company for awhile."

My mouth dropped. I'd asked for a baby brother almost as long as I asked for a horse. My eyes fell to my mother's stomach that seemed as flat as ever. "Can I name him?"

"Oh, for Heaven's sake, Pete. Tell her what's going on." Mama put a protective hand over her belly.

"Chick, your grandmother, Mother Grace, is going to live with us for a little while. We'll need your help for sure and you'll have to be on your very best behavior. Mother Grace can't take a lot of monkey shining."

"How will she get up the stairs?" I had a million questions, but that was the only one I could get out.

"Would you hush your foolishness?" Mama said. "Go get started."

I was so worked up on the morning that Mother Grace arrived that I got two spankings in an hour and was told to sit in my room until she got there. I killed time by pretending I was Mother Grace. I stood at my door with my eyes closed, an umbrella in my left hand as a cane and my right leg drawn up. When I opened my eyes, I scanned the room slowly to imagine what she would see. I saw the yellow curtains that crisscrossed the window, the narrow bed, the bread bag rug on the floor, the baby rocking chair with Raggedy Ann in it with her right leg tucked up under her skirt. I averted my Mother Grace eyes and batted at the chair with the umbrella until I heard the doll fall to the floor. I hopped around the room until I got tired. For the seventeenth time that day, I went through my closet to the closet next door. I practiced opening the door silently and peered into the guest room. Still empty.

At two o'clock sharp I drank in my first sight of Mother Grace. Question one was answered. She wore a fake leg beneath a polyester pantsuit with a striped white blouse. Her hair looked like an SOS pad, bluish and wispy around her head. She was smaller than I thought she would be. I might could even pick her up if I had to. More than anything I wanted to look down, but my eyes never left her lipless mouth. Daddy took her suitcase and Mama said, “Come on in, Mother Grace. Chick will show you your room.”

“What the hell’s a Chick?” She clucked her false teeth. “Where’s the toilet?”

“I’ll show you, Mother Grace.” I held out my hand, but she never took it. I got behind her instead ready to catch her from behind as Mama showed her the way. She zigzagged from the door to the couch to the stairs, grabbing on to anything that would hold her up. I concentrated hard on the hump on her back. She stopped so quickly on the fifth step, I nearly ran over her.

She turned and looked down on me with the tiniest eyes I’d ever seen. “Get away from me. If I wanted something clamoring around me all the time, I would put a pig on a leash and drag him around.” She waited for me to retreat before she continued on. I thought her stub must hurt awful bad.

Mother Grace slept late most mornings and all of us had to creep around until she got up. About the third week I took to sneaking into her closet and watching her sleep. I figured I would be able to see the fake leg propped up against the wall or lying on the dresser, but to my surprise, she wore that thing to bed. As plain as day I saw her two feet sticking up under the covers. A time or two I thought one of them was twisted up pretty good, but it was hard to tell.

Mama stayed clear of her. When Mother Grace weaved into the room, bumping the furniture and dropping ashes on the carpet, she talked to herself. “Look at this place. Filthy mess. Dust an inch deep. I’d be ashamed.” Then from the recliner she’d watch her stories. I’d fetch her something to drink and cigarettes when she ran out. Soap operas were something no one in our house was supposed to watch, so I did my best not to look at the TV, but I learned a lot just listening, and couldn’t wait to hear what was going to happen next. And even though I’d never seen Bo’s face, I loved him.

“Chicken, light me a cigarette.” I never corrected her when she called me Chicken and I never refused her anything. I’d seen it done many times so I pulled a long white Virginia Slim from its pack and put it to my lips. The match flared up on the second try. I drew in as I'd seen folks do and lit it. My lungs felt scorched and full. I didn't want Mother Grace to think I was some sort of stupid kid who couldn't even light a cigarette, so I held the smoke in as I handed it to her. She laughed and held out her fingers for me. I meant to give it to her and then run outside real quick to cough. Instead I started coughing first and dropped the burning cigarette in her lap. It burned a fast hole in her slacks then rolled off into the crack between the arm and seat. "Hurry up, genius before you catch the house on fire." I scrambled to the floor and felt around under the chair. I saw a dark spot growing on the flap sewn under the chair and then a red ring grew out from the black. I grabbed Mother Grace's Coke and threw it on the fire.

I sat there under the footrest of the recliner trying to catch my breath, wondering if I'd really gotten the fire out, wondering if the house smelled like melting polyester pants and upholstery and Virginia Slims and Coke. I looked up and saw her skinny little legs. I slid back a little farther, craned my neck, but the leg eluded me again.

She banged her foot down on the footrest and said, "Get me a Coke and light me a cigarette."

There were no visits from Uncle Junis or Marvin that long summer. Daddy said he wasn't the least bit surprised. Mother Grace didn't even mention it until the first of August. "I know you're getting ready to ship me out of here, but I'm not going. I'll be staying right here, thank you very much. Chicken, get me a Coke and a smoke." I fixed her drink with five ice cubes just like she liked it, grabbed her cigarette case and caught up with her on the stairs. We went to her bedroom where Daddy had put a new 19 inch Zenith.

On the night I finally pulled my last front tooth, I stood there holding it up to the light. I explained how the tooth fairy would probably give me fifty cents for that one because I'd pulled it myself. Mother Grace patted the bed and said, "Settle down. Get your chicken hind end up here before you make me miss *Dallas*."

"What about my tooth?"

She grabbed the tooth and slung it under her pillow. I crawled in beside her just in time to see JR lay a big one on some blonde woman I knew wasn't Sue Ellen.

Mother Grace punched me with her elbow. "Some day you'll be kissing some old ugly boy like that." I made a face and explained to her the dangers of boy germs. "They're dangerous alright," she told me and then laughed. I laughed too, but I didn't know why.

I was too excited to sleep the night before school started. I picked out my clothes and tried them on several times. Mother Grace said my butt was flat and why shouldn't it be since my chest was too. I said, "Thanks," and continued modeling while she watched Johnny Carson.

My eyes weren't the least bit tired when she turned out the light. I stared at the little diamond of light the moon was throwing in through the curtains, and just as the first wave of sleep began to take me, I heard a whimper. It sounded just like a puppy, but it made me nervous instead of excited. When I heard it again, I sat up and squinted at Mother Grace in the dark. She lay there as small as a child with her knees drawn to her chest and her face twisted. She moaned something I couldn't understand. "Mother Grace?" Her eyes opened and I saw fear. "It's ok," I whispered. She took my wrist and pulled me to her as she rolled over and I wrapped her in my arms, my head resting on top of hers. I fell asleep immediately.

I woke up before Mother Grace and the sun. She held my wrist more tightly than ever. I could see the back of her head and the hair that now lay glued to her head and shaped like a triangle from the pillow. I moved my left leg ever so slowly toward her, bumping her right leg that lay poker straight out from her body. It was cold and hard, just like I thought it would be. I took a deep breath and ever so slowly and gently I let my toe investigate. Although it sort of felt like skin, there was no give. There were creases and I ran my toe down one of those to the foot. The heel was rough and the arch was almost flat, I guessed to give her better balance and support. It was amazing, this leg. I wished I could see it.

It was all I could do to reclaim my hand from her grip. I checked under the pillow and found my tooth instead of two quarters, made a note to myself to put it under my own pillow tonight so the tooth fairy could find it, then sneaked quietly through the closet to my room. I pulled a pair of panties from the drawer and studied Mother Grace's picture once again. She was so young. I wondered suddenly how old she was now. I stood on my left leg until I fell over.

There were four cars and Daddy's truck in the driveway when I got home. "What's going on?" I asked.

"Chick, honey. Come over here and sit down." Mama patted her lap.

"What's wrong?" I didn't move an inch.

"It's Mother Grace. She's gone."

"Where'd she go? Did you make her leave?" Daddy pulled me to his chest and I cried. No one in that kitchen cried but me.

"Your Mama found her this morning. She must have gone in her sleep." I could feel his jaw moving against my head as he talked. I wanted to say something smart. I wanted to cuss. I wanted to go watch *Days of Our Lives*.

The next day I missed school to go with Mama and Aunt Gladys to the funeral home. They took a pink flowery dress that Mother Grace would have spit on. While they talked with Mr. Johnson, I roamed around the funeral home basement until I found Mr. Elliott. "How does my grandmother look?"

"She looks beautiful," he said. He leaned down close and spoke in an eerie, quiet voice.

"Will the bottom lid be closed on the casket?"

"Yes. Just like always."

I didn't want to have to say it. "If she's going to have to wear that dress, you're going to have to keep that closed. She wouldn't want anyone to see her leg."

"Her leg?"

"I mean the fake one. I don't guess she'd care about the other one."

He smiled a curious smile. "What are you talking about? She didn't have a fake leg."

The picture in the silver frame on my dresser above the panty drawer was a one-legged woman. If there was anything I knew in my life up to that point it was that. That Saturday, after everything was said and done, I took it out of the frame and looked at it. Really looked at it. And then I saw it. The blackness that fell below her skirt in that picture taken a thousand years ago was suddenly and clearly the shadow of the photographer. A shadow that perfectly masked her right leg.

I slid the picture under the panties in the top drawer. After supper I crawled into Mother Grace's bed with a Coke and ghost smoked a Virginia Slim until I fell asleep to the noise of the TV.

Jackie Rogers

A Science Hill native, Jackie White Rogers spends her days as an English teacher at Pulaski County High School. She is working on a collection of short stories and a novel, *The Missionary*. She has studied with authors such as Silas House, Pamela Duncan, Ron Rash, Lee Smith and Crystal Wilkinson.

Genesis for *Her Leg*

My paternal grandmother, who is somehow attached to all of my childhood memories, was so funny. She loved Johnny Cash and Pete Rose equally, danced to the radio while maneuvering her walker, put lard in her beans and played checkers with deadly competiveness. I was a lot like Chick back then, but she was nothing like Mother Grace. I have a picture of her as a young woman. I study it a lot, trying to find a trace of the grandmother I knew before rheumatoid arthritis took advantage of her. Just like in the story, the bottom part of her leg seems to be missing, hidden by the photographer's shadow. It didn't take long for me to wonder what an imaginative child could do with something as interesting as a relative with a fake leg. Since then I've written a few other stories that involve severed hands and deformed feet. The folks in my writers group are calling this my appendage period.

Tip of the Screw

Lauren Titus

Home Depot sold an overwhelming selection of toilet parts. Even the flappers—the circular pieces that cover the drains of the commodes—were offered in a variety of models. John tapped one of the hanging plastic containers. He'd forgotten to get the part for Karen yesterday, had already been at the job site when she'd called to remind him. She'd been complaining for weeks about having to hold down the toilet lever until it flushed completely and blamed the old flapper, had decided it was too dense to float in the water. Despite her intuitive expertise in toilet mechanics, she refused to buy the part herself. Yesterday, when John admitted that he'd forgotten to pick it up, she'd sighed and the sound came through his cell phone like a gust of wind.

Her father, Dale Senior, was helping them work on her house that Sunday. For the first half of the day, the old man had stood beside John and emphasized the importance of elbow grease, had told him how the rich people mowed their lawns in diagonal rows, and had spit tobacco into an empty beer can. John had worked quietly down his honey-do list in atonement, for forgetting to buy the flapper on Saturday, and for Julia, the younger woman he'd dated during his and Karen's last break-up a few weeks before. Even Dale Senior's soused eyes seemed sharp with reproach. John had planned to go to the store alone, but Karen had squeezed his arm and said: "Take my dad with you."

In the air-conditioning, John's armpits became clammy and his hair pricked against the cotton seams of his T-shirt. Shorn blades of grass stuck to his boots. He stomped his foot, but the grass clung to the leather with dew. John had left Julia and gone back to Karen as soon as Karen had asked him to. He'd thought that had been enough for her, but soon he realized that the girl represented the hundreds of disappointments he'd caused Karen over the past five years. Since they'd reunited, Karen had alternated between being the sweet, fragile woman who had begged for him back and the woman who thought he breathed too loud. But for the first time she had finally decided that she wanted to marry him, or that she would marry him. That day, John was supposed to ask her father for permission, but first he'd have to find the old man in Home Depot. As soon as they'd walked into the store, Dale Senior had wandered off, and they experienced no male bonding over toilet parts.

John hoped he wouldn't have to ask one of the teenage employees to page Dale Senior over the intercom as if he were a wayward child. John took off his baseball hat, ran his hands through his matted dark curls, and put it back on. All the flappers looked the same, except for the packaging. Karen would know, however, if he chose the $2.50 flapper over the $5.99 flapper. She always knew those things, knew when he watched a baseball game instead of going to the Laundromat, knew when his checkbook was overdrawn, and knew when he searched for porn over the Internet. He picked up the $5.99 Super Flapper Ultra, which had a list of its merits streaming down the box under the impressive title that sounded like a feminine product.

Dale Senior had insisted on driving both of them to the store in his new-to-him Chevy truck. It was an automatic, which the old man wasn't used to. He'd grasp at the air between them in search of the stick, only to fall empty-handed to the seat. John jumped a bit the first few times the man's fist slapped against the vinyl.

"I got a tip for you, son," Dale Senior had told him on the way to the store. "If you ever gotta jump a car that has that white crud on the battery terminals, you pour some Coca Cola on it and it comes right off."

"Yes, sir."

"You know what I heard on the news this week?" Dale Senior took a sharp right turn without signaling.

"No, sir. What'd you hear?"

"I heard that woman's pill causes cancer."

John adjusted his seatbelt, not knowing if he was supposed to answer.

"Yep," Dale Senior said. "I sure as hell hope my daughter isn't taking those pills."

Karen had never been on the pill with John. She'd told him it was too dangerous for a woman over thirty who smoked. They'd never used condoms, not even when they first started dating, but for five years she had never gotten pregnant. After the first year they didn't have sex often enough to worry, maybe every other week when she was drunk but not too drunk. Usually they'd lie down in bed and he'd try, but she'd push his hands away.

John realized that the truck had been creeping toward the opposite lane. Dale Senior's head had been turned to John with an expression of expectation.

"No," John said. "I don't think Karen's taking any medication."

Dale Senior returned his eyes to the road and steered the truck back into the lane.

Home Depot's racks of merchandise ran up at least a story, maybe higher. John paced down one of the center aisles and searched for Dale Senior while trying to casually hold the toilet part against his hip. The light fixture aisle glowed yellow in the midst of the florescent store. Fake Tiffany lamps, ceiling fans, and glass chandeliers crowded each other on brass and stainless steel chains. Dale Senior stood in the middle of the aisle with his hands shoved into the pockets of his twill workpants. The lights reflected off the bare section of scalp on the crown of his head.

What kind of instructions would Dale Senior give John when he found out that John was marrying his daughter? John shuddered to think of the procreation methods that Dale Senior had tips on. It was clear that the old man wanted grandkids. That was probably why he'd asked John if Karen was on the pill. Julia had been on birth control, but still insisted on extra-strength spermicidal-lubricant condoms. Maybe it was her generation. She'd been a child in the eighties, during the AIDS scare, while John, ten years older, had already been implementing the coitus interruptus technique with his high school girlfriend. Regardless of her precautions against conception and disease, she'd had no aversion to his body. He'd feel her palm on his thigh under the table, or her lips seeking his when they were alone.

"There you are!" Dale Senior barked across the aisle. "I was going to send out a search and rescue party."

While John paid for the Super Flapper Ultra, Dale Senior milled behind the cashier lanes, hands still shoved in his pockets, back arched forward. The boy at the register rolled his eyes when John had to pay with a credit card. When the transaction was over, Dale Senior waved him to go on. "I'll meet you at the truck."

The heat was close outside, especially after walking through the continuous gale of air conditioning that blew in front of the exit doors.

John scanned the rows and located the truck, which had been parked at an angle over two spots. Dale Senior didn't want to get it "dinged." It was late into the afternoon, and John hadn't had a cigarette since morning, but Dale Senior would be out any minute. A woman was walking down the parking lot with her back to John. Her dark hair was cut above her shoulders and her jeans hung low on her hips. For a moment, he thought it could have been Julia, but the woman was too thin, too rigid in her walk. She clicked a car remote and climbed into a BMW. John realized he hadn't been breathing.

Karen had asked him after dinner one night, "Do you miss her?"

She'd sat across from him with her arms on the crumb-strewn table. A cigarette that he'd forgotten about was still burning. He reached over and tapped the filter. Ashes fell on top of other ashes in the tray.

"Not really," he said, and he didn't miss Julia, not really. He didn't pine for her, didn't know exactly what he'd be pining for. Being with her had never felt real. Maybe he'd even done it to get back at Karen, a little bit, to show her that even in his thirties, he could still find someone else.

"It's okay if you miss her," Karen said. "I'll understand."

"I know," he said, "but I don't."

"Do you think she misses you?"

"I hadn't thought about it," he said, though he had.

"Was she upset when you dumped her?" Karen asked.

"I guess."

Julia had resisted ending their relationship, but her arguments for staying together weren't substantial. She didn't have anything to compete with his five years with Karen, but he didn't tell her that Karen was the reason he was leaving. He just said that he'd noticed some differences between them, that he didn't think they had what it would take to make it long-term. Still, Julia looked at him as though she smelled another woman, but she didn't say anything except "okay." Then, she stood from the kitchen table, took his hand, and led him to the bedroom. He wasn't going to sleep with her, had promised himself that he wouldn't sleep with her. She moved close to him and he could smell the scented lotion on her skin. He kept his arms at his sides, but she slid her hands up his back and down his spine. He dropped his head into her hair and brought his arms around her. He kissed her and then he couldn't stop kissing her. Afterward, she cried. He put his hand on her shoulder, but she stood up and put her clothes on.

"Have you talked to her since?" Karen asked.

"No," he said.

"She's never called you?"

He shook his head. Karen knew that he and Julia hadn't talked, but she kept bringing up the subject in different ways, like if she asked just right at the perfect time, his answer would be different. He knew Julia was never going to call him after she left his bed that night. He knew he should have gotten up, should have walked her to the door, but he couldn't. The weight he felt in his chest as he lay on the bed was more than he'd expected. She left his bedroom and her footfalls were soft and slow in the hallway. He took a breath to call out to her, but held it instead. Julia hadn't untied him from Karen, and he knew then how much he had wanted her to.

The sun was low in the sky and beamed off the car roofs in the parking lot. The asphalt wiggled in a heat mirage. From inside the store, an alarm bled out as the sliding doors opened and tapered to silence as they shut. After a few minutes of leaning against the pillar in the loading dock, John returned to the store. Not far from the entrance, Dale Senior was flanked by two employees. One was a regular employee with the store T-shirt, but the other wore a short-sleeved button down and a thin black tie. John walked to them and saw that Dale Senior's pants pockets were hung inside-out on either side. He stood behind the old man, who held a container of screw tips—Phillips #2. Dale Senior popped the lid and poured out the contents into his palm. The tips fell out like ammunition. The man in the tie peered over the tips in Dale Senior's hand and shifted his weight from side to side.

"You see here," Dale Senior said and picked up a tip from the pile. "This one's old and used. You see the rust on the grooves?"

"Yes, I see that," the man in the tie said. "But that doesn't explain why it set the alarm off."

"Maybe it's the metal screws in my hip."

"Sir, it's not a metal detector."

John tried to back away, but his boot caught on the waxed floor and screeched under the tall ceilings. People who were looking sideways at the confrontation stared at him dead-on. Dale Senior also took note and gestured toward him.

"Ask my son," he said. "He'll tell you I brought these with me. We just came here to buy us a flapper."

The plastic bag that held the Super Flapper Ultra began to slip in the sweat of John's hands. He had put the receipt in his wallet, next to the credit card slip. The manager's shirt and tie made him look like a door-to-door missionary, someone beyond reproach.

"Did your father bring these screw tips in with him?" he asked.

There were eyes on him, the manager's, the kid employee, other customers, and Dale Senior, who winked and nodded his head. John's chest stung and he felt his skin burn hot up his neck. Maybe Karen's father had brought the screw tips with him. Maybe it was a mistake. If he could just believe it long enough for the blood to drain away the blush from his face, he could answer.

In the sixth grade, his family drove out to the Kentucky countryside for his Great Aunt Louise's funeral. In the church, the preacher had pointed a sausage finger to John in the third pew. "Have you been washed in the blood of the Lamb?" Twelve-year-old John turned to his father, wanted his father to tell him if he had been or not, if it was a farming term, if he was supposed to answer. The preacher's face was blotched red above the collar that cinched his neck like a corset. "Have you been washed in the blood of the Lamb?" John's father nodded his head with closed eyes in agreement and shame. John also closed his eyes and bowed his head, but knew it was a lie—that he was lying in church. The heat of all the bodies next to each other, bathed in cologne, lye soap, and pungent sweat made him feel dizzy. He wanted to stand on the pew and list all his sins, confess that he'd cheated on his geography test, that during a spin-the-bottle game he'd kissed two Jews and one Unitarian, and that he thought Aunt Louise, who hadn't been embalmed, smelled like the longest, worst fart in history.

"Sir," the manager squared his shoulders toward John. "Did he bring those screw tips in with him?"

John felt air come in his mouth and dry out his tongue. "Well, if he said he did…"

The manager let out a hard breath, "The security tag hasn't been deactivated."

Dale Senior began to put the tips back into the canister. "They're only, what, three dollars? Why would I steal a three dollar set of screw tips? And why would y'all be selling ones that're old and rusted out?"

The manager gave in and let them go. As they walked out the door,

Dale Senior commenced a tirade. “I should sue this company for harassment. I didn’t defend my country in Korea to be treated like a criminal or like those junkies from Nam…”

Once out of the store and far enough away from the exit, Dale Senior said, “That was harder than I thought.”

John stopped. “You stole those screw tips?”

“Not all of them. I brought three old ones with me and put them in the case.”

“Why didn’t you just dump the news ones out into your pockets and leave the case?”

“Why would I have done that?”

“So it wouldn’t have set off the security alarm.”

“That’s a good tip. I’ll remember that.”

The ride back was uncomfortable for John as he sat and listened to Dale Senior describe the encounter with “those faggots.” He was so enthused with reliving the events that he didn’t reach out and snatch the air for the non-existent stick-shift, or stomp his left foot over the clutch-less floorboard. Eventually, the story grew old, even to Dale Senior. John rolled his window down, rested his arm on the door, and felt the wind trace through the hair on his forearm. The brim of his baseball hat shielded the sun from his eyes, but he could feel it hot on his mouth and chin.

“Dale?” he asked.

“Senior.” The older man swerved to avoid a pothole.

John’s shoulder hit the door. “What?”

“Dale Senior.”

“Yeah, okay, Dale Senior, I wanted to talk to you about something.”

“The Dodgers are playing.” He began to fiddle with the radio. The stations switched from static to gospel to talk radio. “You a Dodgers fan, John?”

“Yeah, sure.” John said, though he preferred the Giants.

“I’ve been a Dodgers fan since they were in Brooklyn.” Dale Senior located a station with the game on and turned the volume up until the deep bass of the announcer’s voice vibrated in the speakers. They were down by four in the eighth inning. The old man kept on looking at the radio as if it were a television, as if his prolonged glances would change the score. He missed a stop sign and screeched to a halt in the middle of an intersection.

The seatbelt crushed into John's hipbones. "Do you want me to drive so you can listen to the game?"

"They must have just put that sign up. It wasn't there before."

There was no point in talking to Dale Senior about marrying Karen if he wasn't going to make it out of the truck alive. They turned onto a narrow street where cars were parked on either side of the road and only one car could pass at a time. As Dale Senior barreled down the street, a Ford sedan came from the opposite direction. One of the cars would have to pull over into a vacant space in the lines of parked cars. Dale Senior beat his fist against the steering wheel.

"Damn!" He jerked the wheel to the right and the truck veered toward an open space by a fire hydrant.

John clutched the armrest on the passenger side door. His arms tingled down to his fingertips. He closed his eyes and waited for the sound of metal crunching. Whoosh. The Ford swept past them, only causing a gust of wind to hit the side of the truck. Dale Senior honked the horn and gave the finger out the window.

"Oh hell, son," he yelled over the radio, "that's two for me today, didn't get arrested and didn't die." He continued down the street, punching John on the shoulder as if they'd just shared a dirty joke. "Excitement like this doesn't come cheap. Let me give you a tip about dodging the law…"

Dale Senior went on, told John about how to suck on a penny to fool Breathalyzer tests. John stared at the road and counted the blocks to Karen's house in his head. There were nine. The engine growled as if it could barely carry its weight, and the rotten egg stench of a broken catalytic converter filled the cab. John felt like the twelve-year-old boy again, stuck in a hot space he couldn't escape with the dead catalytic converter emitting foul fumes like Aunt Louise, and Dale Senior's body just a few inches from his on the pew-like bench seat. What would happen when he asked if he could marry Karen? Maybe the old man would produce a pistol from the deep pockets of his twill pants and shoot John dead and it would all be over. Of course, if Dale Senior shot him with an old, rusted bullet, he probably could have talked his way out of a conviction. Eight more blocks to Karen's house.

Dale Senior turned off the radio and punched John in the shoulder again, "Hey, you hearing me, boy?"

A few yards in front of the truck, a bird flew into the street, low to the ground, almost buzzing the asphalt. Behind the bird, a cat leapt from between two cars and made an arc of white fur.

"Careful!" John pointed to the cat.

It landed in the middle of the street and looked ready to pounce again but whipped its head toward the truck. Its back arched. Its mouth opened and revealed a swatch of pink tongue. Dale Senior jerked the wheel again, but there was no space in the line of parked cars to swerve into. The cat's head disappeared under the front of the car and John heard something like a thud, like an apple that fell to the kitchen floor, and then a slight rise of the truck on the left side. It took Dale Senior a few moments to collect himself, to straighten the path of the truck and slow down to a stop.

"Did I hit it?" he asked John.

"I don't know," John said, but he did.

The men looked at each other. The engine idled, turned, and purred. John felt the vibration in the floorboards. Dale Senior's eyes began to dampen around the corners and his top lip jutted out like an eave.

"Did I hit that cat?"

John twisted in the seat until he could look through the back window of the truck. In the street, the cat was pulling itself toward the curb with its front paws. The tail and back haunches dragged behind—stained with an imprint of dirt on its white fur.

"It's still alive," John said. "Let's just go on home."

Dale Senior cut the engine. "No, that wouldn't be right."

"Come on, let's go!" Even if they took the cat to an animal hospital, it would probably die. "There's nothing we can do now."

The older man opened his door, climbed out, said, "No, I reckon it's my responsibility to take care of it," and slammed the door shut. Something scraped across the bed of the truck, metal against metal. He turned back to see Dale Senior walking away with a crowbar. In a second John was out of the truck, didn't close the door behind him.

"Dale Senior, what're you doing with that crowbar?" he asked.

The old man knelt on the pavement beside the cat, which had stopped moving. He poked it with the crowbar and flipped it over. Its legs fell limp to the side. Its tongue hung out over its fangs. The black pupils in its green irises were dilated. Its claws were extended from the pads on the feet. Even with the fur, John thought he could count its ribs.

"It's dead," Dale Senior said. "No tags. It must be a stray."

John patted him on the shoulder. "Let's go back to Karen's and call animal control. They'll come get it."

Dale Senior extended the crowbar toward John, "Here, hold this."

John took the crowbar and Dale Senior went to the ground on one knee like he was proposing. For a moment his head hung down and wagged from shoulder to shoulder. Then, he reached forward and got a hold of both of the cat's back legs.

"I don't think you should touch it," John said.

Dale Senior lifted the body up by the legs and walked back to the truck. John followed with the crowbar and thought about how bad it would look if someone had shown up at that point, having missed everything else: an old man carrying a dead cat, a younger man walking behind him with a crowbar. Especially in their work clothes, they'd seem like rednecks who'd just caught dinner. Dale Senior laid the cat down in the bed of the truck, took the crowbar out of John's hands, and threw it next to the body. John wished the cat's eyes would close. They stared up into the sky as if asking how it could have happened; what had the cat ever done to the truck, to Dale Senior, or to John? The rest of the ride to Karen's house was silent. They pulled in front of the house. Dale Senior stood beside the car until John found the flapper in the hardware store bag under the seat.

"All right then," Dale Senior said. "Karen should have a shovel in the garage. Why don't you go look."

John turned to him. The sun had descended below the tree line and cast a glare behind the man's head so John couldn't read his face. "I don't think that's a good idea."

"Don't worry. I'll take care of it. I've done this before."

"You can't just bury a dead cat wherever you want."

"Then I won't bury it," Dale Senior said. "You go on in and install the flapper. Tell my daughter I'll be inside in a little while."

Karen was in the kitchen cutting up potatoes. She'd put her hair up with a clip, but a few strands had fallen out and lay against the nape of her neck. The sun came through the window and made her blond hair look red and her pale skin glow. John set the flapper on the kitchen table and came up behind her. At the sound of his boots, she looked over her shoulder.

"What took you so long?" she asked. "Did you get the part?"

"Yeah, I did." He wrapped his hands around her waist and rested his face onto her shoulder.

"Did you tell him?"

"Well, I didn't really get the chance." John went to the fridge and pulled out a beer.

She set the knife down on the cutting board. "How didn't you get a chance? You all were gone forever?"

"Well, I lost him in the store and then…" John twisted the beer cap off and threw it into the garbage. He wouldn't tell her about the screw tips. "And then, on the way back, your dad hit a cat with his truck."

"Is it all right?" she asked.

"No," he said. "It got hit by a truck. It's dead."

"Poor kitty." She turned back to the counter. "I think I'm going to put some cayenne in the potatoes."

"Karen, honey." John took a swig of beer. "He brought the cat with him."

"What?" The knife slammed back on the cutting board and she turned to him with narrowed blue eyes. "You let him bring it here?"

"Well, it's in the back of his truck." He gestured with the beer. A few drops flew out and landed on the kitchen floor.

"Jesus Christ, John!" she said, either about the spilled beer or the cat. He couldn't tell which one.

"I'll get it," he said and ripped a paper towel off the roll to clean up the spill.

"Go out there and tell him to leave it in the truck. I don't want a dead cat anywhere near my house."

John squatted down and mopped up the few drops of beer with one swipe. She was standing over him with her hands on her hips. "Karen, this isn't my fault."

"I know," she sighed, took the paper towel from his hand, and tossed it in the garbage.

John stood up from the floor. "He said he wasn't going to bury it. Let's just call animal control or the health department or something and have them pick it up."

"I don't want a health department van parked outside of my house."

John set down the beer bottle on the counter and took a few slow breaths. "What do you want me to do?"

She fluttered her hands at her sides and brushed back a lock of hair from her forehead. "Just, go out there and see what he's doing."

The bed of the truck was empty except for the crowbar and a blood stain, which looked black in the dying light. John crossed around to the back of the house. The dogs in the neighborhood were baying in their yards. It seemed every house on the block had a mutt going wild, not the usual barks of boredom, but something desperate. Even the next door neighbor's poodle was scraping against the screened side door, shrieking and growling. When John reached the backyard he smelled something burning. Dale Senior stood at the back of the yard, by Karen's compost pit, holding the red plastic container that held the gas for the lawn mower. He tipped the contained and a thick stream of fluid fell onto the earth, where a figure—already on fire—burst up higher in flames.

"What are you doing?" John yelled over the barking dogs. He paced and ran his hands through his hair. His hat fell somewhere on the grass. "That's not the cat, is it? Tell me that's not the cat!"

Dale Senior spit a stream of tobacco beside the fire. "I told you I wasn't going to bury it. You were right. You don't want dogs coming in the yard and trying to dig it up. Boy, is that a mess."

The smoke off the body was thick and opaque, but the fire was dying.

"You can't cremate a cat like this," John said. "Do you know how hot a fire has to be to burn up all those fluids?"

"I got more gasoline," Dale Senior said. "And it's just a skinny little cat."

The fire was finished eating through the fur and skin, was simmering over the muscles and melting the fat. Dale Senior emptied the can of gasoline onto the lit cat, but it was no use. The fire went out and the two men stood staring at the charred figure. It didn't look like a cat anymore. The green eyes had become crisp and black. They had never closed. John took a few steps backward and his throat constricted as he fought the opening of his stomach. He leaned against the shade tree and spewed out the few ounces of beer he'd drunk. It frothed over the roots of the trees and sank into the soil.

Lauren Titus

Lauren Titus earned her MFA from Spalding University in 2005. She lives and writes in her hometown of Louisville, Kentucky.

Genesis for *Tip of the Screw*

Years ago, a boyfriend told me how he and a friend of his had tried to cremate a cat after accidentally hitting it with a car. It haunted me for months. Were they trying to erase their guilt? Were they prone to sociopathic behavior? Did they really think it would work? I couldn't resolve their intentions. I couldn't forget about a dead, half-cremated cat that I'd never seen. There were reasons I was haunted by the story, some of which were beneath the surface of my thoughts. I wrote *Tip of the Screw* to explore my preoccupation with the story and its connotations.

The 30th Annual Naming of Boy Howell

Matt Jaeger

The living room began to fill with guests, mostly members of the congregation, all of whom milled in circles, chewing and talking through their food. Boy Howell, the guest of honor, just a week shy of turning twenty-nine years old, sat by himself in the corner beside a sagging, upright piano. Even sitting, he was taller than the piano, taller than the empty vase on top of the piano, but he sat still, quietly, as if trying to fade into the wall. Over his lap he held a small, Styrofoam plate of finger food, but he stared out the window instead of eating.

A single framed photograph of the family who lived there—mother, father, and son—hung by a string on a nail directly over Boy's head. Otherwise, the walls were bare.

The young preacher, new to the church, had arrived at the same time as a large contingent of his congregation but quickly found himself sharing the green, tweed loveseat with Boy's mother, Bebe. She'd insisted, patting the seat beside her when he introduced himself. Her bracelets and upper arm jiggled. She was a stout woman, nearly as wide as she was tall, and wore a faded flower dress which clung to each of her bulges and crannies—each time she shifted or breathed she looked like an entire garden in the active process of wilting. Her bulk formed a sloping crater in the loveseat's cushions, and as she talked the young preacher draped himself over the couch's arm, struggling, pulling, to keep from sliding into the hole or at least to maintain a hair's width distance between himself and the hulking woman. He gave up and finally resigned to lean against her, sitting flush against her moist, bare arm and shoulder.

Bebe Howell gave no indication that she minded or even noticed. She pulled apart chunks of sweating meat with her fingers and stuffed the shreds in the pouches of her cheeks as if storing them for later. "Do you think it's a sin that Boy ain't got no real name?" she asked, her voice edged with an expectant casualness and mouth half-filled with food.

The question caught the preacher off-guard. He stuttered through the theology of it in his head. He was well-schooled in scripture, could quote most biblical text when prompted with only chapter and verse, but he struggled to think of a passage pertinent to Mrs. Howell's question, wrestled to know the mind of God in the matter, which made him feel increasingly green and ill-equipped.

"Way I see it," she said, not waiting for the answer, "if he should up and die, God can just give him a name, all-knowing as He is. I'm growing real tired of being in charge."

Two more guests walked through the door, a husband and wife, and approached the loveseat as if it was a throne. The woman bent to kiss Bebe on the cheek and handed her a gift wrapped in shiny gold paper with a curly mound of rainbow-colored ribbon on top. "This is for Boy," she said. "It's a silver cup. He can get it engraved whenever he's ready."

Bebe thanked the woman and told her she was sweet. "And your new hair-do," Bebe said, "makes you look a hundred years younger."

"I love it," the woman said. She thumped her husband on his chest with her open hand. "Francis, here, isn't so sure. But he'll just have to get used to it, won't he?"

Bebe laughed and wiped at the corners of her eyes with a food-stained paper napkin. The husband looked at the preacher and winked. The preacher smiled, and wondered if it would've been proper for him to bring a gift as well.

The couple retreated to the line at the food table. Bebe slid the gift under the couch with all the other presents and resumed her simultaneous talking and eating. "I was just sure Boy was gonna die the minute he was born. Doctor said he wasn't developed all the way, and they took him from me. Put him in one of those inkabators like they do chicken eggs. Looked like a little glass coffin is what or one them plastic boxes they put corsages in." She pointed at Boy with her fork. "Except a tad bigger, I guess."

She offered the preacher one of her cocktail weiners. He refused politely.

"My husband, Gerald, started calling him Peter right then and there. He said that Peter meant 'The Rock,' and if we started calling him 'The Rock,' maybe he'd start acting like one." Her voice lowered as if she prepared to tell him a secret. "But they took him from me, and I just couldn't put a name to that sick, little face. I told Gerald we should wait. No sense in wasting a name. See if he even lived long enough to need one." She took a bite of something smothered in gravy. "That kind of stuff's hard on a mother, naming something that's gonna die anyway. You understand that, don't you?"

The preacher nodded, not knowing if he truly meant to agree and then cocked his head in an effort to look supportive, certain that it wasn't right to contradict her.

"I know he's sick now because they wouldn't let me touch him for that first month, let alone hold him. All that lost time. That just ain't right. It's their fault. I told them nurses that a boy needs to be with his mother, needs to sleep on her chest and hear what her heart sounds like and stuff. He needs to do that at least whether he's gonna die or not."

She began to gnaw around the bone of a fried chicken wing, turning it in her fingers like a spit. "I reckon that's why he never took to the breast," she continued. "Them nurses said he'd pick it up just fine, but he always had a fit when I fed him. Oh, he'd suck all right. Like a Hoover. But he'd spit it all up like it was poison or something."

The conversation turned the preacher's face the red of raw beef, and he tried once again to pull himself from her side. She looked at him and smiled. Her tongue flickered like a baited worm from between her lips to lick at the corners of her mouth. Her eyes, too small for her broad face, like glinting black pinheads, yanked him into their sunken stare. "I don't know much, but if there's one thing a mother knows," she said, "it's what her boy needs. Boy should've been with me from the get go. He needed my heartbeat to get him going with the spin of the world, and he needed his mother's milk just like a wanderin' Jew needs manna from heaven. Don't you think so, preacher?"

The preacher dried his palms on the front of his trousers. This wasn't a conversation he'd ever prepared himself to have. He was a bachelor; no children of his own. He'd seen a woman's naked breast only once and that opportunity quite by accident while visiting his aunt as a teenager. He thought of his own mother and cringed with distaste at the image of himself ever breast-feeding, unable to fathom that his mother had ever been that intimate with him. She was a gaunt woman, thin as a wire hanger, who demanded that idle time be spent scrubbing baseboards or reading aloud from the Bible. "Not too loud, though," she would say, "but loud enough so I can hear you from the kitchen."

She'd always handed down commandments in this way.

Bebe Howell jutted out her chins and widened her eyes, awaiting his response. "Sounds right to me," the preacher finally managed. He stuffed a handful of grapes in his mouth, biting them to let the juice escape so he'd have an excuse not to say any more.

"Yep, that's what I think," she said, looking pleased. She tilted in close to him. "Between you and me," she said, "deep in my heart, way down deep, I knew it was gonna be a struggle with Boy even after he got out of the inkabator." She lowered her voice even further. The heated breath of her words slid into his ear. "'Cuz when they handed him to me, his head was still all squished up like a Hershey's Kiss."

She leaned back on the sofa and stared straight ahead. The preacher recognized her attempt at a smile, though the corners of her lips were still turned down. She put her hand on the preacher's knee and squeezed. "That don't mean I love him any less, though," she said loudly, as if wanting the whole room to hear, then used his knee to push herself up from the loveseat and walked away without excusing herself.

If Bebe Howell hadn't pointed him out, the preacher never would've guessed that the young man by the piano was Boy. He'd been told by others that Boy had been sick all his life, but others in the room looked far more infirm. A pair of them, a grayed, stubbled-faced man with no left arm and a pear-shaped woman with a shiny bulbous growth on her neck, chatted in the doorway. A wrinkled shell of a man sat by the door, a metal air tank propped beside him; he alternated between sipping from a plastic cup of red fruit punch and cupping a plastic oxygen mask over his nose and mouth. A sunburnt, greasy-haired girl, probably six or seven years old, scratched at an angry wound on her leg, then reached into a glass dish of buttermints on the windowsill.

Even Boy's parents looked far worse than he. Bebe, through every seeming fault of her own, seemed, at the very least, on the verge of a heart attack, if not a full-blown explosion. The preacher watched her walk from the room. Her ankles spilled over the sides of her soft-soled shoes, and that flowered dress, which looked to have been made from old bedsheets, strained around her rump with each step. The man whom the preacher took to be Gerald, the father, had spent the better part of the early evening bent over the food table slowly sticking toothpicks into cubes of orange cheese. Twice, the preacher caught the old man staring at him. Gerald was tall and gawky-limbed with a long, drawn-out face that looked to have the constant countenance of a man just roused from a deep sleep. His eyes, hardly visible from the preacher's seat, were rimmed with black bags and appeared to have been dropped into their sockets from a great height.

Except for paleness in his cheeks, Boy looked fine. Healthy as a horse, the preacher thought. If good qualities were to be had from his parents, Boy had received them in just the right doses—the height of his father and girth of mother combined to create an enviable goliath of a son. Boy was massive compared to the preacher; his frame completely hid the chair in which he sat which made him appear to be maintaining a hovering squat over the floor, supported only by the balls and heels of his feet. He wore brown hiking boots and blue jeans, and the muscles in his arms bulged from the short sleeves of his white t-shirt. Like the preacher, Boy sported a beard and mustache, though it was much fuller and more even-colored than the preacher's. If the young preacher had passed Boy on the street, he would've thought him to be a truck driver or lumberjack. The preacher knew he and Boy were roughly the same age. Watching him now, the preacher considered Boy a superior specimen, a virtual miracle considering his lineage.

Through the course of the evening, Boy didn't move. All the guests had taken a turn in greeting him. Some had tentatively shaken his hand or patted him on the shoulder. None of them pulled up a chair for a chat. The preacher realized he was guilty of the same, but felt justified because he'd been forced into a similar solitude. Besides Bebe, no one had talked to him either. She now stood in the middle of a large, laughing group of ladies, their collective voices like a pack of dogs. Gerald stood behind her; he held on to the top of a doorjamb and rocked himself back and forth. The plate Boy had held on his lap, now rested on top of the piano, still untouched. He read a comic book, his lips moving soundlessly with the words. The preacher could see the crimson leotard of the hero on the front cover.

"You met my husband yet?"

The preacher jumped in his seat. The voice felt as a slap across his cheek. Bebe stood before him; a lavender flower on her bosom was level with his eyes. He looked up to her face, trying to disguise his shock that such a heavy woman had been able to sneak up on him. She held a plate of food in her hand. The preacher tilted his head back farther to see Gerald's face, and the tall man extended a large, square hand to him.

"This is Gerald," she said. The man's handshake was much limper than the preacher expected.

"Forgive me," Bebe said, rolling her beady eyes. "I got so many names in my head that I up and forgot yours."

The preacher made to stand, but Bebe put a hand on his shoulder keeping him in place. "Jacob," he said. "Pastor Jacob."

She began laughing, holding her stomach as if to keep it from splitting open, then smacked Gerald across his chest with the back of her hand. "I told you he had one of Boy's names. Jacob. I should've remembered. How old was Boy when we give him that one? Fifteen?"

"Seventeen," Gerald said.

"Was that the year he got the gout?"

"Appendix burst. Timothy was the gout. Year after that was Philip, and Boy's retina got itself detached."

"You're right," she said. "Absolutely right."

Gerald nodded once at Jacob and walked away. He sat in the recliner across the room, kicked up the footrest, and leaned back, fully extending himself. His legs hung a good foot off the end of the chair into the middle of the room.

Bebe took up her place on the loveseat again. Jacob slid into her side. She removed a clean paper napkin from her bra and spread it over her lap like a picnic blanket. "Gerald don't look so smart," she said, "but he can remember each one of Boy's names and each one of his 'flictions. His mind is like a mouse trap. I can only remember some of them. Jesus, Gerald even remembers how much Boy weighed when he was born. Can you imagine having a mind like that?

"We always tried to give Boy a good Christian name. Straight outta the Bible. The kind of name God himself would give him," she continued. "You appreciate that, don't you preacher? A good Christian name gives him a strong foundation. It's the least we can do." She popped a raspberry tart in her mouth. "We've named him most of the disciples, I think. Not Judas, though. That would be mean. Probably give him cancer. Except for getting himself sick all the time, Boy's never been a lick of trouble."

She sighed and stopped for a moment. Her shoulders humped forward, and her plate hung loosely in her hands, threatening to topple. She looked at nothing in the room, but her eyes appeared to be searching for something, something far off that she couldn't quite see. "One of these days we'll find a name that sits right with him," she said with a softness Jacob hadn't heard all night.

Jacob struggled to pull his arm from her side. He put his hand on her shoulder. "Are you still afraid he's going to die?" Jacob asked. It was all he could think of to say.

She looked at him and huffed out a deep breath. "Used to be," she said. "Them baby years were tough. Those years I remember. Gerald calls them the Gospel years. First year we named him Matthew, and he fell asleep with a pillow on his face. Year two was Mark, and he got his little neck stuck in the banister. Nearly hung himself. Luke was the year he wandered into the deep end of the neighbor's pool. Luckily, Gerald was in the Navy." She swiped her hand across her forehead in a comic sign of relief. Her old voice had returned, loud and boisterous, any hint of tenderness gone. "And ten seconds after we named him John, he swallowed a quarter."

"Nope, I haven't been really afraid since we got him baptized." Bebe sat up in her seat. "What'd we name Boy that year we had him baptized?" she called across the room. "You hearing me, Gerald?"

"Adam," the old man said mechanically, still prone in his recliner.

She turned to Jacob. "We thought we had a good one with Adam. Boy seemed fine for two whole weeks afterward, so we bought him a suit and got him baptized. Turned out he had hookworms the whole time. We just didn't notice. We took back the name, and them worms cleared right up." She pounded her thick fist on her thigh as she talked. "It may not be proper that Boy don't have no name right now. Way I see it, though, you can't take back a baptism. Washed in water and Boy is clean. Free and clear. All of us. Once a child of God, always a child of God. Don't you think so, preacher?"

Jacob didn't know if she was right or not but refrained himself from shrugging.

"And if he ain't a child of God," she said, "at least he's his Mama's Boy. That's just as good."

Across the room, Boy still sat by piano looking at the ceiling, his thick arms folded across his chest.

An older woman in a turquoise dress and matching eyeshadow approached the green, tweed loveseat. Her hands were clasped in front of her, and she bent at the waist to level her eyes with Bebe. "Is it time yet?" she asked hopefully.

Bebe looked at her wrist. She wore no watch. "It's getting there. I suppose we can go ahead."

The older woman clapped her hands. "Any hints this year?"

Bebe shook her head.

"My money's on Samson," the older woman said.

Bebe drew her fingers across her mouth as if closing a zipper. "My lips are sealed," she said. "And don't go pressing Gerald for information either 'cuz I haven't told him a thing."

"Gerald let it leak last year," Bebe said to Jacob, "and Boy had a seizure before we even told him. Good name, too. Elisha. Almost ruined the party."

"That was a good one," the turquoise woman said.

As she tried to push herself from the couch, Bebe's food plate upended, spilling its contents down the front of her dress. A strawberry lodged itself in her bosom. The older woman in turquoise gasped and reached to remove it. Bebe slapped her hand away. "Leave it alone," she said, and she clapped her hands together. "Help me up."

Jacob stood, and he and the older woman each grabbed one of Bebe's hands and pulled. Bebe grunted until she was on her feet. The strawberry slipped from her bosom and fell through her dress to floor, coming to rest between her feet. Bebe abandoned it there, and leaning back, she walked to the center of the room. "Gerald," she said loudly. "Get over here." Then more loudly she said, "Attention everyone." She waved her hand in the air. "Look at me."

The room trickled to silence, and the guests circled around her. They bent toward Bebe with their eyes wide, mouths open. "Now's as good a time as any," she said and waved Boy over. The crowd began to applaud. Jacob caught himself joining in the clapping and put his hands in his pockets.

Boy stood and crammed his rolled comic into the back pocket of his jeans. Seeing him at full height was impressive. He towered above everyone, and the crowd split in the middle to let him pass. Those on the outside had to press themselves against the wall. Even the gawkily tall Gerald looked dwarfish next to his son.

Boy moved in beside his mother. The top of her head reached the center of his torso. She slung her meaty arm around his waist.

Jacob prepared himself for her speech, but there wasn't one. Bebe sipped at a cup of punch and cleared her throat. "If you please," was all she said.

The wrinkled old man who sat by the front door drumrolled on his oxygen tank.

Bebe reached into the front of her dress and pulled out a small square card, then peeled a piece from the back of it and slapped it on Boy's chest.

The drumroll stopped and all was quiet for a few moments except for wrinkled old man sucking air from his mask.

"That's a good one, Bebe," a woman finally said. Gerald, the father, nodded approvingly. The crowd erupted in applause and whistles.

Jacob squinted to see the letters on the nametag. It read: Hello, my name is Balthazar.

The woman in turquoise snapped her fingers in disappointment. "I never would've guessed that one," she said. "Not in a million years."

Boy yanked the tag from his shirt and stared at it, holding it at arms' length. "Who the hell is Balthazar?" His voice was higher pitched than Jacob had imagined, but still commanding.

"One of the Three Kings," Bebe answered, "and I'll thank you very much not to cuss in front of our guests."

"Heck of a name," someone said. "It suits you well, Boy."

"Strong name."

"Yes, one of the Wise Men."

Boy stared at the name a little longer. "I don't like it," he finally said.

Collectively, the crowd groaned, including the young preacher, Jacob. He felt as if he had been punched in the chest and his stomach began to churn. Boy, too, looked collapsed. He slouched in the gut, his arms hung down at his sides. His pressed lips were ghostly white while his cheeks had flushed a frightening red. He began to cry and looked as if he might throw up.

Bebe took a step back and watched him warily.

"I'd like to be called Gary," Boy said. "You know that."

"It ain't a proper Christian name," Bebe said.

"I don't care about proper. I'd like to be called Gary!" He stomped the ground like a counting horse.

Bebe shook her head.

Boy flexed his jaw and clenched his fists, looking as if he might strike. Bebe's eyes flickered with a fire, and then softened. She smiled and took his fist, rubbing the back of it with her thumb until he opened his fingers.

"I love you," she said, "but you don't get to name yourself. It just ain't how it's done. Naming is a job for God and for mothers, and Balthazar is the name I chose this year."

Boy covered his face with his hands, turned, and ran for the front door, his legs now as unsteady under him as a foal.

Gerald, seeing his son's intended path, opened the front door, and Boy ran past him and down the porch steps. Jacob watched him go. Boy's large body shook with sobs. Only his white t-shirt was visible in the dark as he ran farther down the walk. His cries, like the whining wail of a siren, became increasingly faint.

Jacob himself started to run for the door, but Bebe's thick fingers wrapped themselves over his shoulder and stopped him. "Don't bother," she said. "We used to run after him, too, but it don't make no difference. He won't get far. It's the damndest thing, don't you think? I wish I understood it."

Jacob stooped under her grasp, releasing himself, and Bebe moved to the loveseat she'd earlier shared with him. She let herself fall in the middle of it, not leaving room for a companion on either side. She spread her arms over the back of the small couch. Her stomach bulged in front of her. She sighed with a loud huff, wanting the room to know how broken and exhausted she was.

The guests began to collect their things: their purses and coats and empty platters of food. Several of the women carried stacks of plates and plastic cups into the kitchen. Then they began to leave, person by person, first stopping at the loveseat to pay homage to Bebe and wish her good luck. "We'll be praying for you," the woman in turquoise said. Bebe stayed seated and held out her hand to be shook. Soon, Jacob was the only one left in the room.

Outside, Boy's crying stopped abruptly.

"What's he done to himself?" she asked flatly. "Someone run over him?"

Gerald stood in the doorway. He shielded his eyes, though it was dark. "Tripped on the edge of lawn and hit his head on the fence, looks like."

"That's not so bad," she said. "At least it ain't a disease. That medicine can get expensive."

"Not bad at all," Gerald said. "We've had it worse."

"Yeah, an easy one this year. Maybe the easiest." Bebe considered things for a moment. "You know, I may not have been too far off with Balthazar," she said, her voice slightly perked. "Maybe he'd take to a 'B' name. We've been calling him Boy so long he's probably used to the sound."

"Benjamin maybe," Gerald offered.

"I like Barnabas," she said, "or Bartholomew. And next year we have those mini egg-rolls again. Those things were tasty."

The preacher thought of other "B" names—Balaam, Barabbas, and Beelzebub—but he didn't say them aloud. He didn't dare. It wasn't his place.

Bebe closed her eyes and clasped her fingers over her head. Gerald left the house, and a few moments later came back with the limp body of Boy slung over his back, Boy's feet dragging the ground behind him. The father strained under his son's body, and Jacob ran to help the child to bed.

Boy's bedroom was as stark as the living room, nothing on the walls. The desk was bare, and the wastebasket empty. They laid Boy on his narrow bed on top of the powder-blue comforter. His clothes were wet with dew, and Jacob began to remove them.

"He'll be all right," Gerald said. "He always is." He nodded and walked from the room.

Jacob was left alone to watch over Boy. A purple knot had begun to swell from the middle of Boy's forehead. His breathing was shallow. A beaded sweat had broken out on his face and neck. Jacob removed the comic book from Boy's back pocket and flattened it out on the night stand, then folded Boy's arms across his chest and tucked the sheets around him, tightly.

The young preacher thought it might be proper to close with a prayer, but still unable to think of anything pertinent, he simply wished Boy a good night. He left the room, closing the door quietly behind him, not knowing if Boy was asleep or unconscious. Either way, he thought it a blessing.

Matt Jaeger

Matt Jaeger lives and writes in Paducah, KY, where he also works as the Parish Administrator of Grace Episcopal Church. He is a graduate of Spalding University's Master of Fine Arts in Writing program, with an emphasis in Fiction, particularly short stories.

Genesis for *The 30th Annual Naming of Boy Howell*

It is not often that I can pinpoint the origin of a story. Concepts for stories come inexplicably, usually late at night, appearing as malformed ghosts made up of blinking images from the day's, week's, or year's events. The extent to which these concepts haunt me determines whether I recognize the impetus to actually take the time to create a story from them.

However, I distinctly remember the catalyst for *The 30th Annual Naming of Boy Howell* coming quite differently. That is, I formed most of the plot for the story while watching a Discovery Channel program on the history of Judaism, inspired in particular by a section describing the tradition of naming ceremonies, which in ancient times were instituted to allow a period of time (usually eight days) to ensure the survival of an infant before assigning a name. The result is my bastardization of that wonderful ceremony, which hopefully, within its manipulation, still contains some of the elements which would cause such a tradition to be formed in the first place.

Rabbit Blood

Mike Hampton

My first real love, Darlene, was bound to die in a car wreck. When I was growing up, it seemed that was all anybody could talk about.

Old men would sit on milk crates with their backs against the ice machine out front of Sailor Brothers' grocery store to watch her fly by. Their gray heads would nod one to the other and say, "She's going to catch it one of these days. Yes sir she is."

The worried heads of onlookers would turn in hopes of seeing a county sheriff or state trooper in hot pursuit behind her at last. But no police ever happened to be by to witness her tires screaming against the broken pavement of our little town and I loved her for it.

Darlene would wheel her Firebird up the blacksnake road that led through the hills past my house towards her home. My daddy said she was going to catch the gravel wrong one time when she was speeding up the curves, and flip her car over in the creek before anyone could help her. He had seen that kind of thing happen a hundred times since he worked on the volunteer fire department. But that wasn't what happened at all.

What happened to her had more to do with her ex-husband, Darrell, and her dog, the way she told it. She said it had to do with her daddy, and the state of emotion she had been in. But I think it was because she was a rabbit kind of woman. She had too much of that hot rabbit blood in her.

Before Darlene wrecked her Firebird, she used to pick me up most mornings during the summer when school was out and take me to her tattoo shop. My daddy had to know where I was going, but he never said anything. I was twelve then and old enough to make my own decisions in his eyes. Besides, he spent most of his time shooting pool or talking to his friends down at the fire department.

Her tattoo shop wasn't anything more than a concrete block room with a naked lady painted on the side of it, but it was all she had. She would pick me up because of how good I could draw. My pictures were all over the walls of her shop. "Flash" she called it. When the miners would come in to get Woody Woodpecker drilled into their arms or a big Apache chief, what they were pointing at were my masterpieces.

A19 on the wall was a skull I copied off of a Slayer T-shirt I saw at the county fair. I was spitting up heartbreak over some little girl when I drew it. H11 was a real nice looking motorcycle I drew when I was thinking about how bad I wanted one. Darlene liked all my pictures, but wanted me to learn Chinese writing since it was the big thing. I told her to go to hell, and didn't draw nothing but dragons for a week. No one had any say-so in my work but me. Drawing was something I had always been able to do since I was little. Tooth-marked pencils and Sharpie markers helped me leave my mark on the world.

Darlene wasn't kin to me, but it didn't matter. She lived on the same holler so it was just the same. Her daddy, Lucky, raised fighting cocks just up past Zion Baptist Church. He had won enough money fighting them to get her that Firebird. I told my daddy he ought to raise fighting cocks too, but he said he was a rabbit man through and through. Besides he said, fighting chickens are no good to eat. The way you have to keep them wired up on speed takes all the tenderness out of them. Rabbits were different. You could live on rabbit meat. That is if you got all that hot blood out of them.

For a rabbit man, my daddy did all right for himself. Sometimes he would make as much from them little bunnies as he did from his disability checks. I hated helping him with them but there was nothing for it. He explained the truth of the world good and clear. Sometimes you have to let pretty things go just to get by.

When I was younger, I walked out to the cages with him to help with the killing. My daddy would hold them fat papa bunnies up by their ears. Then he would crack their little heads with a crow bar till there wasn't any life left in them. Most of the time it only took one good stroke and they would jerk, and go off to their reward without as much as a yelp. After he had cracked one he would toss it on the ground, and it was my job to pass him the next. A big brown rabbit. Whack! A fat white one with dirty fur. Whack! He never saw a tear.

The first time I tried to argue with him, saying it was wrong and all since they were helpless, but he told me what he was doing was buying me my Christmas. It was a damn cold truth. My hands went into the cage and I turned my head. The trees were turning gold and brown like rotten apples, and I thought about getting a dirt bike.

"Here, whack this one, Daddy!"

The rabbits were the reason I met Darlene. I would take rabbit meat up to Lucky on Saturdays and he would give me pain medicine in a sandwich bag to take back to my daddy. What he was wasn't a doctor, but someone who knew about pain I guess.

When I met Darlene the first time, she was laying out in her backyard on a towel. She had a bikini on that was the color of dandelion fluff with the straps let down. Lucky wasn't home and her man was off on a long haul, so she was out back working on her tan.

"What you got there all wrapped up?" she asked as I made my way through the yard. The chickens started cussing and spitting at me from where they were pinned up in the yard. Fighting chickens are like that. It's in their blood.

"Just some rabbit meat for Lucky."

"Well he ain't here and I don't eat it." Her eyes were on the tops of the pine trees scraping against Heaven.

"I'm supposed to bring it for trade. We even went and took all the blood out for him." I looked down at the butcher paper all tied up with string.

"What do you mean you even took the blood out?" she asked over her big white sunglasses.

"You can't eat the rabbit blood." I said.

"Why not?"

"Daddy says rabbit blood is too hot. It puts run into you."

"So?" she said.

"It'll make you run too fast for your own good."

I smiled down at where her bikini straps hung loose under her arms. She was the first real girl I had seen that way. By then, she was almost out of high school.

Things could have gone one way or the other, but she wrapped the towel around herself and went inside. I waited in the yard while she got daddy's medicine for trade. Something inside of me made me shake like I was pissing on an electric fence.

"Here you go," she said. "Now don't you sneak around here no more."

"I won't come back again if you don't want me to," I said. The way she stood with her hands on her hips made her look like the girls I had seen on the calendar at the firehouse.

"I didn't say to stay away." She smiled the way girls did in the back of the school bus. "Just don't be a sneaking."

From then on out, Darlene and I were good friends.

Every day I would go up to her house and she would teach me about all kinds of stuff. We would practice kissing one day, then the next she would tell me about how to make a chicken real mean so when it gets in the ring you'd know it's a winner. She told me how love is just an excuse for people to stop living. I told her how drawing a perfect circle is about the hardest thing anyone can do.

She had herself a lot of sweethearts on the side by then. I wasn't interested in that though, since I was still young and kissing was all I could handle. Back then kissing was better than Christmas and dirt bikes put together. I would ride home from the tattoo shop with her in Lucky's truck, its tires kicking up gravel and pine needles, grinning like my daddy with a bellyful of medicine.

It was when Darlene got that Firebird, things started to change. She had quit school by then, since she owned her own business and they couldn't teach her nothing any how. She would pick me up to go draw for her, but we didn't talk much.

Her man, Darrell, had been asking questions about other men and where his checks had been going, she said. He had been talking to a lawyer in town too. It broke her heart. She would just smoke those big long cigarettes the whole way to the tattoo shop without so much as a glance my way. One minute she would say her man was the worst SOB she had ever seen. The next she would talk like he was the hero of us all. Love does that to girls.

Once we got to the shop, she would go off to get her hair done or talk to her pastor. She had papers to sign and a hell of a custody battle brewing over their little beagle dog. I started to do the tattooing for her when I had the chance.

The majority of the customers would shy away when they saw it was only me there with the gun, but not all. If the men were half-lit and hollering when they walked in, every once in awhile I could convince them that I was the man for the job seeing as I had drawn all the pictures hanging up in the shop. I always did my best work on the wild ones who let me drill into them; Jesus on the cross, dogs showing their teeth. None of them ever complained. I would sop the blood off of them with cotton balls while they praised my needlework. Then I would stuff their money in a jar Darlene kept under the table and hope she would be impressed. Most of the time though, she would just tussle my hair and take me home without so much as a "thank you."

Darlene let me practice tattooing on watermelons and cantaloupes out back of her shop when there wasn't any picture drawing to do. She said that was the best way to learn since they got pores like people do. The thing was you couldn't practice stretching the skin on them, though, which was real important. She told me I would never be a real tattoo artist until I learned to stretch the skin no matter how many drunks I needled. I didn't care what she said, though. All she did was trace down what I put on the walls anyway.

With summer ending, I was working real hard on getting my drawing down right. The tattooing was going slow since less and less people wanted a kid near them with Darlene's gerry-rigged tattoo gun. I started thinking about running away from home. Maybe getting an art scholarship to one of those schools I had seen on the television commercials. I was sure I had enough practice with all the wall drawing and needling I had done, so I sent away for an art test. It was for a real art school in Chicago. I had seen its commercial in between Gilligan's Island reruns. It made perfect sense.

Darlene got back to tattooing when the courts slowed things down. That gave me time to sit out back by the rotten cantaloupes, all scarred up with tigers and devils, and practice for my art test. I was torn between the turtle or the pirate. For awhile I just practiced drawing a perfect circle on some old grocery bags. But then I decided on the pirate and spent all day getting his earring and hat to look the way it did on the pamphlet the art school sent me.

I folded my test up real careful and gave it to Darlene to mail for me. It was going all the way to Chicago but she said I had a good chance. I agreed with her. I'd had extra practice drawing on the inside of the songbooks in church.

Darlene's man, Darrell, had taken off trucking long enough to settle things with her once and for all, but he never seemed to make much headway. One night I would see him in her car when she drove by my house, the radio would be blaring and their arms would be gliding out the windows in the breeze, then the next day I would hear her yelling into the phone about how terrible a man he was. He would yell so loud back at her from wherever he was that it would come through the receiver and echo off the walls of the shop. He would name men I had never heard of, call her every bad name he could sputter, but he would never hang up. He would just go on being hateful till she would tear up and slam down the phone. Love does that to men.

The last day of summer, my daddy was sitting on the porch brushing out the fur he had pulled off some bunny after the fact. He watched me walk up from where Darlene dropped me off at the bridge, and shook his head.

"Son, come over here," he said as he wiped his hands clean on his jeans. He had one of them rabbit's shirts dangling in his hands, bleeding in the breeze.

That was when he told me about Lucky's troubles and that I couldn't see him or Darlene anymore. He told me to act like I never even heard tell of them. The sheriff had helicopters in the air. Deputies had been getting medicine from Lucky. He had heard all about it at the firehouse.

The next morning cruisers from the county and the state filled up the parking lot of Zion Baptist church. Reporters had driven in from Hazard for the Mountain News. All I could hear were sirens and the sound of those fighting cocks tearing at their cages to get at the police. By the time it was dark outside, everything was still as Sunday morning again. Out barefoot in the yard, I was spitting up heartbreak all over again.

Staying away from Darlene was something I couldn't do. I still had all my good drawings up at her shop. I wanted to know if she had heard back about my art test. I wanted to make sure she was all right. That was the way I loved her.

It took a while for me to figure out which school bus went by her shop, but when I did I went to see her. It meant walking home and catching hell, but it was worth it.

That morning I snuck some rabbit meat out of the freezer for Lucky. I figured he would be missing it when they sent him away. It thawed out in my backpack by the time the school bus got to her shop, but I figured it would still be all right. It just looked like those bags you see up on poles in hospital shows.

The shop was unlocked and empty. All my pictures were gone, and the only thing left was her tattoo rig lying by the trashcan with the battery missing. There was nothing there for me. I left the meat by the door of the shop and started down the road feeling like a fool.

At home, the porch lights were burning bright. Lightning bugs kicked along the tobacco rows. My daddy sat on the porch waiting for me, but went inside once he saw me cross the bridge. He knew where I stood and there was no use talking about it. Besides, without his medicine he was in no shape for fighting. Since Lucky had been taken away, he spent most of his time on the porch staring down the road, as if he thought Lucky might drive past at anytime. Sometimes he would stay up all night heartbroke and hoping.

Under the covers that night, I prayed for Darlene and the Art Institute of Chicago. Beagles howled off sad in the dark. My daddy's emergency pager from the firehouse started to beep so loud it made me have to pull the pillow over my head just to get some peace. I already knew what had happened.

Sunday morning I walked to church alone. My daddy had been up all night and didn't want to talk about it. He always spared me the stories about picking up heads off the highway or fishing somebody's kid out of a silt pond. No matter how bad I begged to know who got killed, he saved that for the Lord and the newspaper.

I walked to church, and as soon as I got within eye-shot of the doors Darlene's man Darrell took me by the arm. We were on the road before he said word one to me.

"We ain't together," Darrell said. "It was my damn dog in the first place. I told her. She should have stayed in school. I told her."

He was talking to the steering wheel as much as to me, rolling his window up and down for no reason at all.

When we made it to the hospital he told me what room she was in. He wasn't about to see her for fear he'd kill her. That was why he brought me he said. I walked in the closest thing to kin she had.

In the room they had her hooked up to all kinds of machines. She was covered with stickers. Her nose was raw and red. Her eyes looked like someone had just snuck up on her. The rest of her was all different colors of blue and green.

When she could, she told me about taking too much medicine for her pain and all, about wanting to steal her dog back from Darrell, about what they were charging Lucky with and losing control of her Firebird at the tree line. None of it made any sense.

"Why'd you run all the way out there to steal back a damn dog?" I wanted to say the things her daddy would have if he could have been there, but I was too hot at her.

"I don't know," she said. "It just came over me last night. I got all hot blooded at the world."

She told me she threw away my art test. She told me I was just a dumb kid. She told me about losing her tattoo shop to the bank. She told me to leave her be.

"Did you find the rabbit meat I left for your daddy at least?" I asked.

"Yeah," she said; "it was rotting out front of the shop. I told you I don't eat it."

Her eyes started to move away as sleep came over her. I pulled her arms over her chest like the angels in the church. With the marker I had brought for the songbooks, I started to draw on her while she slept. I stretched her skin tight like a real artist and drew a chicken like her daddy had on her face, standing strong and mean against the sun. I put a little heart on that chicken with my initials in it. The sun behind it was as close to a perfect circle as I've ever come.

After seeing her in that bed I never passed another bunny to my daddy, dirt bike or no dirt bike. There are things you can't explain in this life. Mysteries like perfect loves and people born with hot rabbit blood in their veins. Damn cold truths.

Mike Hampton

Mike Hampton holds a B.A. in English from the University of Kentucky, and a M.F.A. in Writing from Spalding University. His work has appeared in *3AM Magazine*, *Me Three*, *The Southeast Review*, and *McSweeney's*. He has completed his first novel, and is currently at work on a short story cycle which includes the story featured here. He lives in Cincinnati, OH with his wife, Allison.

Genesis for *Rabbit Blood*

Whenever a member of my family had a child, my Mamaw would make a quilt for the baby. This quilt was made up of scraps of materials that were carefully hand-sewn together to create an interconnected pattern. I still have the one she made for me, and it stands to remind me of the world of my childhood.

My approach to storytelling is much like my Mamaw's approach to quilting. I take scraps of memory, questions and curiosity, and sew them together as best I can without letting the stitching show.

Rabbit Blood is composed of several scraps of memory left from my childhood in eastern Kentucky. At one time my father did raise rabbits, attend Zion Baptist Church, and serve as a member of the volunteer fire department. One of my neighbors raised fighting chickens, and another's teenage daughter drove too fast up the holler in a sports car. Also, I once knew a woman who opened and closed a tattoo shop in under a week due to her problems with an ex-husband and drugs. These singular events are tied together and exaggerated in the narrative to compose the story as it appears in this anthology. This story, like my Mamaw's quilt, is a tribute to a world I remember fondly.

Creases

Jess Stanfill

As Billi Jo Hayes chews on her upper lip, she watches her mom, Sandra, leaning over the kitchen sink and realizes she has never washed dishes with her before. She imagines that it is something that most girls have done with their mothers so many times that they don't even give it a second thought. And yet, it has taken Billi twenty-four years to get to this place of realization. As she sits on the cool linoleum, she looks up at her mom washing dishes and watches for traces of herself.

Billi doesn't ask Sandra to come over to wash her dishes. "I'm baking brownies for my students and need a cup of powdered sugar for my frosting," Billi explains over the phone.

"Can't you run over here and get it yourself?" Sandra asks. Billi's apartment is only a couple miles from her parents' home.

"I've already got my pajamas on and stuff. I look like a wild Indian."

"Do you need it right this minute; or can you wait till 60 Minutes is over?"

Sandra enters the apartment without so much as a tap on the door and floats into the kitchen with an unopened bag of powdered sugar in one hand. Billi is startled at her sudden appearance and jumps. "Would it kill you to knock?" she asks.

"You need to keep that door locked. A bunch of riff-raff out there," she says, and scowls towards the door as if she expects they have followed her. "And kids running around everywhere, little ones even, when they ought to be in bed. I don't see how you put up with it." She lays the sugar on the table. "I wouldn't stand for it." She starts to settle herself onto a chair, but Billi stops her.

"Not that chair," Billi says. "The legs are wobbly." Sandra takes another seat at the kitchen table.

"It's not like I have a choice," Billi adds. "Besides, they don't bother me."

While Billi stirs together the ingredients for cream cheese cherry icing, she searches her mind for small talk to make with Sandra. The cherry juice turns the cream cheese pink; the icing looks nothing like the picture on the box of brownie mix. She hadn't expected her to stay, and she doesn't know what to say. Sandra has brought her own can of Dr Pepper with her, knowing Billi wouldn't have any. Without being asked, Billi gets a glass from the cabinet, puts ice cubes in it, and hands it to her. She knows Sandra doesn't like to drink from a can. Sandra tilts the glass towards the light to check for potential spots, then pours her drink in. The fizz sounds louder than usual and reminds Billi of the Alkseltzer her dad used to drink all the time when she was a kid.

"That doesn't look right," Sandra says, eyeballing the icing.

"I know." Billi smoothes the icing over the cooled brownies, then dabs her finger into the bowl. "It tastes good, though."

"Huh! It doesn't look good." Sandra pauses for a moment. Her eyes scan the pictures on the fridge and settle on a smeared set of small hand prints on a pink piece of construction paper. "When do you get Sunny back?"

"Tomorrow. I'm going to pick her up on my way home from school. I told Darrell to have her ready this time. Last time I picked her up, Lisa was there cooking dinner and then of course Sunny wanted to stay." Billi stops herself, shocked at how much she has said.

Sandra looks at Billi, but she turns away. "Do you think they'll get married?"

"Probably. I don't see why not; they've been dating almost a year now."

"I'll never understand it. You leave him, now he's ready to remarry, but you've not been on a date in a year. What sense does that make?"

"I reckon it don't make none," Billi says. She can't come up with an answer for herself, so she doesn't bother trying to explain it to Sandra. She has to get out of this conversation; it's choking her. "I bought another box of brownie mix to make with Sunny," she says in a steady voice. "She loves to help me cook." Billi hates the way she feels like she has to prove to Sandra that she's a good mother. She knows she shouldn't have to prove anything to her, and she feels pathetic for not being able to stop herself.

Sandra stands up and steps to the sink. She sweeps a hand out in front of her and points at the kitchen sink. "Will you look at this! Why do you let your dishes get like this?"

"I don't know. I hate washing dishes. They make me sick," Billi says.

"You going to wash them for me?" she asks, not expecting her to.

Sandra turns on the faucet, runs her finger under the stream of water to test its heat, and squirts dishwashing liquid into the sink without saying a word.

Billi covers the brownies with clear Saran Wrap and places them in the refrigerator beside a half case of beer. Her mouth is dry; she starts to reach for a beer but grabs a Diet Pepsi. She lowers herself onto the floor close to Sandra's legs and looks up at her as a child might do. The kitchen table seems too far away for her to sit at; she doesn't want to sit there and stare at Sandra's back. She examines her from head to toe and says a silent prayer that she should be as pretty when she reaches that age. Sandra's hair is still brown without a trace of gray, all one length, and falls into a casual bob just above her shoulders. With a damp hand, she pushes the hair behind her ears.

"Be careful," Billi says, tracing the tight, square design in the linoleum with her index finger. "There's knives in there."

She sits on the floor watching Sandra for awhile, but then feels guilty about sitting around while she washes her dishes. She gets up from the floor and goes into the living room. Wanting to play something Sandra will like, she scans her CD rack and pulls a case away from the thin, metal bars that hold it. She puts in a Rolling Stones disc, hits the shuffle button, and goes back into the kitchen. The sounds of "Get Off My Cloud" fill the small apartment and she sees that Sandra is smiling. That smile is something she always looks for—the flash of perfectly straight teeth beneath thin lips—but seldom catches. Billi wonders if she is remembering the way they used to dance around the living room to that song when she was little. Sometimes it seems easier to remember only the bad memories, and she tries to focus on the good every chance she gets.

She steps back up to the sink beside Sandra. "Here," Billi says, "I'll rinse and dry."

"Don't," Sandra says when Billi begins to twist the silver knob marked with a blue C. "You can't rinse in cold water."

"Why not?"

"You need hot water to get them good and clean."

"It'd have to be boiling to kill bacteria," Billi says as she turns the water as hot as it will go, letting the water run over the dishes, rinsing the suds away.

"I don't see how you've made it this long," Sandra says, "without washing dishes."

"I've washed plenty of dishes."

"Maybe some but not plenty."

Billi feels strange standing this close to her mom. They are side by side at the sink, and her kitchen seems smaller than ever. She shifts her weight back and forth on her feet and glances at Sandra's hands, ghostlike beneath the murky surface. She watches them for a moment and wonders what they feel like. She can't remember ever having touched her hands, although she knows she must have as a child. She looks at her own white hands, which the hot rinse water has turned pink. Then, she looks back at Sandra's hands rising from the dishwater and then submerging again. Her hands are wrinkled, and it surprises Billi. She has never noted any wrinkles on her face, but she looks over at her just to make sure. No, not hardly any wrinkles there. Billi is relieved. She thought maybe somehow she just hadn't noticed, but that isn't the case.

"What are you looking at?" Sandra asks.

"Nothing. I was just thinking of this song. Remember how we used to dance around in the living room?"

"Of course I remember," she says without looking back up. She scrubs the surface of a heart-shaped plate decorated with princesses and hands it to Billi. "I don't suppose you ever dance with Sunny."

"Of course I dance with Sunny. We dance all the time," Billi says, and it's true. Sunny loves to dance. Billi feels like the look on Sandra's face is filled with doubt, but she bites her tongue. She doesn't have to prove anything to her, she tells herself.

"How come your hands are wrinkly, but your face isn't?" Billi asks as she stacks the wet dishes in the dish drainer.

"What kind of question is that?"

"I don't know. I mean, I've never noticed you have wrinkles on your hands before. You don't have none on your face." Billi feels stupid now. Sandra is looking at her hands as though she is ashamed of them, and Billi hopes she hasn't hurt her feelings.

"I guess I've got wrinkles on my hands cause I've used them all my life," she says. "When you spend your life at home with your kids, you do plenty of cleaning." This comment hurts Billi; it echoes what her mom is always saying, that Billi should stay home with Sunny instead of finishing college. She says Billi is missing the best part of Sunny's life, and she is often scared that what she is saying may be true. She looks at Sandra's hands obscured beneath the surface and they look smaller. When she brings them back out of the water, they return to their normal size. Her hands are red from the warmth, lined with tiny wrinkles, and sturdy looking. Billi looks at her own hands, pink and thin, and feels like a failure.

Looking at her own hands, Billi remembers when Sunny was just a tiny baby and how she would sit examining her hands.

"Look, Mom," she had said, excited over her new discovery. "You'll never believe this. Sunny has the exact same creases on the palms of her hands as I do."

"They're the same as mine then," Sandra said and held both of her hands out, palms up. Billi looked at Sandra's palms and then back at her own. Then she looked at Sunny's again. All exactly the same. Except Sandra's hands looked stronger. Billi wondered how she knew the lines were the same. Had Sandra looked at their hands when she was just a baby, searching for similarities?

Sandra lifts an ashtray from the counter and heads for the trash can. The ashtray is a green ceramic number that reads Ireland on its side.

"I don't know why," she says, "you let everyone smoke in here. Doesn't make no sense to not smoke yourself, but to let everyone smoke this place up. You'd have a decent place if you didn't let those friends of yours trash it."

All Billi can smell is apple-scented dish washing liquid and brownies. "I don't let my friends trash it up." She watches the butts tumble into the trash can. She wants to tell Sandra that those ashes were left behind by Dwight, but she doesn't. She doesn't want to try to explain the guy she has met to anyone, especially her mom. Can't even imagine how she'd go about it. She wonders what Sandra's reaction would be if she told her Dwight is a coal miner.

She had first spotted Dwight down at the Kentucky-Tennessee state line at her favorite honky-tonk, The Creek Bank. He was standing near the bar with a striking, black-haired girl in skin-tight jeans hugged up beside him. When the girl left, she walked up to the bar, right beside him, and asked the bartender for a beer. Dwight turned to her and said something, but she couldn't hear him over the band. The girl on the stage was singing a cover of The Dixie Chicks' "Cowboy Take Me

Away." Billi was pretty drunk, and as he took her arm, leading her away from the band, she thought he sure was good-looking. He wasn't much taller than her, maybe 5'10", and slim. She liked the way he was dressed better than most of the guys at the bar; she knew that he had left his black, button-up shirt untucked in an attempt to hide the fact that he cared about what he was wearing. The top button of his shirt was undone and exposed a square, silver chain around his neck; any other guy would have had on a gold rope chain, if any necklace at all. His hair was short with a just-cut look and appeared light brown to her—the color Sandra would call dark blond. Beneath small, wire-rimmed, silver glasses were blue eyes as deep as any lake and full of just as much life. While she talked to him, she decided he was pretty nice, too. He asked her about herself and seemed surprised to find out she was a college student, a graduate assistant studying English.

"What in the world are you doing at a place like this?" he asked, but didn't wait for a real answer. "You don't much seem like you belong in here."

"I belong here as much as the next person," she said, and took a long swallow from her beer. The truth was that she didn't feel like she belonged anywhere. "You're the one who don't look like you belong here. You're not from around here."

"No," he agreed, "I'm a county over." He smiled at her, and she sensed that he meant to come off as holding back, but she had felt confidence flowing from his body as though it had materialized into a warm, invisible blanket. His teeth were perfect—just as they should be in a perfect face—beneath pouty, full lips that most girls wish they had. Billi considered his looks for a moment and then began to reevaluate her own appearance. The black-haired girl was prettier, she thought to herself, and wondered if she'd come back.

"Well, what do you do for a living?" she asked.

"I mine for coal."

Billi let the words soak in for a minute, chewing a little on her bottom lip. The way he had phrased that struck her as odd. She smiled back at him. "You mean, you're a coal miner?"

"Yeah," he said, amused with her smile. His eyes looked even deeper than before, his lashes darker, almost black. "That funny to you?"

"Hell, no," she said, and killed the rest of her beer for show. "You're talking to a coal miner's daughter."

That was the first night he spent with her, leaving behind only his cigarette butts in the ashtray and the smell of his body on her pillow. The next weekend had been the same, except there was a phone call in between.

Dwight does strip mining, which is real different than the deep mining her dad used to do before his accident. But Billi's afraid if she tells her mom about Dwight, she'll never hear from him again. She's been waiting for his phone call. It makes her feel strange; she's not had much interest in dating since she left Darrell a year ago. That would be her luck, she figures, to never hear from Dwight again. She wouldn't want to try to explain that to her mom. She knows Sandra would never say, "What happened to that nice Dwight guy you were telling me about?" No, she'd just assume that Billi had slept with him and he'd never called her back. Billi knows what Sandra expects of her.

Sandra sets the ashtray down on the counter beside the sink. "I'll wash this last so it doesn't get the water nasty." She goes back to washing the dishes in the sink.

And just like that, Billi feels words rising in the back of her throat so all of a sudden that she thinks she might very well vomit. The words don't even make it to the tip of her tongue, but instead settle in the back of her throat, making it hard to swallow. She wants to say, "Do you really wish I'd never been born," but she doesn't. She's afraid of what the answer will be. Billi picks up a faded dishtowel and begins to make circular motions along the inside of a bowl. She tries to remember how old she was the first time she heard those words but can't. Then she tries to remember the last time her heard them but can't remember that either. It's been a long time. She wipes the droplets of water from the bowl, but then continues to wipe its dried surface.

"I think that bowl's dry enough now," Sandra says. "As Tears Go By" is playing in the living room, and Sandra begins to hum along. Her hand rises out of the water. Her index finger is hooked around the handle of a blue coffee mug that says I'm a Kentucky Wildcat. As she reaches it towards Billi, time falls away, and all she can see is Sandra's finger around the trigger of her dad's pistol.

Billi had sat on the floor with her knees pulled up tight to her chest. Tears burned her eyes and her right cheek was red, still stinging. Sandra had said she was going to kill her; it was the first time she had ever said that, but the words weren't making sense to Billi. She couldn't even remember what they're fighting about. All she could do was cry, as the words "I wish I'd never had you, all I ever wanted was two kids" boomed through her head. By fifteen, Billi has heard this so many times that she hadn't waited to hear the rest.

She heard Sandra choking on sobs in the next room but couldn't make out what she was saying to herself. It sounded like she was hunting for something, tearing the room apart. But Billi couldn't imagine what she was hunting for.

Sandra appeared in the doorway then, blocking the light from the hallway. In one hand, she had Billi's dad's pistol; the other hand was closed tight. Her face was red, and tears streamed down her face like a flash flood. For the first time ever, Billi was really scared of her mom. She was crying too hard to understand what Sandra was saying, but she knew she had to get out of that room. Sandra stood in the doorway, sobbing and ranting. The only place Billi had to go was in her bathroom. As she pulled the door closed, she saw bullets spill from one hand as though in slow motion. Then she saw Sandra's finger, firm and solid, hooked through the trigger of the pistol. The image burned a permanent place in Billi's memory. She slammed the door.

She hugged herself as close to the white bathtub as possible, as far from the door as she could get. She waited for bullets to blast through the door. But then Sandra had begun to speak, and between sobs she explained that she was going to kill herself, that everything was all Billi's fault, that she had ruined her life. She told Billi she hoped she would be happy. Billi screamed and pleaded with Sandra until she couldn't breath. Fear and hurt filled her until nothing else existed. She was no longer scared for her own life, but instead, she was afraid her mom would die before she ever got to tell her she loved her.

Billi can't remember how it ended. Their sobs twined together—despite the locked door between them—until everything else vanished. All Billi can remember are Sandra's hands, the pistol, and the sounds of their tangled sobs; then the memory of that day blends into the shadows of her memory never to be spoken of again.

"Are you going to rinse this," Sandra says, holding the blue coffee mug, "or just stare at it?" She looks at Billi as though she doesn't know what to make of her, and sits the cup in the empty side of the sink. "Rinse that, will you?"

"Yeah," Billi says, and holds the cup underneath the hot water, swirling the water around the inside of the mug before placing it in the dish drainer. She wants to push the bad memories out of her head. She wonders why she didn't tell Sandra she loved her the day she had the pistol. She wonders why she never has. It seems the more she tries to put the past behind her, the more memories come back, and the more they confuse her. She's about quit trying to figure out where she went wrong. She can't remember back that far, she tells herself.

Now, when she does think about her relationship with her mom, she wonders how much Sandra is right about. Sometimes she tells herself that her mom is wrong, completely wrong about her. And she thinks for the most part this is true; she's proved herself. But then she thinks about how people say that a mother knows her child best. She takes a deep breath. She hopes everything Sandra has said about her isn't true. She doesn't mean it anyway, she tells herself; she only says that stuff when she's mad. Sometimes she's nice—most of the time, even. She releases the breath, careful not to draw attention to the sweat that she has felt pop out on her face.

"You want to come over tomorrow and help me and Sunny make brownies?" Billi asks. "She'd get a big bang out of that."

"I suppose I could," Sandra says as she sweeps her hand along the bottom of the sink, pulling out the last of the utensils. "Damn!" she says, and yanks her hand out of the sink so fast that water splashes onto Billi's shirt.

"What is it?" Billi asks, too scared to look, knowing Sandra has been cut but asking anyway.

"I cut my finger on a damn knife. I thought I'd got them all out of there." She is holding her index finger in the palm of her other hand. Her hand is closed and her knuckles are white. Billi imagines the creases are filled with blood, standing out on her mom's soft palm like the squiggly red lines on a road map. A thin ribbon of blood escapes her closed fingers and drips down her wrist. "Quick. Get me a towel."

Billi rushes to the linen closet, while "Paint It Black" is blaring in the background, and hands her mom a dishtowel.

"Not a white towel," Sandra says. She seems to have decided her cut isn't too bad, but Billi's stomach still feels queasy. Billi stares at the blood along Sandra's wrist as she hands her a navy blue dishtowel. She glances down at her own wrist, at the faintest scar imaginable, and can't hold back a cringe.

"It's not that bad," Sandra says, misinterpreting the look on Billi's face. "Quit looking like that. Doesn't look bad enough to stitch, but I could definitely use a Band-Aid."

Billi goes to the bathroom to get a Band-Aid from the medicine cabinet. She catches a glimpse of herself in the mirror, but slides the glass open so she doesn't have to look too long at her own tired and empty blue eyes. When she returns, she finds Sandra sitting on the wobbly chair at the kitchen table. She is sipping her Dr Pepper, although the ice cubes have melted and it looks watered down and flat. Billi wants to go to the fridge and get a beer, but she doesn't. She hands her the Band-Aid, then sinks onto the floor beside her despite the three solid, empty chairs at the table.

"I'm telling you what, Billi Jo," she says as she wraps the Band-Aid around the cut finger, "if you ever get out of this little place, I hope you get yourself a dishwasher. I don't think I'll be doing much more of this." She waves her bandaged index finger at Billi, and a small smile slides across her face, then is gone.

Billi searches her mom's face for traces of herself but can't find any. She wants to reach out, take her mom's hand, and study the creases of her palm, but she doesn't. "I will," Billi says, looking away from her mom, rubbing her scarred wrist, studying the tight square pattern on the linoleum. "I'm sorry. I never meant for you to wash my dishes."

Jess Stanfill

The daughter of an Appalachian coal miner and a liberal Yankee homemaker, Jess Stanfill grew up in Pine Knot, Kentucky, in a house her father built. Books and storytelling were the cornerstones of her childhood. A graduate of EKU, Jess is currently working on a collection of short stories.

Genesis for *Creases*

Creases is from a short story collection I've been working on for what seems like forever now. Way back when, I read Steinbeck's *Pastures of Heaven* and fell in love with the format: chapters that could be read consecutively as a novel or individually as short stories. Later I noticed that Mildred Haun's *The Hawk's Done Gone* and Gurney Norman's *Kinfolks*, among others, follow a similar pattern. I like the idea of opening a book up to any chapter and finding a complete story within, while also knowing that the story is part of a larger whole.

In 2002, I wrote a short story in which Billi Jo Hayes is the main character. Shortly after, I wrote another story whose character had a different name. Realizing the characters were for the most part—if not entirely—the same, I changed the second character's name to Billi Jo as well.

Then I wrote a third Billi Jo story. Then a fourth. And so on. Eventually, as my Billi Jo stories started to pile up, I began to envision them working either way—as short stories or as a novel when read as a whole. Although I write other, non-related stories and such, somehow I seem to always come back to Billi Jo.

In many ways, she's a lot like me. But at the same time, she is most definitely not me. Writing teachers tend to always say, "Write what you know." That's what I try to do. Billi Jo and I may share similar backgrounds, but she finds herself in situations I've never been in. So, where do the stories come from? My observations, my imagination, and so on. I was raised in a family that loves to tell stories, and I learned to listen closely at a young age, not just to my family alone but to every person I encounter. There are stories everywhere, and I store these stories inside my head. Sometimes they leak out through my finger tips.

Tabernacle of Love

Bev Olert

Burgess Bledsoe turns off High Street and gently glides the custom-painted midnight blue Camaro into the McDonald's parking lot. In the last hour they have circled down Main Street to the tobacco warehouse, up High Street, then back through the McDonald's parking lot at least a dozen times. Cruising is still the Saturday evening slow dance of youth in Limestone.

With each lap Burgess turns the volume on the stereo higher, trying to drown out Tela, his girlfriend's cousin. She lives in horse country, but twice a year her parents dump her on Stacy's family while they run off to some place with a nice beach. Hawaii, Tahiti, even Spain. Burgess is worn out by her non-stop jabbering about her friends and the mall and the damn sushi place that serves beer to minors over by campus. And those nasty clove cigarettes. He won't let her smoke them in the car. He can still hear her voice, pinched and whiney, over the Led Zeppelin.

"And in Lexington there is this bar, The Court House, and on Sundays they open just for teens, like juice and soda only, and they get the best bands to play, and all my friends and I meet up there and dance. It beats just riding around town in a car all night. No offense," she says. A few more times through town and Burgess figures he will have the music so loud that she won't be able to talk anymore.

"I just love the mountains," she says. She takes a deep gulp of air and starts back in. "You look just like Jim Morrison," she says, mostly to Curt, Burgess's friend. She reaches around the headrest to rub his shoulder and touch the back of his hair.

"I've been letting it grow long this summer," he says, never turning around.

Good God, is this girl actually trying to hook-up with Curt? Burgess thinks as he adjusts the rearview mirror to get a better look at Tela in action. Instead he catches his own reflection, his coppery blond hair spiked and cropped in a short buzz cut that all the seniors on the team wear. His high cheekbones are tanned with a few tiny freckles. His deep-set green eyes are rimmed with the faintest flecks of gold.

"Anybody want anything before we head to the movie?" he asks as they inch toward the speaker of the drive-thru window. "Four large Sprites," he says at the black speaker, pulling on to the pick-up window before he gets his total.

Stacy leans forward, rubs his arm and says, "Park on the side. We want to hit the little girls room."

Burgess Bledsoe and Curt Hardwick step into the thick hot night and help Stacy and Tela out of the low backseat. They watch the two girls as they walk off, their long brown hair swinging below their shoulders, matching Daisy Duke cut-offs, hips keeping time with the flip-flop, flip-flop of their sandals on the black asphalt. The two could pass for sisters.

Burgess watches as his friend sets up a bar in the front of the car. Curt reaches under the front seat and slides two pints from their brown paper sacks. "I had to drive thirty miles to Sterling just to get the Sloe gin," he says. "You can't get that at the bootlegger." Curt had also picked up a pint of Maker's Mark for himself. Burgess won't touch a drop of the alcohol. In training. A full-ride in basketball to Eastlake State in the fall. It's not U.K., but still, State is not bad at all. At least Gravesville is wet. There are several decent bars on the square, all within walking distance from Eastlake State's campus. Not like Limestone College. Here it is dry, not a legal bar or liquor store in the entire county. As Curt always says, why bother going to college in a town where you can't even party? It defeats the whole purpose.

Curt pops the lids off two of the Sprites and doctors them up with the gin until they are both a rosy pink. "For the ladies," he says before opening the whiskey for his own drink. He stirs with his finger. "Here come the girls. I'm gonna jump in the back. I've got something to stick in that Tela's mouth that will shut her up." He laughs at his own crudeness and takes a long drink off the pint of Kentucky bourbon.

Tela crawls in the back seat with Curt. "We don't have any drive-in movies in Lexington, but the new multiplex by the interstate has twenty movies in it, and you can order food that they deliver to your seat, and these little tables drop down from the back of the seat in front of you, like on an airplane," she says. They all nod even though none of the three has ever been on an airplane. Burgess parks the freshly waxed Camaro in the back row and adjusts the radio to the station where they can hear the movie.

"Nice car, Burgess," Tela continues, "Did you get it for graduation?"

"It's my brother's."

"And he lets you drive it? Must be nice."

"He's in the Army now, stationed down in Texas." Burgess misses Brooks, but taking over his old room and the car and Curt, Brooks' best friend, has made it a lot easier. Brooks didn't have much choice about the Army. He barely made it through high school. It was either join the Army or go to work at the gate factory. But Burgess, he has basketball. His ticket to college and out of the factory. He has earned it too. Even during grade school Burgess was up before daylight to practice his free throw or nail his lay up. You got to go the distance, Coach always said.

Curt is lucky, too. His dad owns the Chevrolet dealership, so he has a good job running the service department for him.

Burgess and Curt actually share joint custody of the Camaro while Brooks is enlisted. Curt drives Burgess the two-hundred mile round trip to Eastlake State College, three days a week, all summer so Burgess can attend his developmental classes, or he won't be ready to start college on his scholarship in the fall. Even though he was the leading scorer in the region, Burgess barely made passing grades in the basic classes. He has never taken algebra or chemistry. But State is catching him up on his English and history and biology over the summer. And Curt is tutoring him in life-skills on the side.

"We've got to go," Stacy says abruptly after the first movie.

"The best movie is always the second one. Curt's never even seen the Blair Witch," Burgess complains as he fires up the engine.

"I can't help it, it's all those stupid church burglaries. Daddy is all worked up; he says there are devil worshipers in Limestone, so now I have an eleven o'clock curfew." Stacy slurps the rest of her Sloe Gin Fizz through the straw. On the ride home, she and Tela both suck on cherry Lifesavers to cover the alcohol.

They park in front of Stacy's house and the two couples smear each other with frantic kisses until the porch light flips off and on in parental Morse code, and the girls peel themselves away. Burgess walks Stacy up to the door as Curt and Tela climb out of the backseat. "I'll be here all week," Tela says pressing his hand.

"Cool," says Curt, easing himself into the driver's seat, his well practiced I don't give a damn look in place.

The gibbous moon hangs like the slightest sliver above Lumen Lake. Curt edges the Camaro into fifth gear and shoots through the curves on the backside of the lake like a slalom skier. They are headed for Rooty Hill. It has become the Saturday night routine. Except usually Burgess picks up Curt after he drops off Stacy. Curt never has a date unless Burgess can import one for him. Curt has a reputation that's too big for a little town like Limestone. Trouble. No decent parents will allow their daughter to go out with Curt Hardwick.

"Too many mommies and not enough Daddy in that house," Burgess's mother always says about "poor little Curt." She was a friend of Janet Hardwick's, one of the first to die of brain cancer in Limestone. Curt was only four then. There had been three other Mrs. Hardwicks since, each younger and blonder than the one before. Every one of the three ended up with a Chevy convertible as part of their divorce settlements.

About a hundred people, even little kids, have died of all different kinds of rare cancers, blood cancers, brain cancers and bone cancers mostly. Cluster cases are what the researchers from Lexington called it. The basketball team sponsored a fundraiser for a little boy from Mussert Flats who was about to die from leukemia. They played a game against the local radio station personalities, but the catch was that they all had to ride on donkeys. Even the little sick boy was laughing.

But nobody knows what is causing the cancers. Some people think it is the chemicals that they release from the smokestacks of Burlcroft twice a day. Other people swear the mill lets fabric dye run off into the creeks that feed the reservoir. Curt is sure it is Paraquat poisoning. "My dad says the government tested it in the Daniel Boone Forest the summer before my mom got sick," he told Burgess the first night he brought him up to the fire tower on Rooty Hill.

Burgess loves to climb the fire tower. It had been Brooks' secret place. Brooks brought Curt there when they were seniors, and then Curt brought Burgess out and they climbed it the night Burgess got his scholarship offer. Now it is the best part of their weekly ritual. Climbing the fire tower and reading Brooks' letters.

Brooks sends Curt letters for Burgess that he doesn't want their mother to find and read. Burgess climbs up the two-hundred-foot ladder first with Curt right behind. They settle on the benches at the top, which are built around all four walls of the lookout tower. The wind whips through the worn wooden slats that form the eagle's nest. Curt cups his hand around a joint and repeatedly flicks his lighter trying to get it going. Burgess squints in the dim moonlight at the loose scrawl of Brooks' handwriting across the lined notebook paper:

Lil' Bro,

It is so damn hot here you cain't draw a breath that don't burn your lungs. It has been 13 days now that the temperature's been over a 100 degrees. Me and Harrison, another PFC from New Jersey, had a two-day pass so we used Keely's car and drove down and crossed the Border at Nuevo Laredo. I have always wanted to see the Rio Grande River, but it was the biggest disappointment because it was just this little dirty trickle through a marshy swamp. No bigger than Fleming Creek and half as clean. Just think about it. The only thing that keeps us from being Mexicans is this little dirty dribble and a couple of strings of barbed wire. Nothing really.

We parked Keely's car and walked over to Mexico 'cause neither of us wanted to spend our money on the international insurance, so we just walked across, and even in civvies they knew we were military by our hair and the men came up from every direction and said, "You want to go to Boy's Town? I take you to Boy's Town for five dollar." And that got Harrison riled up because that is what they call Juvie Hall in New Jersey, but in Mexico that is what they call the whorehouse. They take you to Boy's Town in this wagon that is pulled by a horse with bright paper flowers wired on his bit and harness and it cost five dollars each just to get out there. Then when you do get there, the downstairs is like one of those cowboy saloons that you see in the old black and white westerns, or remember the saloon in Gunsmoke reruns? But all they play is that fat-bellied Mexican guitar music and everyone drinks tequila and beer with lime and salt. You have to pay to dance with the girls and after about a dozen dances, you can rent one of the rooms upstairs for twenty bucks. Harrison and I split a room and took turns, fifteen minutes each. Now get this, I went first and I picked this girl who looked about sixteen, with long black hair and this tight red mini-skirt.

When it was Harrison's turn, he takes, I swear now, this fat hag that reminded me of Aunt Shirley, at least thirty-years-old, and she weighed at least as much as me, but Harrison was tequila drunk and said he was too drunk to finish, and he was also too drunk to notice that she stole a hundred bucks out of his wallet. He had a bad rash by the time we crossed back over the bridge to Texas. It got so bad he had to go to the infirmary for some pills to clear it up. He tells everybody that he got it from drinking the water, but they are all calling him Bare-back Rider and the Itchilada Lover.

Study hard this summer so you can play ball in the fall. I hope you go post-season so I can catch you on one of those televised games on ESPN2. Take care of my baby, oil change every 2,000 miles in the heat and humidity. Keep her off the gravel roads—paved only. Don't let Curt get you in any trouble. I'll call you on your birthday at the end of the month.

Hang loose but keep tight,
Yo big bro—Brooks

The cherry glows orange on Curt's joint, lighting the palm of his hand like a jack-o-lantern as he protects it from the wind. He passes it to Burgess, who reluctantly takes a long draw then holds it, resting his head back on the railing. The fire tower is Burgess's safe place, his escape from his local star status, a place to tempt the fates. "This is the last week I can smoke," Burgess says. "My piss test is at the beginning of next month."

"Pee-Free," Curt grunts, holding his hit. "I got Brooks high the night before his Army test, and he did the Pee-Free on the way to Lexington and his test was clean as a whistle. You have to drink the amount of water it says, not any juice or anything. Citrus throws it off." They stared across the swaying tops of the pine trees at the glow of Limestone where it snuggled up against the foot of Boone Mountain.

Burgess likes the way his mind floats free of his body when he smokes. He can see himself as someone else, someone without all the worries and pressures that come with playing ball for a college. He isn't worried about the ball playing part; that he can handle. But the thought of all those books to read and papers to write makes a knot dig into his stomach. Burgess looks at his hands in the dim light of the moon. They seem detached from his body, like a hand tool that he just gets out for specialized jobs. The span of his grip is massive; he can grab a basketball and palm it the way other guys grab a baseball. What did that anatomy tutor tell him? The hands have over a thousand nerve endings, their wiring more complex than the most powerful computer.

Burgess likes hanging out with Curt, playing bad-boy, making people talk a little. Plenty of time for talk in Limestone. He can be himself with Curt. Curt doesn't expect anything from him; he never tries to impress Burgess. Curt doesn't really look up to him at all. To Curt he is just Brooks' little tattletale, punk brother. And that takes the pressure off. Smoking pot makes him see this about himself.

"It's the witching hour. Midnight," Curt says, lifting his eyebrows twice, real quick, as he starts back down the ladder. "Time to roll." Burgess feels a rush of pain across his gut. He doesn't want to go. He wants to sit in the tower until daybreak, or his birthday, or until after school starts. He knows what comes next and he is going to get out of it. He is not going to go with Curt this week.

"I need to get on home tonight," Burgess says when they are both back on the ground.

"I need to get home, my daddy's a-scared of the church robbers," says Curt, mimicking both Stacy and Burgess at once. "What's a matter, wuddle Burgie; don't be a feared of that mean old satanic cult. I promise not to let them get you." Curt is wild-eyed, mocking, looking over and watching Burgess as much as he is watching the narrow road. The Camaro lays out a jet stream of gravel dust behind them.

"No, really, take me on home and you just keep the car tonight," says Burgess, keeping his eyes on the road. "We've got to go all the way to Hampton's Cross tomorrow for a family reunion. I promised Mom."

"I promised my mommy. Burgess is Mommy's good boy," Curt mocks; the whiskey and weed are running a mean streak on him tonight. Burgess hates when Curt takes a mean turn. "What would your momma think if she heard her Burgie had been a real bad boy? Huh, Burgess? What would all your momma's rich kin in Hampton's Cross think if they knew how their little superstar spent his summer vacation?" Curt has amazing control over the car as it hugs the curves down the side of Boone Mountain. Burgess keeps his eyes forward, refusing to acknowledge Curt's mania.

When they reach the paved road that winds along the banks of Lake Lumen, Burgess hopes Curt will turn right, head back into town. He has the munchies. He wants to go home and eat leftover meatloaf on light bread, with a little ketchup, and a cold Coke from the can. And fall asleep in his waterbed with the television on MTV.

"Sorry, college boy." Curt gives Burgess his best Jack-Nicholson-crazy-look and turns the car left, away from Limestone, toward the dark hollows on the backside of Lumen Lake. "This just ain't your lucky night."

"Go where you want, I'll just sit in the car. It's not like you can make me go in."

Curt isn't listening. He turns up the radio and sings loudly to *The Ballad of Curtis Lowe.* Curt takes the empty pint bottle from the whiskey and flings it out the window at a road sign, smashing it right into the center, glass tinkling to the black asphalt. A slight bump in the pavement is the only hint they have crossed out of Quarry County, east into Redbud County. The road narrows and the curves tighten as they head up the dark side of Squire's Peak. Does he know where he is going or where we even are?

Without hesitating, Curt jerks the wheel left and they cross the center line and drive in the wrong direction in the other lane. With two slight taps on the brake and another quick left, Curt has the Camaro gliding down a secluded gravel fire road. Burgess will not give Curt the pleasure of hearing him ask, "Where the hell are we?"

Out his window Burgess can see the flatland bogs, fog floating above the water like cottonmouths gliding down Licking Creek at sunset in the thick of summer. The road jags through a rock tunnel. The headlights spray the damp gray blackness of the blasted and cut limestone. As they emerge from the other end, the gravel runs only in the treads. Grass and weeds and blue cornflowers grow in between, where road should be.

"I towed a Caprice Classic from out here the other day," Curt finally says.

They pass a family cemetery on a small rise. It has a chain link fence around it. Curt drives extra slow. *Not a single house on this road, just a cemetery*, Burgess thinks, *probably moved the graves when they built the lake and flooded all those little towns.* The road narrows again and dwindles to dusty ruts. Around the next curve the road winds into a pine thicket where the hot summer air hangs thick with the smell of Christmas. The headlights sweep across the clearing and rest on a tiny white church covered with thin strips of aluminum siding and a rusting tin roof. A stubby cupola pokes awkwardly from the roof. Burgess can read the sign someone has hand painted above the door, the black letters with small drips of paint tracking down the door trim. Tabernacle of Love.

"We need to bring Tela and Stacey out here this week. Really turn this place into our little Tabernacle of Lovin'," says Curt, giving a few thrust of his pelvis toward Burgess.

It really started as a joke the first time. Just a stupid joke that got out of hand. It was midnight of the night Burgess got his scholarship; it was their first night at the fire tower, the first night he smoked, and when they got back to town, everything was closed. But they had the munchies.

"I know where we can eat free," Curt had taunted. "You wanna bet?" He just kept saying, "You wanna bet?" And then he pulled up at the back of the oldest church in town. "It's not breaking and entering if the door ain't locked, buddy," Curt told him, laughing and throwing open the back door of the fellowship hall of the Highland Baptist Church in downtown Limestone. It was Vacation Bible School week. They walked right in the back door and helped themselves to almost a dozen hot dogs, micro-waved and on buns with mustard and ketchup and they drank lemonade straight from the Tupperware pitchers chilling in the refrigerator. While Curt used the church phone to call one of those 1-900-kinky-sex-lines, Burgess took an entire pan of frosted brownies out to the car. Homemade by the Ladies Circle said the handwritten card attached to the baking pan.

That is how it started. And that is how it would have ended too, except for one little thing: three lines on page four of the Limestone Standard the following Thursday. LOCAL CHURCH BURGLARIZED said the small headline at the bottom of the page. Pastor Stephen Coons of Highland Baptist reports that someone entered the locked fellowship hall sometime Saturday evening, overriding the security system. The perpetrators ransacked the supplies for Vacation Bible School, taking many items. The suspects are still at large. And that little blurb in the paper is all it took to get Curt going. That is when the experiment, the joke, whatever it was, began.

"They lied," Curt said the next Saturday night, the article from the paper clipped and in his wallet. "We didn't take nothing; just a little snack. They said taking many items. Wonder what they would report if we really did take something?"

Without more discussion, they drove to the new Second Christian Church out on the interstate connector and parked under the side portico. "I'm not going in unless it is unlocked," Burgess had said. And he had made that his rule ever since.

But Second Christian was unlocked, and they went right in and made themselves at home. Curt went straight to the church office and rummaged through the drawer on the secretary's desk. "Thirteen bucks and a roll of stamps in petty cash," Curt said, shoving the wad in his pocket. "I bet they'll say it was a thousand dollars or something." Then Curt called a girl he had met in a bar in Huntington, but he woke her up and she hung up on him.

But it was Burgess who mis-stepped. Burgess was the one who started the destruction at Second Christian, not Curt. They were creepy crawling the Sunday school rooms. That is what Curt called it, "Creepy crawling, just like Charles Manson and the Manson Gang. He was born in Kentucky, you know, not too far from Limestone." They were going through the classrooms one by one. They opened closed windows. If chairs were on top of the table, they would put them under it. If they were under the table, they would put them on top of the table. They hung a daguerreotype of Alexander Campbell upside down.

And during the creepy crawling, Burgess's size-thirteen, high-top Converse accidentally crushed a cheap, thin, hard plastic bank, molded to the shape of a loaf of bread. It crunched and splintered under his athletic build, not into crumbs but plastic shards. That crushing sound was an instant invitation to Curt to seek and destroy the other dozen plastic bread banks. In a few quick moments the Week of Compassion Offering, carefully collected by the fourth grade class to save the starving sub-Saharan heathen children, was scattered over the tile floor, reduced to piles of plastic shrapnel and dirty coins.

When the paper came out the next Thursday, they had made the front page. SECOND CHRISTIAN SECOND VICTIM IN STRING OF CHURCH BURGLARIES. Curt was jubilant. "*The building was vandalized and large sums of cash were taken*; can you believe that crap? Let's go."

Burgess tries to remember which was next, the Catholic Church or the Church of God. The Catholic Church he thinks. Curt was drunk that night and all the statues of saints made him uneasy. There was a rack of candles where you could light one and say a prayer. They blew them all out and moved them all over the sanctuary. On the way out, Curt mistook the fountain of holy water for the urinal, and when he tried to make it flush, the entire pedestal crashed to the granite floor. ALTAR DESECRATED AT ASSUMPTION CATHEDRAL, the Standard reported. *Possible work of Devil Worshipers' Cult.*

Curt became a lion on the stalk. He even went to the library at Eastlake State while Burgess was with his tutor. "Look at these books; this is how real devil worshipers do it," he said, thrusting a book with a diagram of a pentagram toward Burgess when he returned to thc car.

"I hope you didn't check those out on my card."

"Do you think I'm some kind of idiot? I threw them out that window on the second floor," he said, pointing to the back of the library. "Then I run around real quick like and grabbed them out of the bushes. They are gonna think we are real devil-worshipers." The power was infectious.

All summer, the two of them have held the entire town under their spell, and their secret binds them together. They didn't even tell Brooks. Everyone in town holds fear tight, like the hot summer air singeing their lungs with each breath, while Burgess and Curt unfold their days in work and study. And at night, they rein their unholy terror on Limestone.

Burgess serves as the tether, the anchor that keeps Curt from going too far, from real destruction. Burgess finds it fascinating how fast and far the rumors fly from the truth. Maybe in college he will research this. There must be some kind of rumor phenomenon in small towns that has been studied and documented. This sounds like a good topic for one of those college compositions.

A bard owl calls from a high tree as Curt kills the headlights. The Tabernacle of Love burns in silhouette. It looks like the negative of a photograph against the dark thicket of pine. "I've got fake blood from that costume shop in Gravesville. That'll freak out these old country boys," he laughs, throwing open the car door. The sallow interior light makes Burgess reach for his eyes, too bright, too fast. He opens his door and unfolds his long legs from the low car.

"We'll just squirt a little of this around," Curt says, pulling the tube of fake blood from his pocket. "Then we'll lay out some of these creek rock in the pattern of this Egyptian eye. See what they say about that.

We might have to drive over and get a *Redbud Times*. Standard might not cover it outside the county." Curt scrunches his eyebrows together like he is thinking real hard, preparing a plan.

They feel along the inside wall for the light switch, but can't find one. Curt makes his way to the front and lights the candelabra next to the pulpit. "This place is so country they don't even have electricity," he says, laughing as if amazed at the quaintness. "I bet there's an outhouse in the back."

This church feels sad to Burgess, a poor church with the cheap brown sheet paneling like they put in mobile homes. The windows have a dimpled, plastic adhesive layer the color of mustard that adheres to the clear glass. Faux-stained glass. His grandmother has the same pattern of sculptured carpet in her living-dining room combination, but in avocado.

"Don't get that blood on the carpet; it won't show up. Red on red," Burgess says, thinking of what it will cost the poor church people to get it cleaned. He looks at the old hardwood pews with no back pads and no seat cushions. All the churches in town have luxury pews, padded with cushions and upholstery. Even leather at the First Baptist.

"Check this out. Jack-pot," Curt yells. "Oh, get a load of these."

Lining the back of the altar are three small camelback chests, spray-painted with gold glitter paint. Small luggage locks clench the lids down. "The anointing of God is real!" is painted across the top of one of the boxes. "Mark 16:18" is painted in the center one. "In my name they shall cast out the devils," says the third. Curt rocks the center chest back and forth, and they hear the clinking of coins inside. He lets the heavy box down with a thud.

"They're too country for banks. Don't trust 'em. They just keep their offering right here on the altar where God can pick it up his-self," Curt says, laughing as if he just figured everything out for the first time.

"I ain't stealing no offering money," Burgess says.

"We're just gonna bust them open and squirt the fake blood on the money. Get it? Blood on the money? It'll be like we are making some kind of statement. I'll be right back." Curt runs down the aisle and out the old wooden door yelling, " I got just what we need."

Burgess plops down on the edge of the altar. He is tired. The hot, stale air smells of cucumbers. Tiny beads of sweat pop out on his brow and he licks his salty lips. His shadow startles him, splayed large across the back wall of the sanctuary, grotesque and wraithlike in the flickering candle.

"These are just perfect," Curt says holding a slim screwdriver in each hand. He tosses one to Burgess. "Race you."

With a couple of quick pulls and a pick, the cheap locks spring in unison, and the boys throw open the lids. The inside of each lid is lined with red velvet. Velvet covers the tops of the chests, with a slit in the fabric where the offering is dropped in.

"They're too heavy to dump, just pull out the bills, the blood will show up better on the bills than on the change," Curt orders, and they each reach through the gathered velvet to retrieve the dollars from their chests.

"Holy crap. I snagged my finger on a finishing nail," says Curt, his mouth wincing in pain, bottom lip drooping.

The instant Burgess feels his hand around its cool leathery thickness he remembers about the cucumbers. "Be careful playing around that old well. And stay away from the woodpile," his granny used to tell him and Brooks when they were little. "If you smell of cucumbers in the air, scat. That's the scent of a copperhead."

Adrenalin pulses through his temples, and as Burgess tries to jerk his arm back through the velvet casing, he feels both fangs of the pit viper sink deep into the delicate flesh between his thumb and his palm. The venom flashes up his arm like heat lightning. His muscles ripple in spasm down his body. Another strike hits his little finger before he pulls his arm back through the velvet cover. Still attached to his finger is a baby copperhead, no more than seven or eight inches long, its tail still yellow, and the color of sulphur. Fiery pain crawls up his arm and lodges in his neck. The taste of metal coats his tongue. The venom of the copperhead is already dissolving the muscles in his hand, like sugar in hot coffee.

"A Diamondback got me. It weren't no Timber rattler." Burgess can hear Curt yelling, but it sounds like a whisper by the time the words reach his ears. As Curt stumbles forward, his knee catches the lid of the chest, turning it over beside him. A cluster of snakes roll out in a ball, disentangle and scatter for the darkness of the sanctuary.

To Burgess it feels as if the flicker of the candle is breathing him in and out. Dimming as he exhales, blazing each time he draws a breath in. He wants to cool his arm. He wants to sink his hand into the cool backwater of the bogs. He makes his way toward the door. He wants to run. His heart is pumping, but his legs are moving slowly, as if he is wading in deep water. He looks back at the altar and sees Curt crawling off the edge of the steps, trying to make his way toward the doors.

Once outside the night air washes Burgess cool and crisp as he sinks to his knees in the thick grass. It is dew covered and slick. The sliver of moon winks down at him, growing rounder, whiter each time he blinks back. He hears the thump, thump, thump, of his heart pounding blood against his temples—the sound of the solitary player, staying after practice, going the distance.

Bev Olert

Bev Olert is an eleventh-generation Kentuckian and grew up in rural Bourbon County. She has a M.A. in English and has lived in San Antonio and in Baltimore. She recently moved back home to horse country where she lives with her husband, their teenage son and three spoiled dogs. She currently teaches theater and film.

Genesis for *Tabernacle of Love*

I didn't set out to write a story about beer-boys and devil worshipers and the evolution of rumors in a small town, but that is exactly how it turned out. In 1979 when I enrolled at Morehead as a freshman, one of the big rumors around town was that there were "devil worshipers" practicing somewhere out around Cave Run Lake. Over the next few years I heard several fascinating variations, such as it's really a coven of witches, or avoid the Debby Hill area after midnight. With each new crop of freshmen in the fall, this rumor, like the phoenix, would rise up from its own ashes and start a new life.

I left Morehead for several years, traveled, spent a great deal of time on the West Coast, but in 1987 I moved back to finish grad school. I rented this tiny cottage on a lane at the end of Lyons Avenue. My new neighbors where three local boys who had just graduated from high school and were living on their own for the first time. Our houses were so close together that I could hear every word they said. I spent most nights that summer with my windows open while I fell asleep listening to the guys next door tell each other about their day. The general topics of conversation included: hot girls they had seen, but didn't actually know or speak to; the effects of nitrous oxide on an eight-cylinder verses a six-cylinder engine; and always, who's turn it was to run to the bootlegger for beer. I loved to listen, not just to their stories, but the way they told them, their voices and their accents. I loved the way they bantered back-and-forth, one-upped each other and the way they cussed a living blue streak. Their vernacular and the colloquialisms entranced me.

For obvious reasons, I dubbed them the beer-boys, a title they embraced and a moniker they are still identified by today in certain circles. We got to be good friends and they liked to take me out ridge ridin', cruising the gravel fire roads that skimmed the mountains above downtown. One evening we were going out to the lake to watch the sunset from an obscure chunk of shoreline that the locals call The Rocks. Along US 60 stood an old cinderblock building with a saggy roof. Someone had hand painted, rather sloppily, a sign over the door that read "Tabernacle of Love." I said, "That is the saddest church I've ever seen."

It was quiet for a minute or so and then one of the beer-boys said, "You know, I always heard there was a cult of devil-worshipers out at Cave Run."

Alas, this rumor did not end there. Fast-forward to the fall of 2005. I am again living back in Kentucky, but an hour away from Morehead. I ran into a former student who had just enrolled there. I asked her how she liked Morehead and she ran through a quick litany of all the things she loved about it, then got very serious and said, “You know, I heard that there are devil worshipers out at Cave Run.”

This story is my version of how that terrible rumor may have started in another small mountain town.

Canvas

Melissa Bell Pitts

The elevator rises to the maternity floor and lands with a gentle thud. For a moment, Sarah Jane Abernathy fears that she and John are stuck inside. She locates the emergency phone, but then the metal doors open to a lobby with brown carpet and white concrete block walls.

Sarah Jane tries to follow John, who has exited the elevator, but she can't move. Her bare legs under her denim skirt feel webbed together as if a spider has slipped between them and woven them tight with invisible threads. She presses the "door open" button and leans into it.

"John," she calls as he takes long, purposeful strides.

He turns and faces her, a good six feet away. "Sarah Jane, what's wrong?" He is wearing navy shorts and a white tee-shirt, and his slightly sunburned forehead is crinkled.

"I can't."

John steps inside the elevator and reaches for her elbow. He looks almost the same as he did when they married ten years ago with the same athletic build from his days as a soccer player and his dark hair still close cropped. "We're supposed to be there in five minutes. Alice and Bill are expecting us." John helps her off the elevator and guides her to the blinding white wall to her right.

The hallway smells like just opened Band-Aids, and that smell swirls under her nose with peach fragrance rising from bath items packed into a basket she holds in her right hand.

"I think I'm going to be sick," she says. "It's just too much. You know I don't like hospitals. Nothing good ever happens in hospitals." She has not been on a maternity floor since four years ago when she and John tried several in vitro fertilizations that didn't work. A pregnant woman wearing a "Baby on Board" tee-shirt with a big red arrow pointing south waddles past them. Sarah Jane glances at her Birkenstocks and steadies herself by holding onto John's forearm with her free left hand.

"It'll be okay," he says, stroking his hand up and down her arm. "This is the closest we've ever been." The lines on his forehead soften. "Remember, this is a good thing: the baby is fine, and Alice is fine. It's just how they do it; the baby's here, so we need to be. Would it help to think it's a new hospital? The IVF's were in Louisville."

"Maybe. It's not just being in a hospital. I'm afraid they'll change their minds, you know, like Sherry and Tom did. This is when they usually do it, you know, at the hospital, after the baby's born. What if we say something wrong?"

"We just have to do the best we can," John says, touching the tips of her fingers with his and looking at her with his almond eyes. "I'm nervous too."

"You are?"

"Sure. It's not every day you get to meet the baby who may become your daughter. I just hope she doesn't get Bill's nose. He's got a honker."

Sarah Jane laughs. "Honey, that's the least of our concerns."

"Aw, come on," he says, placing one hand above hers and one below.

"Oh, all right, coach. Could you at least walk a little slower?" Sarah Jane hears a faint train whistle in the distance and considers it a signal to walk again. The threads seem to have loosened. She takes small steps.

John has, in fact, slowed his gait, and they walk side by side with their hands entwined. Neither one speaks. Sarah Jane thinks the possibility that Alice and Bill might actually go through with their adoption plan may be nearly as frightening as the possibility that they won't.

They pass the nurses station and head down the corridor. "Is Meredith going to be here?" he asks.

"I don't think so. I think we're on our own," Sarah Jane says, pushing a stray blond curl behind her ear.

Sarah Jane and John met Meredith Kincaid three years ago when they signed up with her adoption agency, New Beginnings. Meredith interviewed them individually and as a couple, checked their backgrounds (credit, police, FBI) and required them to get physicals with a seal of approval from their family physician. She visited their three-bedroom brick ranch to make sure it would be safe for a child. Prior to the home visit, Sarah Jane and John cleaned every inch of the house. Sarah Jane even scoured the trash can.

Once they were approved, Meredith showed their information to birth parents who wanted to consider an adoption for their baby. Sarah Jane water colored daisies with yellow ochre and cadmium yellow centers on the cover of their picture album, and she and John wrote letters that tried to show how much they wanted to become parents. Then they waited. And waited.

"It was always you-all," Alice told Sarah Jane during their first meeting in Meredith's conference room, nearly three months ago. "We knew right away," Alice said as the five of them gathered around a shiny cherry conference table that engulfed the room and made them seem small. She and Bill said they chose Sarah Jane and John because they had college degrees, had been married a long time and had extended family nearby. Sarah Jane and John smiled at each other with relief upon first seeing Alice and Bill, who were so fresh faced and cute. They reminded Sarah Jane of her and John when they were younger and had their lives ahead of them. Sarah Jane and John were further relieved when they learned that neither had any serious medical risks in their family histories nor any "double threats" as they called couples with the same diseases on both sides.

During meetings at restaurants (Bucca de Beppo, La Casa Fiesta and Tandoor), Sarah Jane and John learned the primary reason Alice and Bill were considering adoption. Both Alice and Bill are first generation college students of devout Georgian Baptists. Neither one told their parents of the pregnancy and had avoided the out-of-state trips home with school and work excuses. Alice seemed especially fearful of her parents' disappointment.

"Mama would kill me if she knew I got pregnant before I graduated," she told Sarah Jane as they waited for her ultrasound in a black and white tile room. "I swear, I think she'd switch me to death." She continued with how her mama used to pray: "Don't let our Alice have a baby before it's time, please Dear God, let her get that cap and gown first."

Sarah Jane told Alice, "I know you think adoption is right for you now, but you won't really know until the baby is born." A part of Sarah Jane doesn't want to pressure Alice to place the baby with them. She tells herself, "this is their only chance to raise this baby." But another part of her wants to scream out, "I really hope you all will."

Sarah Jane and John stop outside hospital room 337. John knocks, three times, not too loud and not too soft. Just the perfect amount of pressure, Sarah Jane thinks.

"Just a minute," a voice she doesn't recognize calls out.

Through a slight opening in the door, Sarah Jane makes out the vague outline of someone in periwinkle blue scrubs tending to Alice in bed. A baby whimpers.

"She's here," she mouths to John.

She never imagined she and John would be in this position, waiting outside Alice and Bill's hospital door to meet their baby, like some vultures. Dr. Taylor, her fertility specialist, told her getting pregnant was a numbers games: the more you try, the better your chances. Sarah Jane thinks getting pregnant is more like an algebraic formula, x + y = b. She failed algebra, but John aced calculus and is an accountant, so she thought he would make up for her shortcoming. They tried it all: artificial insemination, ten times; super stimulation, six times; and in vitro fertilization, three times. No matter what they did, her x and his y chromosomes never equaled a baby. The doctors had no explanation, but she thinks it must be an x factor. Sarah Jane has decided adoption is an even more complicated equation because then you have two x's, two y's and only one baby.

When Sarah Jane told her mother about their struggle with infertility, Vonda said, "Honey, not everyone is meant to be a mama. Maybe this is just God's way. You couldn't even remember to feed the dog when you were in junior high. You've got John and your painting. You should just be happy." Sarah Jane read *When Bad Things Happen to Good People* to feel better about God and his not punishing her. As the years passed and they still didn't have a baby, she wondered if Mom was right.

Alice calls out, "Come in." A heavy set nurse with shoulder length hair lumbers toward the door.

John squeezes Sarah Jane's right hand briefly before they enter the room. Alice is propped up in bed with three pillows behind her back. The baby lies asleep curled up on Alice's chest and belly, cocooned inside a faded pink and blue plaid blanket. Bill lounges in a blue leather wing chair on the other side of the bed, near the window. The late evening sun coming through the wooden blinds casts a warm light on the three of them.

Sarah Jane holds up the basket. "For you," she says before walking over to the metal food table next to Alice's bed. She pats Alice's firm shoulder and places the basket beside a bouquet of white roses they had a florist deliver earlier. "We're thinking of you," they finally decided the card would read.

"Oh, goody," Alice says, rising up a bit. "I can't wait to take a bath and I love peach. It reminds me of home." Her cheeks flinch when she reaches over to turn the basket around. The baby continues to sleep. Bill clears his throat.

"Are you okay?" John asks.

"I'm pretty good," Alice says.

She looks the picture of maternal health: full breasts covered in a white eyelet gown, slightly freckled face with its high cheek bones and rounded eyebrows free of makeup, strawberry blond hair a little messy. But she still looks beautiful. Before they met her three months ago, Meredith described her as someone who could be on a milk ad. Mary Cassatt would have loved her.

Sarah Jane envies her fullness, her wholesomeness. She casts a furtive glance at her own chest, flat by comparison. Once her breasts had filled up a little and hurt with every step. When she took off her bra there were red marks on her chest. Her stomach pooched a bit, and she was six days late. She debated over how she'd tell John. Would she wrap a silver rattle or cook a dinner with baby peas and baby carrots as side dishes? She was leaning toward the rattle, deciding the small vegetables would be too subtle. That night, though, she dreamed of the red-splattered fluid she always saw before she got her period.

Sarah Jane has been painting that image over and over the past seven years. She begins the same way: she loads her number seven brush with a thick coating of vermilion and runs her fingers through the end, splattering paint onto the canvas and herself. Then Sarah Jane pulls her one-inch brush out of her painter's apron, dips it in vermilion, and paints random tracks to cover the canvas. Her tears usually begin to flow during the laying of tracks. Finally she dips number five into black and attacks the canvas with its tip, splaying the brush as she pounds the black into various abstract forms. She has ruined numerous number five and number seven brushes. Sarah Jane considers she must have fifty of these types of canvasses. For now, they line the walls and are staggered in rows on the floor of the room that they hope some day will become their nursery. John calls it "the red room."

Alice's maternity-ward room is nearly void of color except the blue wing chair and a long blue floral dress hanging on the wall. Sarah Jane assumes Alice was wearing it when she went into labor.

"I couldn't believe you called us while you were in labor," Sarah Jane says. She is standing next to John near the foot of the bed. "You sounded so calm, like it was no big deal. 'Oh the baby should be here in an hour.'" Alice did not want them in labor and delivery, though they would have liked to have been there. Meredith said, "This is their time. If it works, you'll have the rest of her life."

"She did great," Bill says. "She didn't hit me once." He looks tired, with dark circles making his deep-set eyes look even deeper, and his dark curls are rumpled as if he hasn't combed them since yesterday. "My hand is still sore, though. She about squeezed it off. Thank God they didn't let her wear her rings."

"Do you want to hold her?" Alice lifts the baby up and extends her arms out to Sarah Jane.

Sarah Jane hasn't held a baby since 1998 when John's brother and wife had their son. She puts one hand under the baby's head and supports her body with the other one. She prays, "please don't let me drop her" as she carries her to a cushioned chair near Alice. Sarah Jane feels nauseous but tries to hide it.

"She's perfect," she says. Sarah Jane wants to hug the baby close, to tell her how long they have waited to meet her, how they want to love her and protect her, but don't know if that's what will happen and how she wishes it wasn't so confusing and that no matter what, they want what's best for her. But she knows she cannot say these things, not in their presence, because the situation is too tenuous. John is standing beside her, touching the baby's dark, fuzzy head and smiling with his lips closed together, the same way he smiled when they toasted each other at their wedding reception.

She tries to live in this moment, to take the baby in: the way she smells like a mixture of honey and milk, the way her lips are crinkly and tender like Kiwi, the way her breaths are short and quick, and the way she moves her hands slowly, as if they are still in water.

"I can't see I had anything to do with her," Alice says. "She's got Bill's eyes and nose. Neither one of us is taking credit for her mouth."

"She's beautiful," John says and rubs his forefinger up and down her nose.

Sarah Jane is not good at telling who a baby looks like. She does seem to favor Bill with her dark hair and olive skin.

Bill discusses her APGAR test results which were all high. As soon as you get out of the womb, the tests begin, Sarah Jane thinks. Bill is studying to be a biologist, which should have helped prevent a pregnancy, but he is only a sophomore. Alice was on the pill.

It is enough for Sarah Jane to know the baby is healthy. She can tell the birthing was hard. She uses her pinky to trace a red line that zig zags down the baby's forehead. The skin around her blue gray eyes is swollen. She thinks her nose looks fine. Sarah Jane is glad she weighs eight pounds. She seems less fragile that way, not like a five-pound baby.

It is hard for Sarah Jane to comprehend that she is sitting here, holding this newborn baby who may become their daughter. She, Sarah Jane Abernathy, who has not even been able to watch a Pamper's commercial without crying. For a brief moment she closes her eyes and allows herself to imagine plaiting fine silk hair into braids, first steps and first teeth, finger paints, visits to Santa and Christmas cards with their family portrait on the cover, pink leotards and little tights, rocking chairs, *Make Way For Ducklings*, *Wynken, Blynken and Nod*, and *Beatrix Potter*.

John interrupts her reverie.

"We better go," he whispers to Sarah Jane. "We know you all must be tired," he says aloud.

The next day John taps on the fully open hospital door. When he and Sarah Jane walk inside, Alice and Bill are lying in bed with the baby cuddled up asleep between them. The television blares.

"Oh, hi," Alice says, sitting straighter in the bed and covering the baby's feet. "She's staying with us." Alice pauses. "I don't want her to be alone in the nursery."

Sarah Jane's pulse quickens. She and John are intruders in this picture, like that segment she used to watch on *Sesame Street*. "One of these things belongs with the other one. One of these things doesn't belong. Now it's time to play our game." She sees a big X drawn over her and John.

The chair they sat in yesterday is covered in clothes: Bill's jeans, tee-shirts, baby blankets and a white knit cardigan sweater she assumes is Alice's.

"She definitely prefers to be held," Alice says as she lifts the baby into the crook of her arm. In one day, she knows her and we don't, Sarah Jane realizes.

"She looks pretty comfortable," John says. He doesn't look the least bit worried. She knows he would say she worries too much, but she feels a definite shift in mood today. She thinks maybe Alice and Bill are just stringing them along and wishes she could be the one in that bed with John by her side. Then they wouldn't have to deal with Alice and Bill's changing whims. Then there would be no question over who will take the baby home and who will get to keep her.

Bill climbs out of bed and grabs a canned Pepsi out of a blue cooler. Sarah Jane didn't notice them having it yesterday. He does not offer them one. Bill stands still briefly, cracking open the Pepsi. "She's one of the biggest in the nursery," he says. He walks to the window and closes the blinds.

Once when Sarah Jane was small, her father gave her pull-down blinds to paint on. She pretended they were her canvases, just like his, and put every color in his palette on them. She'd been painting ever since. But when she couldn't get pregnant, her painting was limited to the vermilion abstractions. Any time she tried to paint a new image, the whiteness of the canvas, like these white walls, mocked her.

Bill walks away from the blinds and gets back in bed with Alice and the baby. He lifts the blanket to uncover the baby's toes. "She's got my toes, big and funny looking. Poor thing," he says with a laugh.

Sarah Jane is always amazed when Bill laughs. He keeps his upper body completely stiff, but his head moves back and forth like he's a bobble doll, a goofy, dark, curly-headed bobble doll.

Alice removes the blanket completely, holds the baby up and smoothes down her v-neck white tee-shirt. The baby pushes Alice's hand away and begins crying. Maybe she doesn't know everything, Sarah Jane thinks.

Alice wraps the baby back up and rocks her back and forth in her arms. Sarah Jane smells a sweet stench and realizes what is wrong.

"Do you-all want to change her?" Alice asks, holding the baby out toward John and Sarah Jane.

"Um, sure," Sarah Jane says. But, she thinks, "Oh God, another test. We're not ready." She read you're supposed to practice changing a diaper on a doll or something. They never did because they thought the more ready they got, the more disappointed they'd be if it didn't work out.

Sarah Jane carries her toward the metal food table at the end of the bed. Today it seems to be a makeshift changing table as it has a stack of diapers with baby muppets on the bands and a plastic container of baby wipes. When Sarah Jane lays her flat on her back, the baby cries and kicks her feet. Her cries go up a decibel when the diaper is removed. Poop fills more nooks and crannies on this baby's bottom, legs and vagina than she ever imagined possible. It is the consistency of oil paints when they first come out of the tube, and it is a color she's never seen: a combination of burnt umber, crimson Alizarin, a dab of yellow ochre and a pinch of Hooker's Dark Green.

She and John work in tandem. She wipes and he takes the dirty wipe away and hands her a new one. The baby cries and kicks continually. Sarah Jane worries the baby will kick her feet into the poop and start flinging it. She feels Alice and Bill's eyes on them. Finally the slimy substance is removed. John hands her a clean diaper.

"I don't think that's right," John whispers when the diaper is on. His upper lip is covered in little beads of perspiration. Sarah Jane studies the diaper. She realizes that the cut out scallop is most likely an opening for the umbilical cord and not the butt crack.

She removes the tabs and tries to reverse the diaper, but the tabs won't stick anymore. The baby is now flopping like a fish, kicking so hard that she lifts up her back. Her cry is now a wail. Sarah Jane wonders, how could I ever think I could be a mother? I'm an idiot. I'm sorry, baby.

"Alice holds the baby's feet together and lifts her butt up at the same time," Bill says.

Of course she does, Sarah Jane thinks. But she tries it. Sarah Jane gathers the baby's feet together and stretches her left fingers to wrap around her ankles and lifts while using her right hand to get the diaper underneath her. She pulls the tab that sticks the side of the diaper to the front of the diaper, but it tears off. She considers the possibility that these are trick diapers, like those birthday candles. She hands the now ruined diaper to John, and he hands her a new one. This time John reaches over to help pull the tab around to the front and it sticks. She does the other side. Finally the baby is diapered, scallop in front and both side tabs attached.

"We'll get better," Sarah Jane says turning her to Alice and Bill, who have confused expressions on their faces. Three diapers for one bowel movement equals a failure.

Bill looks at Alice with raised eyebrows and opens his lips slightly as if he is going to say something, but Alice shakes her head "no". Bill closes his lips and clears his throat. Silence fills the room.

"Hey," John says. "There's a lot of pressure here. It's more than a diaper change—we all know that. We know it's hard for you-all, but it's hard for us too. It's just part of the deal—we know—but let's not deny this is pretty tense."

"Yeah, you're right man," Bill says. "We just want to make sure she's in good hands."

Alice suggests they give the baby a bottle and, thankfully, John offers to do it. He takes her over to the clothes covered chair and clears a spot, so he can feed her.

Sarah Jane stands near him. She's glad they can do something to make up for the diaper change. She's also glad John was so direct. Somehow it helps to have some of what they're going through out in the open. Sweat drips down her neck, and she lifts her pony tail up and down to cool it. She shifts her weight from one leg to the other, but it is as if they can no longer support her. She holds onto the back of the chair.

"What name are you-all thinking of?" Bill asks.

"Grace," Sarah Jane says, too drained to even hesitate before answering. She doesn't say it, but now they call her "Maybe Baby," and Sarah Jane's her Maybe Mother.

"Grace," Alice says slowly as if it is a two syllable name and she's trying it on her lips for size. Her full lips turn up slightly after she says it.

The next day, Sarah Jane points to the brass numbers on the nearly closed hospital door while John's hand is mid knock.

"John," she whispers. "This is not good. Three + three + seven equals thirteen. It's not lucky."

"Sarah Jane, you think too much for your own good," John says and completes the knock.

Sarah Jane takes a deep breath. It is as if all of the years of walking this line between hope and despair are in this moment and she knows that on the other side of this door with those unlucky numbers, it will be decided one way or another and it's always the way she doesn't want it to be, and it will be so much worse this time after holding her, smelling her, imagining her as their daughter, but maybe…She thinks of the gold-starred car seat strapped in the back seat and the white lacy bassinet waiting in their bedroom. She and John bought them last night at Target, although she felt like a fraud even walking down the baby aisle with her flat belly. She'd prayed they wouldn't see anyone they knew at the checkout counter. She could not deal with questions. Not now.

Bill calls, "Come in." She considers his tone a bit dejected as if he is tired of dealing with them.

John turns the door knob and opens the door. As they step inside, Sarah Jane closes her eyes briefly. She feels as if she is inside a tunnel, uncertain of when her eyes will adjust or of what she will see. She blinks and opens.

Bill and Alice are sitting on the end of the completely made bed. Meredith, tall, thin, wearing spiked heels, sits in the blue leather chair. The baby is not in the room. No clothes are scattered about. The metal food table sits in its original position next to the bed without diapers and wipes. Two navy Samsonite fabric suitcases and the blue cooler are tucked in the corner.

"The baby's in the nursery," Bill says, matter-of-factly.

Sarah Jane's chest muscles tighten, and she begins steeling herself for what they have to say. They're not going to do it, she thinks, and they don't want the baby to witness a scene. I'll be brave about it. I can fall apart later, she tells herself.

Alice is holding the diaper bag the hospital gives to new parents. It is yellow vinyl with cows jumping over the moon, and Alice keeps looking down at it.

"We need to talk," Bill says.

Sarah Jane involuntarily tightens her leg muscles, and one behind her knee pulses in and out.

"We know we said before that if we go through with it, we would only want pictures and letters, but we've decided we want to see her—at least a few times a year," Bill says.

"Well, how would that work?" John asks.

Sarah Jane tries to look at John with eyes that say, "It's OK. That means they want to do it, honey. We're going to be parents."

John nods his head slightly at her, as if to say, "I know, but I need this answered."

"Lots of couples keep in contact," Meredith says, standing up and shuffling some papers. "A lot of them meet in restaurants, some even go to each other's houses. It's just whatever everyone is comfortable with. I'll help you-all work it out."

Alice gets up and walks toward Sarah Jane.

"It's for you," she says of the diaper bag, tears streaming down her cheeks and her chest heaving.

"I'm so sorry. I'm so sorry you-all have to go through this," Sarah Jane says and she begins crying too. Why should this young couple, almost babies themselves, why do they have to deal with this? She feels so confused. It's not at all how she thought she would feel.

"It will be easy to tell her how special you are," she says and reaches out to hold Alice's cold hands. Alice holds her hand briefly and turns around.

"You-all have our number," John says. "Call us if you need anything."

Alice cries even harder. Bill walks over and picks up both pieces of luggage. He tucks one between his elbow and hip and the other in his hand. The cooler has some sort of handle and wheel system and it rolls behind him like an ultramarine blue wagon. Alice's shoulders shudder, and her head bends low as they leave the room.

"It's hard to be happy when they're so sad," Sarah Jane says after they are gone.

"It's bittersweet," Meredith says.

A nurse leans over Grace in a clear bassinet centered in what they call a holding room. She is the only baby in the room, which has several oak rocking chairs scattered about.

"Are you the new parents?" the nurse asks, smiling.

"They sure are," Meredith proclaims.

Sarah Jane hesitates before she answers. She digs the tip of a fingernail into the back of her hand to be sure she's not in a dream. After she sees the crescent indention, she answers, "Yes."

"What are you naming her?" Meredith asks.

"Grace," John says, "after my grandmother. She practically raised me. Sarah Jane loves her too."

"It's lovely, and she's beautiful," the nurse says.

John leans over the other side of the bassinet. "She's so tiny—those fingers."

The nurse explains some general guidelines on caring for an infant.

"Remember with girls, always wipe front to back. You don't want her to get a yeast infection."

"Now another tip I tell all new parents. One of the easiest ways to change her diaper is to hold her ankles together and lift. They're wiggily little things, otherwise."

Sarah Jane and John smile at each other.

"We know," he says.

It occurs to Sarah Jane that Alice may have received the same advice. She thought Alice just knew intuitively—some kind of hormonal thing. Maybe she'd had to learn too. She gently lifts Grace from the bassinet. "We'll learn together," she says looking at Grace and John. For the first time she feels ready to take on parenting and adoption with all of their risks.

Sarah Jane knows Alice and Bill can change their minds. They can't legally sign away their parental rights for ten days and by then, she and John will be helplessly in love with Grace. But the odds that they'll changes their minds are small. Meredith and all of the adoption books that Sarah Jane has read say that what birth parents decide in the hospital is key. Somehow, actually holding Grace, who is so small and nestled on her chest, makes Sarah Jane less fearful.

Meredith hands John her camera.

"Come on, Dad."

Sarah Jane rocks Grace while John clicks from various angles. Grace sleeps through most of it, but for a moment she opens her eyes and looks at Sarah Jane, really looks at her. Sarah Jane reaches her pinky out to Grace, and she wraps her tiny fingers around it and holds on.

"It's a lot to take in," Sarah Jane says. She thinks of Grace and how new the world is to her, the sounds, air, colors, her and John. Cold air from a vent above blows on them, and she cuddles Grace up closer. Sarah Jane feels a bit raw herself, like a freshly peeled orange.

"Hey," John says, pointing to a large red butterfly print on the wall. "That one looks like your paintings in the red room."

She sees her canvasses in her mind's eye, their jagged reds always with a dark center to them. Now that he's pointed it out, she can see a connection. She carries Grace over to look closer at the print. It's an African butterfly named The Scarlet Nymphalidae Cymothorheinoldi.

Sarah Jane looks down at Grace and holds her close to her chest. She realizes that if she and John had not been through all those losses over the years, they wouldn't be here in this moment. They might have never met Grace. She knows now that she's been too limited in her perspective about the whole process.

Sarah Jane begins to cry and shifts her weight to her right foot. As she does, Grace's face emerges from shadow. Sarah Jane's mind floods with images of Grace as she grows. She understands now that Grace is no more part of a fixed algebraic equation than she or John. Grace is light and shadow and soft colors that kaleidoscope into one another and dissipate as new colors and shapes emerge.

"Why the tears?" John asks as he walks toward them.

"It's...she's just so beautiful," Sarah Jane says. She imagines painting this moment with the three of them standing together, John's head slightly above hers, and they're both looking down at Grace filling their outstretched arms and a slightly open door in the background. It occurs to Sarah Jane that she'll only need scant amounts of vermilion mixed with Chinese white to paint their lips.

Melissa Bell Pitts

Melissa Bell Pitts lives in Lexington with her husband and their son. Her work has appeared in *I to I: Life Writing by Kentucky Feminists and Limestone*. She received honorable mention for creative nonfiction at the Kentucky Women Writers Conference. She is a Phi Beta Kappa graduate from the University of Kentucky, where she received a master's degree in English. A former newspaper reporter and technical editor of *The Journal of Consumer Affairs*, she now writes short stories.

Genesis for *Canvas*

I had just sat down on the couch while our son played with Tinker Toys in the next room. For some reason, I imagined these names: Sarah Jane and John Abernathy. They sounded refined, but I knew they were in some sort of trouble that money and refinement could not help. Initially I imagined Sarah Jane as an overly nurturing person who couldn't have a child, so she focused her maternal instincts on her husband, dog, doctors, most anyone she met and drove them insane. A few days later, I realized Sarah Jane was intuitive about her failed attempts to get pregnant; she dreamed of red splattered fluid before she started her period. I knew then that she was an artist, and her math phobia began to emerge. John was a little bit harder for me to capture. At first he was not as supportive of the adoption or Sarah Jane. I spent some time trying to understand his past. Much of what I learned about John did not go into the story, but it helped me to understand how he would react within this story, and he grew to be more supportive and enthusiastic.

Fault Lines

Wanda Fries

When Carlos Helton rounds the corner of his house Wednesday morning, he finds his brother Billy's Taurus parked in the driveway. Through the screen door, he hears his wife, Sue, singing, but not straight through and effortlessly, the way she sings when she works. Between phrases, Billy stops to give her instructions, giving her the pitch on the piano one note at a time.

On the top step, Carlos bends to take off his boots. Letting the screen door shut softly behind him, he sets them on the newspapers Sue has laid out for him, the only thing out of place in the spotless room. The old upright piano stands catty-corner at the far end of the long kitchen. Billy sits on a ladder back chair in front of the piano. He has a gold sweater draped around his shoulders with the sleeves tied in the front. Sue leans across him, looking at the music. Her hand rests on the chair back, her forearm just touching his shoulder.

"That sure is some pretty music," Carlos says, and they both turn around.

Sue lets go of the chair suddenly and slides both hands into the pockets of her jeans. The eye shadow she has on makes her eyes look green. Carlos tries to remember. Did she put on make-up early this morning, or did she wait until she saw Billy's car at the bottom of the hill? And why does it matter? After all, Billy is his brother.

"You scared me to death," she says, pushing a dark strand of hair behind her ear. She smiles, blushing, looking up at Carlos. "Does it really sound good? Billy wants me to sing this song Sunday by myself. My first solo."

Billy stands, too. The hand he holds toward Carlos is long-fingered, the nails shiny and even. "How's it going, buddy? I see you're up with the chickens."

Carlos raises his own hands into the air to show how sticky they are from the tobacco. Then he backs to the sink. Sue keeps dishwashing liquid on top next to the faucet, and Carlos squirts some into the palms of his hands. He doesn't like his brother being here much, and it makes him feel awful to admit this, even to himself. Billy is between jobs, and has come home for the year while he works on his master's thesis. With Daddy in Lone Oak Assisted Living, this seemed a good time to come home. At least, that's Billy's story. Carlos thinks there's more to it than Billy's letting on.

When Carlos finishes at the sink, Billy has sat down again, his long fingers splayed to make a chord at the piano. He sings the notes in falsetto, to show Sue where she went wrong. Carlos pours himself a cup of coffee and listens to them. The cup clatters when he sets it in the sink, hard, but neither of them turns around.

"Guess I'd better get on back to work," he says. "Sue, I need you down there, too, as soon as you can get away." He pauses at the doorway, but Sue keeps looking at the sheet music. In farewell, Billy turns his head sideways toward Carlos and wiggles it up and down, chording with his left hand, while he traces the pattern of notes for Sue with his right.

Their sons are working down the hill in the barn. The old building is dim and dusty, even with the big front doors propped open to let in some light. Near the stripping tables, Andrew, the youngest boy, draws back a tobacco stick, aiming it at his brother like a spear. Carlos reaches over the boy's shoulder and takes the stick from him. "Quit," he says, though talking to Andrew is like talking to a rock. Even when he was a baby, he could scream in his crib for hours. The books Sue read said that if parents left a baby to cry it out, the baby would last maybe thirty minutes. Well, the experts didn't know Andrew. Now, sixteen and six foot three, he still wants to be up all night, raising who knows what kind of hell and getting into who knows what kind of trouble.

Sue is always after Carlos to talk to Andrew, but what would he say? The truth is, Carlos was a lot like Andrew when he was young. When he wasn't working on the farm or at football practice, he spent every spare minute running with some of the other football players, drinking beer and fishing down at the river. They'd listen to the old stuff on somebody's tape player—Jimi Hendrix and Charlie Daniels and Lynard Skynard—and talk about getting laid. Talking was all most of them knew how to do. Carlos hopes that Andrew is all swagger and talk, too, and that, sooner or later, Andrew will just grow out of it, the way Carlos did, when a two-hundred and fifty-pound linebacker put an end to Carlos's football scholarship and Daddy's dreams, and Carlos finally had to grow up and figure out how to make a living.

Jon looks up gratefully at Carlos. Then, with fingers almost as nimble and quick as his father's, he bends over the table to tie a handful of leaves together at the top and bottom with strips of tobacco. From the house, they hear Billy playing the piano and Sue singing.

Carlos takes an armload of tobacco and flings it into the truck bed hard enough to send dust swirling into the air. He is always hard to live with during tobacco season. It's even worse this year with a depressed market, a note due at the bank at the end of December, and Billy making Sue dissatisfied, just when Carlos thought she had finally settled in.

But Carlos loves this place, and no matter how hard it is to make a living here, he can't imagine being anywhere else. It's not as if he hasn't tried. After he and Sue got married, he left the farm to take a job as an assistant manager in a department store chain. The store had transferred him to three different cities in six years when his father called to tell Carlos his mother was dying. Probably, the doctor said, from breathing his father's cigarette smoke for so many years. But his daddy maintained right up to the funeral that the doctor was full of horse manure. "Think about it," he said, in the car on the way to the cemetery. "It don't make no sense, does it? I'm the one been smoking. If it was tobacco give a body cancer, don't it seem like they'd be burying me?"

When they do bury his daddy, will there be anybody left who understands the way Carlos feels about this place, or about anything else? He tries and tries to explain to Sue, but it just wears them both out. Carlos thinks talking is over-rated. Some things you just have to know in your bones.

Daddy was against Sue from the beginning, but Carlos believed that when Daddy really got to know her, he would love her just as Carlos did. Not that Carlos himself understood why he loved her. She wouldn't give Carlos the time of day in high school, but the more he pursued her, and the more she said no, the more he wanted her. He took another girl to the senior prom, a prettier girl, to tell the truth, but he spent the whole night looking over the girl's shoulder, trying to catch glimpses of Sue looking awkward and too tall in a blue satin dress. Some of her dark hair had slipped free and waved around the edge of her shoulders when she danced.

Then, her sophomore year at college, Sue came home at Christmas and gave him a call. "You still want to date me?" she said. He could have sworn she was crying.

"I do," he said.

"You know where I live?"

"In town? In that white house on the corner of Elm St. and Blair?"

"That's the one. Pick me up at seven."

Sue didn't go back to school in January, and by March, they were married. This was entirely Sue's idea. Carlos would never have dared to ask her. Loving her was like waiting silent and still in a deer blind. He had wanted her so long, and now she had come home and offered herself to him. After all his patience, why take the chance of making the one wrong move that might chase her away?

Daddy was breaking up dirt in a sheltered spot to plant winter lettuce when Carlos went out to tell him he had a new daughter-in-law. Daddy kept digging the whole time Carlos was talking. When Carlos finished, Daddy stopped and leaned on the handle of the shovel. "I'm telling you," he said, shaking his head. "She won't like it out here." For the first time, Carlos wondered if he had made a terrible mistake.

Daddy was right, and when Sue wanted Carlos to leave and take a job in the city, he left. She mesmerized him, that's what she did, but there was something about her, about the way he could never be sure of her, that made him like it. Besides, by the time he knew—at least in his heart—that he would never be able to keep her, they had Jon to think of. Then it didn't seem either of them had a choice, and he could relax his hold on her, his way of watching her, always at the edge of his consciousness, the way farmers keep checking the air for signs of rain.

On the way back to Knoxville after his mother's funeral, Carlos said, in a low voice to keep from waking up the boys, who were asleep in the back seat, "The farm's going to be a handful with just Daddy left. He's not getting any younger. I know he could use some help."

"He can hire help."

"Hired help will steal you blind, you don't have somebody looking out for you."

Sue studied her hands, turning her wedding ring around and around on her finger. The knuckle above it had thickened until she needed soapy water to get the ring off. "It's a wonder he's lasted this long. Not much of a life, is it, living hand to mouth and every year going more in debt than out? I don't think I could stand it, Carlos. I couldn't stand it for a day."

The next morning, without talking to her first, Carlos gave the store notice and called from a pay phone, asking Daddy to get the old rental house cleaned up. Carlos was bringing his family home.

It's warm in the barn this time of day, even in late November, and Carlos swipes his hand impatiently across his forehead, smearing the dirt and sweat. It's not as though he hasn't tried to be good to her. Reaching for another bundle of hands Andrew has tied, Carlos says, "Jon, run up to the house and get your mother. We could use a little help down here."

When Sue comes to the barn twenty minutes or so later, she glares at Carlos. "I was coming," she says, low, when her work brings her close enough for him to hear. "You didn't need to send Jon after me."

"Hey, don't start in on me," Carlos says. He spits tobacco juice on the dry dirt beside the truck tire and watches it gather like a glob of mercury from a broken thermometer. "I didn't say a damned thing. But tell me this. If Billy is so damned smart, what's he wasting a year of his life here for? This ain't exactly no music capital of the world."

In January, Billy lands a job with a high school one county over, replacing a chorus teacher on pregnancy leave. His fiancé moves down from Louisville to live with him, and that, Carlos figures, will at least do him in with the Baptists at the little church they attend, where Billy directs the choir. But it seems Billy can follow his own rules. Even Daddy makes over Billy. At church, when Billy parks his new car next to Carlos's beat-up old pickup, Daddy tells everybody he can get to stand still long enough to listen how Billy went off to college and made something of himself. But Carlos is the one who has to pick Daddy up at the nursing home and bring him to church.

And anyway, who stayed? Carlos wants to ask Daddy. Doesn't that count for something, too?

When Lisa has been there a few days, Sue invites the two of them for supper. Lisa is short, pear-shaped, and skinny, except for the span of her hips. At supper, she scoots up close to the oak table and leans forward to slide a wedge of glazed ham from the platter onto her plate. "I just love good country cooking," she says.

"I'm glad to see her eating," Billy says. He smiles at her, the caps on his teeth as white as the rims on their mother's good china. "She doesn't eat enough to keep a bird alive. I'm glad she's moved down here for good so I can take care of her."

For good? Carlos thinks.

Lisa blushes and reaches a tiny, red-tipped finger over to press his hand. "Oh, you are so sweet. Don't you think he is so sweet?"

Carlos smears butter on an ear of corn. He can think of other words for Billy, but he keeps them to himself. This must be what Sue means when she says Carlos doesn't know how to show his feelings. Well, she might be glad of that tonight, if she could guess even half the feelings he's been holding in.

"Sue," Carlos says, between bites. "Sue here can eat me under the table." Sue narrows her eyes at him over a forkful of slaw, and he realizes at once he's stumbled. He knows she worries about her weight, though she doesn't need to. He heard her tell her friend Brenda at church Sunday it didn't do her any good to go on a diet. For every twenty pounds she lost, she found twenty-five. How could he forget that? Why can't she realize he's just teasing her?

"I don't mean anything bad by it," he says, trying to repair the damage, but digging himself in deeper with every word. This is one night he just can't seem to shut up. "Sue's a strong woman. She can lift as much as Andrew can. Me, I don't have any use for a woman who won't eat."

Lisa smiles at Sue and pats her on the arm. When she speaks, her voice is condescending, not about Sue's weight, but about Sue's stupid husband. "She has to feed her voice. Billy says she is just the most amazing singer. It takes strength to sing."

After supper, Carlos finds a deck of cards in a drawer in the kitchen. He flips through them to pull out the jokers. "You all play spades?"

Sue's frown—the one she's worn all evening, from the first moment Carlos opened his mouth—deepens. "Not everybody wants to sit around and play cards all night. They might just want to talk. Or Billy might play the piano and we could sing?"

But Billy looks up at Carlos and taps the table once with his index finger. "Deal 'em. But remember how I used to beat you two out of every three."

Carlos gets Lisa for a partner, and she turns out to be a pretty good player. She puts on big round glasses to read the cards, and she keeps up with every trump that's played. He and Lisa win the first two games, and Carlos looks over at Billy. "Now who used to beat who two out of three?'

Before the third game, Sue gets up to slice the chocolate cake. She carries the slices to the table on clear pink dessert plates, Depression glass, he thinks she calls it, and he can't get over how pretty she looks tonight. Her dark hair falls softly over the collar of her red blouse, and her dangly silver earrings glitter in the bright kitchen light. Compared to Lisa, she looks so womanly, with a woman's breasts, not those flat little things that look like fried eggs, or that short raggedy hair that looks like a girl's head got caught in a hay baler. She tilts her head toward Carlos. He wants to say something, but he's just like a boy with a weight on his tongue, and he looks down at the table as if he's waiting for his cake.

Billy tilts his chair back, his hands laced behind his head. "I've been meaning to talk to you, Carlos. There's a developer in town looking to buy up some property out this way to build a new subdivision. Says this farm could bring top dollar for housing lots. Or we could develop it. All you'd have to invest would be the money for water lines and roads."

"It's a farm," Carlos says. "Hard to farm on pavement."

"But it doesn't have to be a farm. It's land. You can use it for whatever you want to. Besides, Carlos, how long do you think you can hang on out here? Tobacco's your biggest cash crop, right? I mean, come on. Tobacco's been on its way out for thirty years. What are you going to do for labor when all the Mexicans and Guatemalans start working in that new chicken-processing plant?"

"We'll figure something else out. Anyway, it's no concern of yours, Billy. I'm the one working the farm. You're the one with the job in town."

"But when something happens to Dad—and you know the way his health's been—it would be a concern to me. I wouldn't make you sell the farm to buy out my half, but I'd sure try and get you to think about it. It seems like a no-brainer to me. You can work yourself to death like Dad, or you can make some money and get out."

"That's what I've been trying to tell him," Sue says. "He loves this place, but there's no future here."

"Did you know this whole county is on the New Madrid fault line?" Billy asks her. "When the last big earthquake hit, in the eighteen hundreds, it made the Mississippi River run backwards. You'd never know it, would you, just by looking, how unstable the ground is underneath? Let me tell you, nothing lasts forever, not even land."

Carlos picks up the cards dealt for him and fans them out in his hands. He tries not to think about fault lines and bulldozers, about Sue in her red blouse, or the way she looks at Billy as though he hung the moon. He divides the cards up first by color and then by suits. He studies the cards and his heart sinks. Not much to bet on here, now that Billy has finally shown his hand.

He wants to tell Billy that Daddy won't leave Billy half the farm, that he'll talk to Daddy, get him to make out a will so that the land passes to Carlos, who will keep it for his sons and Billy's, who haven't been born yet. But while Carlos has been working the dirt on the farm, what has Billy been working, especially considering the condition of their father's weak, old heart?

When Billy and Lisa leave, Carlos puts on his coat and goes to the barn to check on the animals, his flashlight bobbing circles in front of him in the dark. He keeps the milk cows in the barn at night, and he pats the flank of each one as he passes.

At the house, Sue has already gone to bed. He undresses and scoots in beside her. He puts his arm into the curve of her waist. She moves away, and he could pretend to miss her signal, but for some reason tonight, he doesn't want to roll over and let it go. "What did I do?" he says, stubbornly, his hand shaking her by the hip. "Just what in the hell did I do?"

She pulls away from him then and turns her pillow to its cold side, punching it into a wad before she lies back down. "Nothing. You didn't do anything. You never do."

Carlos rolls over on his back and looks up at the ceiling, white and ghostly from the porch light. "Did you know Billy in high school?" he asks. "He went around in that silly white band suit, waving that baton. One son of a bitch was dumb enough to ask me to my face if I knew my brother was a queer. I'll bet you didn't know that, did you? That everybody thought Billy was a queer?"

Sue sighs, but she doesn't sound angry, just tired. "I hate it when you talk like that. I don't know what you think it proves. Besides, what does Billy have to do with anything?"

He sits up in bed and puts his feet on the cold floor. "You tell me."

"You know you're making a fool of yourself? God, Carlos. Billy's your brother. And anyway, he's crazy about Lisa. They act like two teenagers." She waits a moment or two before she speaks again, and when she does, her voice sounds light, as though she is pleased in spite of herself. "What in the world would Billy want with me?"

Carlos gets up and slips his pants on. Even in the dark, he can feel her smiling. He doesn't know if she is smiling because she sees how Billy looks at her, no matter what kind of show he thinks he's putting on, or if she is laughing at Carlos and his jealousy. But God help him, if he doesn't get out of here fast, he'll knock the smile right off her face.

He wakes up the next morning in his recliner, freezing. He tiptoes into the bedroom in the dark to shut off the alarm before it goes off and wakes Sue. His work shirt from the day before hangs on the post at the foot of the bed. He slips it on and is out of the house before she even knows he is gone.

He drives out to the creek to repair some fences. He doesn't finish until it's nearly dark, but instead of turning up the long driveway toward the lighted windows of his house, he stays on the blacktop and drives. He drives every back road in the county, but they don't seem as much like back roads anymore. How did he miss it when acres of houses with paved, winding streets took over so much of the good farmland? He feels as if he went to sleep in one place, where the land stretched green for miles around him, folded here and there into hills, and he woke up to find himself lost in a country full of strangers, where all the landmarks have disappeared.

He shakes his head at his own stubbornness and stupidity. Billy's right. What kind of crazy dream has Carlos been living in? The boys work the farm because they have to, but Andrew will be gone as soon as he's old enough to go. Jon keeps his head buried in a chemistry book and says he wants to be a pharmacist, to spend his whole working life in a space about the size of a horse's stall. Why would they want Carlos to fight Billy to keep the farm in one piece? If he asks them, they will tell him to sell off the land and put the money in their hands.

He doesn't head home sometime until close to ten. Billy's Taurus glimmers in the moonlight near the house. Carlos pulls the pick-up truck next to Billy's car. He opens the door and stands for a moment, watching Sue through the kitchen window, Billy behind her. She looks like she's been crying, and for a moment Carlos's heart races. She's right. He is a fool. She's worried about him. He should have called her. But what would he have said? Billy puts both hands on her shoulders, the way he has more than once before, even while Carlos has been in the room with them, kneading the tension out of her neck, then working his hands from her neck to the tops of her arms and back again. Then, suddenly, he wraps his arms around her waist and pulls her close to him, leaning his cheek against the top of her dark hair.

She stops him. Later, Carlos will remember that she stops him. She takes his hands, unclasps his arms, and moves away. But he will also remember what he can see from the window, though from behind her Billy doesn't—the misery and longing on her face.

He doesn't start the truck when he climbs back into it. He leaves the headlights turned off, puts the truck into neutral, and coasts to the bottom of the hill before he cranks up the engine. He drives a short distance and turns up the road to the other side of the farm, to Daddy's house. The road here is rough, and the truck bounces along. The old moon bounces along, too, low in the sky above him, like a balloon on a string.

At the end of the road, Carlos sits in the truck and studies the old house. When Daddy built it, in the late sixties, it was a house he was proud of, with five good rooms to raise his sons in. Now, Carlos knows, most mobile homes have more square footage and at least two baths. He tries to imagine this house sitting in the middle of a new subdivision where it's against the deed restrictions to hang clothes on a line or park a pick-up truck on the street.

He sits a little longer in the dark, but he has already made up his mind. Then, the plan and action forming together, he takes a five-gallon container from the back of the pickup and splashes gasoline on the weatherboard siding, working his way around the perimeter of the house. He takes firewood from the shed and heaps it on the front porch. Then he pours gasoline on the pile of wood, too.

When the first container is empty, he goes to the truck for another. He carries it inside the front door, into the living room, and sets it down. He takes the family photos off the mantel and carries them out to the truck. Then he gets the photo albums off the bookcase and the bills and papers from Daddy's roll top desk.

When he returns to the house for the third time, he stops and tries to think what else he should carry with him. His football trophies that

Daddy still displays in a glass case he had specially made? What about his mother's furniture, darkened by dust and age? But he decides to leave it all behind. No point in carting out junk he'll just have to get rid of later. Billy and Sue have been giving him the same message over and over. He may be slow, but he finally gets it. There is nothing worth saving here.

When he has stacked the photographs and Daddy's papers neatly in the passenger seat of the truck, he goes inside the final time. In the living room, he pours out the gasoline from the second container, walking in circles around the braided rug. When the can is empty, he leaves it in the center of the circle and goes out again. This time he slams the door hard behind him. At the bottom of the porch steps, he kneels in the dirt, takes out the small flashlight he carries in his pocket, and searches the ground. When he finds a stick dry enough, he holds his lighter to the end until it catches fire. Then he tosses the lighted stick onto the porch, and in a few seconds, the wood there catches, too.

He backs the truck a safe distance from the house, and gets out. He is dead tired, but he stays to watch the fire, wondering, as if he's back in high school trying to solve an algebra problem, how long it will take the house to burn down. He knows it will take a fraction of the time it took to build it.

But it burns even faster than that. The place is past saving long before the trucks from the volunteer fire department arrive. He starts walking toward the fire, but a fireman takes him roughly by the shoulder and pulls him back. They don't even bother to get out their gear.

Carlos sits on the ground, and then looks up, surprised to see them. When he wipes the smoke from his eyes, he realizes that he has been crying. The tears drip off his chin like sweat.

Wanda Fries

The granddaughter of coal miners, Wanda Fries was born in Harlan County but lived in Cincinnati, Cleveland, and Chicago until the first grade when her father brought the family back to Pulaski County for good. Twice the recipient of the Kentucky Arts Council's Al Smith Fellowship, Fries' stories and poems have appeared in various journals, including *The Michigan Quarterly Review, Sojourners, River City Review, Wind*, and *Appalachian Heritage*. A teacher at Somerset Community College, she lives in Somerset with her husband, Denny, a geologist, and their two teenagers. She is currently working on a novel.

Genesis for *Fault Lines*

I grew up in rural Pulaski County, and though my father was a preacher and an electrician, our neighbors were mostly small farmers. On Sundays, they filled the pews of the Baptist church where my father was pastor. They sold us milk and vegetables and employed my brothers to work in tobacco, their primary cash crop.

By the time I went to college in the seventies, high interest rates had made the loans the farmers relied on to stay solvent from one tobacco season to another even harder to repay. Some of the farmers' wives took "public" jobs in town to supplement their family incomes. They sewed "suit coats" at the Palm Beach factory or worked for the state as health aides or housekeepers at the Oakwood residential facility for the mentally handicapped. In search of an easier and more secure livelihood, some of the children left home for college to become teachers and pharmacists. As the county's population increased, developers bought up acres of farmland for subdivisions.

Though I intended to focus this story on the fault lines in a marriage, as I worked on various drafts, I became more and more aware of how drastically the rural areas of my childhood had been altered by "progress." It is always easy to sentimentalize hard work and "family values"; still, it is remarkable how quickly and without much opposition the change from a land-based to a jobs-based economy came.

Why are some people connected profoundly to a place, while others, raised in the same environment, cannot wait to get away? (I must confess that I was the latter.) As the story became fully realized, the conflict centered less on the marriage itself and more on the returning prodigal, who sees nothing but profit in selling the home place, and the older brother for whom the family's land represents not just his livelihood but the measure by which he defines himself.

These days strip malls and subdivisions stretch along our highways. In Pulaski and other Kentucky counties, "the future corridor" (as the signs say) of I-66 will claim even more land. Even if the politicians and chambers of commerce who optimistically predict region-wide economic benefits are right, those benefits will be at best a mixed blessing. For men like Carlos, I am afraid, the time of small rural farms and the families who worked them for generations may have already come and gone.

Stuck

Todd Hunt

"…what most people fail to recognize is that all of us, as bearers of souls, have a responsibility to strike out with our lives and merge with the world. The most wicked sin is for one to travel through life without ever making an attempt to touch anybody, or to shrink back from the efforts of another. Nature is a force that demands the coupling of souls, and it can reward with chains of fruitful, exploratory lives. It can also assure the hermit an eternity with himself …"

"Bull!" Caynefield said and stabbed the eject button. The cassette was white and featureless, except for a thin marker scrawl: *Living Again. And Again.* The old, smoked-out lady behind the counter at the truck-stop in Spartanburg had given it to him. Although he'd seen her every week for years, today was the first time they had exchanged any words beyond "Thanks." He didn't like people, and kept his own counsel. Playing with her wet, stringy hair, she had said something that lodged in Caynefield's head like a wine headache.

"Stupid reincarno."

He roared out of the under-mountain tunnel and gasped as he glanced west. A purple mist floated down from the heights of the Cherokee National Forest. Caynefield eased the pressure a bit on the accelerator, even though he was already going to be late in Asheville with the load of turkey necks. He'd been back and forth on this curvy stretch of I-40 with his rig Boomer for seventeen years and seen a lot of mist, but none of it had ever been purple. The fog flashed intermittently, like a fluorescent Easter egg.

"Oh, no!" he whispered.

He slowed Boomer down some more and a red Honda flashed by on his left, bleating its horn as it disappeared around a sharp corner. Its passage sucked the mist down onto the road; ethereal fingers clutched futilely at the small car. Caynefield cursed as he barreled helplessly into the miasma. He stamped the brakes as Boomer's tires shrieked against the chafing asphalt. The indigo haze puffed out of the air-conditioning vents like ink, filling the cab. It smelled maddeningly sweet. He opened his mouth tasting saccharine, which faded to a bitterness that made his eyes involuntarily squeeze shut.

When Caynefield opened his eyes, the mist had completely vanished. He could only begin a surprised grunt when his halting truck collided into something. Soft. Yielding. A small doe hurtled through the air and landed in the unkempt grass on the interstate shoulder. Taking off his cap, he scratched a zit on his scalp. "What the hell is this? First I see stuff like I was still playing with the Dust, and now I've gone and smashed another damn deer."

He jumped out of Boomer and stood dead still at the echo his boots made against the pavement. The sound lingered for thirty seconds, finally disappearing into the panoramic valley beyond the shoulder. Thc morning sun shone low in the east, but its light was cold. The interstate was barren, and he felt no vibrations in the road beneath the soles of his feet. Caynefield listened for something, but the surroundings offered nothing but the clicks and pops of the cooling engine, and the ghostly moans in the ear of silence.

A rustling in the grass startled a shout from his throat. The deer was still alive. He went and knelt down beside it. This was the fifteenth deer he had hit, and her moist, walnut eyes made his stomach hurt. Her hindquarters were ruined, and her head spasmed on the neck like a strummed guitar string.

"I'm so sorry, beautiful. I didn't see you come out in front of me." He touched her head gingerly, and the doe surprised him by pressing her nose into his palm to lick his fingers. Something about her profile, her gaze, stirred recognition in him. The idea was ridiculous, but how ridiculous compared to a mist that tasted like coffee-sweetener? "Why is it so quiet, beautiful? What happened here?" Her movements slowed gradually, and Caynefield did his best to comfort her, scratching her neck, her shoulders and forelegs. His left hand froze on the doe's left foreleg. A dark, red birthmark, the shape of a vinyl record, wrapped around the leg. Complete with a small circle in the center.

Hands shaking, he unbuttoned the cuff at his left wrist and folded the sleeve back, revealing an identical birthmark. His tongue felt gritty. Suddenly, he was looking at his own downcast face. He scanned the pitted complexion and peaked nose; the chapped lips moved around words he felt his tongue forming. "I'm looking at me." Just as fast he saw the animal again. The doe raised her head and licked the shape on his arm then collapsed into the deep grass. Caynefield jerked away from the carcass and stood up.

"No, Caynefield. No way. You don't believe in that stuff. That's for cigarette-stinking crones."

He turned to go back to the truck, but Boomer was gone. He blinked as a green sedan emerged from nowhere, horn blaring. The car slid and crashed into him. Air whistled through his hair and he landed on his back, realizing he couldn't feel anything below his waist. Blood gushed from his mouth like a broken water main. A woman stood over him, clutching her hands around her neck and crying. The unmoving sun lit up her chestnut hair from behind, making her look like Mary in a stained glass window. As she fell to her knees, Caynefield recognized her walnut eyes. Same as his own. The crone's words reverberated in his memory: "I think you need to listen to this tape, truckie. I been looking at you for ages and don't know nothing about you. You're a lonely soul, and the hand behind this world gets impatient with lonelies. Likes to put them away. If you keep up the way you've been, you're liable to run into a soul trap. Ain't nobody going to miss you, as it is right now. You might like your own company, but it'd be a terrible thing to spend forever seeing all the great things you could've been. And seeing how you wasted it every time."

"I couldn't see you through the mist. There was this purple mist," the woman sobbed. She wore a sleeveless blouse, and he found the vinyl record mark around her slender forearm. Instantly he saw his dying face through her eyes. Lifting his own arm, he spit out blood and said, "I'm you today and you're me tomorrow. Get in your car and drive through the trap. Then go kiss a stranger."

She covered her mouth in astonishment, but didn't move an inch. "Why did I just see my own face? You've got the same mark as me…"

"Please, leave. Or our corpses will clog this road." Caynefield's eyes fluttered shut as another frightened horn emerged from the mist.

Todd Hunt

Todd Austin Hunt was born in the Smoky Mountains the year his father took off work to become a writer and was raised in Paris, KY. He discovered Stephen King at age 13, which warped his brain for the better. A graduate of UK and EKU, he's been publishing stories since 2003.

Genesis for *Stuck*

A very wonderful friend and I have repeatedly had an argument regarding the importance of the author's background and circumstances surrounding the understanding of a fictional work. I insist that Roland Barthes was right, that a short story rises up like a newborn spirit, cognizant of self and independent of the writer. I insist that readers who peer too closely at the writer will vanquish that spirit with the shadow of the writer. My friend, a talented, young poet, believes that the connection between writer and work is an ethereal cord impossible to sever. Thus, she thinks my head is clogged with romantic horseshit.

She's probably right.

That said, this little story did not emerge from a vacuum. Like the main body of my work, *Stuck* is a fantasy; however, the idea rose from the stage of my mainstream existence. In the spring of 2003, I was new to graduate school and once again returned to my home state of Kentucky. A year before, I had been living in relative isolation, and at Eastern Kentucky University, I came into a horde of friends. The disparity between the two lifestyles presented to me how light an individual soul is, and how vulnerable that soul can be to the currents of time if always alone.

Around this time, I watched Richard Kelly's jolting film, *Donnie Darko*, which deals with themes of isolation, as well as time travel. Good stories or movies often serve as springboards for new ideas, and I wondered, can a person be damned for touching no one?

So, the idea stuck, and I remembered the beautiful drive on I-40 through the Cherokee National Forest the summer before. The story was written in delight, as my best stories are. It was lucky to receive an Honorable Mention in the 2003 Ray Bradbury Writing Contest.

In hindsight, I recognize that I carved out more of myself in creating Caynefield than I had imagined at the time. Essentially, this writer's not dead.

And my friend is right.

Discussion Questions

An Otherwise Flawless Canvas

1. In her genesis essay, Zaring says she "wanted to show that the decision to remain childless isn't always cut-and-dry." How does she accomplish this purpose?

2. Anna Jarvis, the recognized foundress of Mother's Day, later regretted originating the national holiday because of excessive commercialism. How do you feel about what often happens to the spirit of our holidays?

3. How does Zaring use the border status of Kentucky—the most northern southern state and the most southern northern state—to symbolize Diana's dilemma in the story?

4. What do you make of Diana's decision at story's end? Are you sympathetic, or do you disagree?

5. How does Zaring use the swing set to reinforce Diana's struggle?

A Place to Cross

1. Why is it important that Ben tell the story in his own words rather than having it delivered by a third-person narrator? How can the method of narration affect a story?

2. Croley chooses to tell his story in the present tense. What effect does this technique have on the reader's engagement?

3. Why do you think Croley chose this story's title? What significance does the title have relative to the story's theme?

4. Croley says his story is about "unconditional love." How does he portray this quality in the relationship of Ben and Deb?

Her Leg

1. Rogers' story depicts an incident from the past filtered through the memory of a young girl. What do we learn about the narrator from the way she recounts the events?

2. The story centers around the unique, somewhat strange relationship between Chick and Mother Grace. Can you recall a relative who was a bit eccentric, a bit out of the ordinary in appearance or manner?

3. What do you think of Chick's final actions in the story? How has the incident changed her?

Tip of the Screw

1. Titus transforms an incident from the past by creating a different backdrop and situation. How does she use a macabre event to reveal character? What do we learn about Dale Senior, John, and Karen through their reactions to the incident?

2. Titus uses verisimilitude, the accumulation of precise details to create a semblance of reality, to pull readers into the scenes of her story. Is she successful in making the story come alive? Which details seem most realistic to you?

3. Why do you think so much of the story occurs in the Home Depot? What does the setting accomplish for Titus' treatment of character? Of plot?

The 30th Annual Naming of Boy Howell

1. *Nomen est omen* (name is destiny) is a concept that has strongly influenced cultures for centuries. How does Jaeger use this concept in his story? Is his use straightforward or ironic?

2. Jaeger uses dialect effectively throughout the story. How does Bebe Howell's dialect contribute to her characterization?

3. What do you make of the story's ending? What do you think Jacob will take away from this strange evening?

Rabbit Blood

1. An initiation story is one that involves a character (usually a young one) in a potentially maturing situation. Sometimes the character gains an insight; sometimes, not. Do you think the young narrator of *Rabbit Blood* learns anything about life by story's end? Does he mature in any way?

2. Do you think your understanding of this story would be different if it were told in third person rather than by the character himself? How?

3. Dramatic irony occurs when the reader knows more than a character or narrator. What effect does your knowing things about the situation (e.g., Lucky's "medicine" is some type of illegal drug) that escape the narrator have on your interpretation of the story?

4. Hampton claims that his story "is composed of several scraps of memory left from my childhood." Do you think creating fiction by weaving memories from different events and real-life characters would be difficult? Why?

Creases

1. Stanfill says that the protagonist of her story is "a lot like me." What dangers might writers encounter by modeling characters on themselves? What strengths might they gain?

2. John D. MacDonald, the novelist and critic, says that story is something happening to someone we have been led to care about. What makes the reader "care" about Billi Jo? Do you care enough to want to read other stories about her?

3. Stanfill makes use of what Stephen King and contemporary writers call "brand-name realism" in her story. That is, she inserts names of real products (e.g., Diet Pepsi, Band-Aid) and personalities (e.g., Rolling Stones, Dixie Chicks) instead of using generics. How does this technique affect the reader's perception of the characters and action? Does it make the story seem more real? Will this technique cause problems for the next generation of readers?

4. At several junctures Stanfill refers to specific music in the background? Are these tunes randomly selected from her "jukebox," or do they have any special relationship to the characters and events? Do they add to your understanding of the story?

Tabernacle of Love

1. Olert's story treats a series of events that grows from an almost innocent occurrence to a tragic culmination that takes two lives. What does this story say about evil and its cumulative nature?

2. Was the story's ending a surprise? How does Olert cleverly prepare for the twist at the end?

3. What role does Brooks play in the story? What keeps him from being simply an extra character padding the narrative?

4. How does the story picture small-town Kentucky? Do you agree with the portrayal?

Canvas

1. How does Pitts' use of the present verb tense affect the story? Does it make the narrative more immediate, or does it seem mechanical?

2. Does Pitts do an effective job of transmitting Sarah Jane's fears? Do her emotions come across as genuine?

3. Have you ever encountered a situation to which you did not know how to react? How did you handle your emotions? Were you fearful or did you react with confidence?

Fault Lines

1. What is the real conflict in the story? Is it between Billy and Carlos? Carlos and Sue? Or is it between two sets of values represented by the characters?

2. Why do you think Sue marries Carlos? What is it that truly makes her unhappy in the marriage? What do you think will happen to their marriage?

3. What do you make of Carlos' final action of burning down his father's house? What about the things he removes before the fire?

Stuck

1. Hunt claims at the end of his genesis essay that his poet friend is correct about an unbreakable connection between the writer and the work. Do you agree, or do you believe that once a writer produces a work, that writer surrenders any claim of ownership to readers, who are free to find in it whatever they may?

2. Does Hunt's story lead you to agree with Stephen King that horror grows best out of the ordinary, the everyday?

3. How does Hunt use details from several senses to draw the reader into his brief, but powerful tale?

Recent Kentucky

POETRY

with Introductory Comments by

Frank X Walker

With the ever-increasing popularity of performance poetry and open mic readings at cafés and bookstores all over the region, poetry and poets seem practically everywhere. In fact, almost too many people leave inspired from many of the public venues that feature live readings, go home, scratch out their best first effort, and proudly proclaim membership into the circle of poets. But not unlike other art forms, great poetry and accomplished poets are still the products of discipline, passion, and good old-fashioned hard work. The poets assembled in these pages didn't just luck up on well paced, rhythmical, image-rich verses that will please the readers and listeners when read aloud. They have spent time, and some even decades, polishing their craft. And it shows.

The poets in these pages are the sons and daughters of accomplished Kentucky writers. They have grown up with the books and pencils and journals. They've fallen asleep and been "awakened" at readings. They are graduates of Kentucky's Governors School for the Arts, the School for Creative and Performance Arts and other scholastic programs that stress the importance of creating opportunities for instruction for students identified with particular gifts and talent as creative writers. They are products of one of the new graduate programs in creative writing now available in the state. They are rural and urban, multi-gendered and fairly representative of the diverse population that continues to use poignant, image-driven, economical verse as their primary means of communication. They know and respect the power of the word. They buy books and read classical and obscure contemporary poets. They know what Barbara Kingsolver meant when she said, "the first draft is a necessary evil." They worry over line breaks, clichés, metric feet, double entendres, alliteration, and internal rhymes. They are students of the word. They are not accidents. They live. They breathe. They are real poets.

I am proud to have had the chance to help select and introduce to the reader the poets and powerful voices assembled in these pages. If this book can be considered the barometer, the future of poetry in Kentucky, indeed in the region, is in great hands. Having taught all over the country and being intimately familiar with the literary activity in this region, especially as it relates to poetry, I can say with all the confidence that these pages represent some of the best work by the Commonwealth's best emerging writers, period. Enjoy!

Living Among Us

Tammy Ramsey

My friend has just read the biography of Gordon Cooper,
a former astronaut who contends he's seen UFOs.
My friend says he is convinced.
Of what? I ask, and in his most certain voice, he answers:
That we have already been visited and they live among us.
I can tell he is serious, and it scares me just a little.
But the skeptic in me shrugs her shoulders.
This guy's no slouch, my friend says. He knows what he saw.
A night or two later, a documentary about crop circles
parades scientists, horticulturists, agronomists,
each who says there is no human explanation.
My seventh-grade science teacher, without batting an eye,
told us repeatedly that a spaceship set down on his land,
leaving behind a field full of silver metal.
Why is that so hard for you to believe? he asked us.
I'm telling you the truth. I saw it.
There was more to his story too,
something about dead cows and government cover-ups.
The most troubling part was that our teacher
looked like he might have ridden in on the ship himself.
He was bald, with an oddly round head
and facial features and expressions
that somehow didn't seem just right.
I'm not sure how it happened, whether some of us
finally got so tired of his stories that we reported him
or whether someone told on us for all our mocking.
However it came about, the principal
appeared unannounced one day in our science classroom.
He scolded us for starting the rude joke
that our teacher was an alien.
He didn't rebut the spaceship stories,
even defended them, saying
Only the one who saw it knows what he saw.
He knows what he saw, my friend says again,
convinced Gordon Cooper wouldn't lie.
Look around. Why is it so hard for you to believe?

Whitewash

Bianca Spriggs

She still washes her whites
on a tin scrub board in the creek
that runs halfway through her back yard
and halfway through what is now a park.
The park is on a plot that used to be a jail
for brown people and a gallows.
And country folks used to bring fried chicken
and fried pickles and peach cobbler
and watch their kids splash
each other in the shallow end,
their voices skipping like stones over water
rippling in the direction of convicts with brown skin
that soon ceased to be flesh and God-breath
dissipated back into just some clay.

She still squats to sit on a large stone
facing the park and new courthouse,
bare feet flexing on smaller stones.
Finding crevices to poise in,
she scoots her skirt back above the knee
or ties it in knots on either side
and bends at the waist,
stretches her back
in a down and up rhythm.
She sits with scrub board
between her thighs
conjures the soil
from dripping whites
into a wash tin with detergent.
Sometimes the suds lather
over its sides to be lapped up
on the creek's banks

making rings that are rainbow
with chemical additives and soap.

She still washes her whites
on a tin scrub board
rubbing them free
from sediment and sins,
wringing out the echoes,
baptizing her fabric
over and over in one half of a creek
whose waters are bordered by
grasses and stones and roots and branches
that used to sip up blood and skin and lives.

Human Kindness

Sherry Chandler

Betty's voice, tethered helium,
bounced in the slightest breeze. Even listening,
she made little gasps and moans. Her laugh
gurgled like cherry wine from a jug.

Betty had a roving eye. It twitched.
Mom said men were apt to see a wink.
How much a mistake was that? Mom said
affairs, fancy word for a country woman.

Mawmaw Reenie, ramrod straight and starched,
rouged and powdered, every black hair permed
perfect: I don't know how, even to
this day, to picture her unbuttoned, pinks

and browns of babes and breasts and nipples. Yet
Mom tells me it was so. Aunt Rosal, after
seven children, sick, Reenie, seventeen,
with milk for two: my mom and Betty.

At 2 A.M.

Sherry Chandler

Bladder eased, I crawl between the sheets.
You reach an arm to pull me in, thirty
years a habit. I settle in your warmth for sleep,
but voices whisper ice a decade old.

Mama on a February day.
He asked, he said, come to bed with me
and warm my back. He fights for every breath,
all day, all night. But I could not
lie down and warm his back.

This love stuff's worthless. Dad in June
walks emphysema's pace through prized
tomatoes, grown by will, strength long-since gone.
Family's the thing. Don't let your mother fool you.
Her heart's as strong as yours. When I am gone,
she'll have this place, but she takes care of me.
That's the deal. I need to die at home.

The thaw comes with your breath
upon my nape. The sneer and the lament
fade as his grave sinks before the double stone
and she sleeps still
in my narrow childhood bed.
On Sunday afternoons, grandchildren toss
coats on the walnut marriage bed, log cabin
quilt tucked in with mitered corners.

Botany Lesson, A First Date

Karen George

From bench to bench they moved,
the first too hot in direct sun,
the second too cool in total shade.
Facing the river,
they settled beneath a horse chestnut
whose leaves, like a sieve, filtered all
but the leanest rays of light.
Leaves' shadows washed back and forth
across their faces and arms.

Stiff as the wax paper she unwrapped,
she bit into the bread,
wondered if she could swallow.
The wind muddled everything.
With one hand she anchored wax paper,
napkin, bag of chips in her lap.
The other raised sandwich,
sliding lettuce and tomato,
to her mouth.
She needed a third hand
to keep hair out of her face.

She let go of the need
to find something to say,
invoked the whoosh of autumn leaves
as conversation.
She gave up trying
to hold her abdomen in,
her shoulders back,
her chin up.

After lunch, they followed the river's flow,
talked of trees they passed under.
Lowering a scarlet oak branch to her height,
he ran his finger
along the toothed lobes of leaf.
He raised a sassafras twig to her nose,
handed her acorns, chestnuts, locust pods.
His fingers touched the small of her back,
to guide her,
as they turned upstream.
"End of the botany lesson," he said,
pressing a winged pair of maple seeds
into the palm of her hand.

Sports Chat with the Nine Muses

after Albert Goldbarth

Tom Hunley

"Let's sing of heroes like Jackie Robinson," says Clio,
muse of history. "1947. Segregated schools. Separate restaurants.
Water fountains labeled 'colored.' Number 42 showed America
that white people and black people could be teammates.
And no one could steal a base like that man."

"Pete Rose stole bases as well as any mortal," says Melpomene,
muse of tragedy. "Used to slide head first, the same way
he leapt into bets. Why isn't the league's all-time best hitter
in the hall of fame? So he was no boy scout. Babe Ruth drank."

Calliope, muse of epic poetry, says "Speaking of scandals,
Rosi Ruiz barely broke a sweat in the Boston Marathon.
No wonder, she skipped the first twenty five and a half miles.
And she rode the subway for most of the New York Marathon."

"Marathons are so long and boring. So's baseball," says Thalia,
muse of comedy. "Give me a blooper reel any time, a basketballer
dunking in the wrong net, a field goal kicker missing the ball, falling."

Erato, muse of love poetry, says she doesn't watch sports.
"But I watch movies about sports. Especially if they're really about
love." Did you see The Cutting Edge? This washed-up hockey star
helps an ice skater go for the gold in paired figure skating."

"My favorite film is Saturday Night Fever, says Terpsichore,
muse of dance. "Is disco a sport?" Everyone shouts "No!"
except for Erato, who loved that film. "What about poetry slams?"
asks Euterpe, the muse of lyric poetry. This reminds Polyhymnia,
muse of songs to the gods, of Saturday night preach-offs in the South.

Urania, muse of astronomy, praises midnight bowling.
"The way those balls spin and glow in the dark,
it's like all of space lights up with planets and stars,
and hero or goat, highlight or blooper, picked first or left standing
against a wall with the too fat and too brainy, you know it's not
whether you win or lose, because we all win for a short while,
then lose for a long while, and the game will keep going, on and on,
until Zeus tucks the sun under his arm, says 'I'll take my ball and go home.'"

My Father's Necktie

Tom Hunley

married at eighteen a father at nineteen
mortgaged by twenty-two he didn't have
an office with diplomas certificates news clippings
and I never saw him strangle himself
with a necktie at least not the kind you unknot
at the end of the day I often heard him curse

the grime he couldn't quite wash off
of his hands I heard him snarl
at my mother and at his invisible necktie
which kept getting tighter and tighter I
heard his footsteps the creak of the door
echoed by years of a silence he fathered

a silence split by my mother's voice calling him
a bastard and by the dirty murmurs of her
other men my father told me I would understand
one day he tried to wash his hands
of all of it all of us
though we clung to his skin like scabs

Milch

Joanie DiMartino

Goodwives spoke of 'white meat:' milk,
mammary glands, breasts, nipples, with these they fed
their young.

They feared buttery spells from impish
churns, soured mother-teats; left divers
accounts of their bristling
dread of dairy magic.   Kitchen witches, accused,

once blamed a spectral succubus for spilled
cups and watery cheeses, the night orb
a single pale drop: curdled, evil eye.

The slender maid on the milking stool
enchanted with rhythm against her pail: a steady
incantation of liquid,

like colostrum, the woman-cream,
transformed into a superstitious witch's milk: rich,
forbidden.

Animal Husbandry: Winter

Leatha Kendrick

In the suburbs it is leashes and feeders,
shivery walks, bags of thistle seed and leaning
to scoop the poop. Perhaps a caged bird singing

only in late sun at the glass where transference
of cold to study and heat to backyard air is
clearest. My cat, content in every weather, gazes

transfixed at the finches safe on the bush, or
coils at my crossed feet as we absorb a fire's
whisper, and yarn pulls across her back, my hands,

into caps and shawls. The dog, on the other hand,
chafes, tosses his bone, runs in his sleep. Outdoors
he prances like a sleigh horse, digs in his heels

as if he is a sled dog, pulling ten times his weight,
bolts at every bird or squirrel out for free lunch.
it's not much, such keeping as I do, compared to

mucking stalls or carrying water endlessly to the trough,
even to the nightly stop you used to make
at our red barn, my love, to feed the cattle, check

the burgeoning nannies, intent to drop their kids
in January. Your red and black wool shirt,
the flap-eared cap and your boots stiff with cold

recalled sets of uncles, grandfathers and my own
father stomping into kitchens years and years receding
from us. Leaving that life was a breeze—periously

easy. We'd just as soon not mess with all that now.
even the dog's too much sometimes. Not human enough—
too prone to animal need, which is why I keep him near:

to be forced out into the cold when I don't
feel like it, to feel the frozen ground underfoot,
the intractable wind, the need to feed and be fed

by what is alive. To remember how alien and utterly
familial each creature is—not us, nor made by us.

Not for Nothing

Charlie Hughes

My first car was a '53 Plymouth
my father bought when I was just sixteen.
Rings shot to hell, it cranked and ran ok,

but burnt more motor oil than gasoline
and belched, smelled, and smoked like Krakatoa.
I drove it like a demon through high school,

its white wall rubber thin as onion skin,
inside the trunk a case of 30-weight,
a bald spare tire, sometimes a beer or two,

and always followed by that sulfurous fog.
It knew as well as I the road to Beth's,
took me to my job as plumber's stooge

and every week to town on Saturday night.
At Sam's Pool Hall I'd shoot nine-ball 'til one
with guys who didn't give a shit for nothing,

and all with better wheels than my old lemon.
I sold the smoker for a hundred bucks
before I left for higher education.

Breadbasket

Charlie Hughes

Twelve hundred calories today —
My belly has all my attention.
This little Buddha beneath my belt
should belong to a woman. I love
my stomach if only for this single thought.
I would cup its loveliness in my palm,
slide my hand over its velvet
and into the bright ringlets below.
I would drink from its navel
the wine of sweet kisses
and taste the salt of inland seas.
Its rise and fall would be my bread and cheese
and it would know the meat of my life.
I would rest my head upon its shores
and listen to the rush of tides,
the gurgling of deep streams.
It would be my pillow
in the night, and in the morning
waken me with the rocking of gentle laughter.

The Tattooed Lady's First

Erin Keane

At fifteen I believed I moved in a rarified
bubble, all feeling contained within,
the dichotomy of in and out sharp,
a line in the crackling dust of a dark
television screen: me vs. all. That summer

I grazed on fudgesicles in the shadow
of an abandoned power station, dragonflies
zipping in tandem through skeletal metal:
tumbling trapeze act, wings beating
a rivergreen trance. Mating in thick
August air, they hovered my sticky hand,

the clacking of Walkman cassette reels
unnoticed. I played one song ten thousand
times, my theme, headphones keeping it
private, between my ears—an illusion
of singularity, of experience. They flew off,

skimming a stagnant puddle, the fallow
transformer dull under dwindling light,
not humming. I didn't have words
for the pins and needles. A mosquito

lit down and sipped from my thigh.
I fingered the welt, blood drops
smearing my leg. The red against white,
almost membrane, almost a wing.

I knew a place. A guy with forearms
graffitti'd like boxcars. Somewhere
they won't see, I whispered. All you
have is your skin, and what it covers.

That Old Green Light

Erin Keane

All things pale & blooming with eyes sealed against
mid-day light. Playing coma never was such fun: night
creeps, the guestroom candle sputters. Might I be found
out. The day goes. The moon hide-and-seeks with digital
bedside numbers, red blink vital signs in two/four time.
It is always midnight, if not noon. The downstairs party
swells, a beast, all murmur & assignations, so many
flowering branches artful in a vase: how some palms find

pliable waists to cup. Let fall the underwear like wilted
Kleenex. Stockings will crash on certain rumpled white
linens. Door ajar, my slant hall view. Voices lull & am I
the sole survivor? Breath held, believe that you might
climb the stairs in slow-mo, lit by trembling sconces,
full of nothing better to do, you emperor of this & that.

Etymology of a Flood

Erin Keane

Recognizing order
is like opening
a dam in a river.
— Lu Chi's Wen Fu

Searching for carnival, I find Carna:
goddess of family, of hinges. And,
but, so, yet. To the movable joint. Scan
down. Carnifico: decapitate, to mangle.
A head at the hinge. A family at its head.

Enter the carnificina, a hangman's office.
What records must he keep on file? Limatulus:
striving for polish, rather refined. Pencil
licked, tucked behind ear. So much, a sigh,

hinges on the tilt of a head. Carpo,
carpere, carptum—to pluck, to pluck
off. Ligare: we bind. Lacrimula, little
tears track like floured feet. But. Yet. And
knowing order means opening a dam—

a goddess, unhinged, mangles Broadway,
plucks the agape girl in her stripey shirt

from father's mythic hand and O, and
O, the Hundred-Years Lachrymosa. So
repeat the soggy scene. Ad infinitum,
the cycle. What is handed back? Refine
the narrative. Drain the river. Reperio,

a sandy bottom. To discover. Bright
as a fresh coin, your loss. Repetentia:
faithless memory—a sandwich in two
right triangles. Three sides to every story.

Demergo: let's play tea party. Sink.
It will happen, the diminish. Work.
Plunge your hands, sift shell from
bone, demand it all back, back, back.

Priscilla Johnson Still Has Hands Like Leaves

Erin Keane

—after the painting by Alice Neel (Speed Art Museum)

Priscilla, by now you will have a Zoloft script that
won't quite do, a hypnosis tape
to cure that pack-a-day, some downtown boyfriend

Julian who will always be too
young for comfort, but he will be smooth,
Belgian, and you have had a thing

for Belgians since Richard's mother, the painter,
brought a poster back
from Brussels, a Bergman film with two

titles: L'Oeil du Diable,
Het Duivel's Oog. You considered—to have two
names, or two tongues: one

plush, one slender. Priscilla, you will still hate
the Beatles, but you'll like
that you're the only one. It is enough to love,

to nurture the small dislikes,
even this far from '66. And your clothes, they
will not have changed. Acid—

green shift, needing a steam in the worst way,
puddling on your sharp frame,
severe toes tipped like weapons: Italian leather

kitten heels pointy, tearing
up the carpet. You used to pose like a sour
Holly Golightly, one arm

vertical, wrist cocked, as if to wield a slim,
stemmed cigarette holder, but
you were 16, and even now, you still can't smoke

in front of anyone's mother.
So your thumb bent your middle fingernail
until it snapped, brittle snag

catching the upholstery. But, like now, you did not
care, in fact enjoyed leaving
a line of yourself traced in the arm of a chair.

The Lion Tamer's Résumé

Erin Keane

At least in this gig, you wear a gun,
pressing your thigh like a trained
Great Dane ready to snap. A needle-
sharp mind's an asset, memory is gift—
recognize the mouth twitch and know:

to crush or caress, this means another night
on the road. A trade to teach a daughter,
unlike my rank years on the girl show,
grinding, scissoring legs. Work strong,
the bally urged, barking my wiggles.

County-wide farmers stared. One girl's
work is another girl's past. No ladies,
no babies—just me, whiskey-soaked,
hand-made tassels twirling Girls! Girls!
Girls! Big tent's green light taunting.

I play the night over and over: get out—
no daughter of mine echoing, uncovering
behind a trailer for the boss. No tits, but
you'll do. A gun. A whip. Are you in
or out? I stuck my finger in his mouth.

Sex Under Glass

Libby Falk Jones

You made the date a month ago, now wait
for your escort, a woman in a
white coat. The mammography suite's
inviting, rug over hospital linoleum,
magazines stacked in baskets, a lace doily on the table
with the self-examination brochures. In the curtained booth
you strip waist up, don a printed cape
that you'll soon shed. Through another door, then
ritual conversation and notes on a form, the thick metal pole
looming. Full frontal, you embrace the metal,
curl your nude torso around the glass tray. She heaves
your breast out full, a pull as relentless as your
first baby's jaws, then the top tray presses down to fondle
your cells. Head bowed, arms stretched,
you lean into the cold stem, hear
the penetrating buzz, a Venus de Milo shot
with microns of light. "Hurt me a little,"
moaned the heroine of the porn novel you devoured
at the Rexall drugstore book rack,
your thirteen-year-old body tingling.
The glass withdraws, your breast throbs on the plate.
Three more times her cold fingers, the dry thrust,
smoothed only by held breath, an empty mind.
Hours later, your breasts quiescent, a white-coated man
will lift the charcoal mounds to the light,
trace their paths, pockets, craters,
the complex stuff of the body,
you hope his probing eyes and fingers
caress no tenderness.

First Spring Back in Kentucky

Libby Falk Jones

How could I have forgotten
the middle of April:
redbuds' sly glances,
floats of pink dogwood blossoms
outside the window
where I stand with my tea,

halleluiah chorus of crabapple buds,
bees wakening from their white sweet dream,
frilly hats on tips of shagbark hickory branches,
more shades of green
than in the biggest Crayola box.

I need to remember
to applaud the peony stalks that crack the earth,
unfolding fern fronds,
to welcome even the weeds,
traces of mint on my fingers,

imagine the river birch
Mother hoped to stay home for—
leaves thin, silver in evening light.

After Handwashing

Sam L. Martin

This stream
carries the caress
of my calloused fingers,
entices the church pianist
bathing in her cloistered creek.
She divines
a sweating, smiling man
offering her spiced wine,
then returns
to her immersion,
exalted.

Liberated

Sam L. Martin

Through fog
the morning sun debuted
as a blood blister
thumbed behind bare trees
by an injured god.
You did not notice.
You sipped bottled coffee,
chanted convictions
about your freedom,
as usual,
your oval phrases
reminding me
of last night's love.
Later I learned
your music,
a crimson lullaby
clotting
in the brain
of our unborn son.

Relics

Andrea O'Brien

A medallion of saints—the relics
of six dead men and women,
each the size of a thistle seed—
nestles among hairpins and earrings
in a dresser drawer. Each name
has faded, each fracture of bone
yellowed. Each aches for the return
to whole. And the other fragments?

Embedded in the altar
of a church in Baltimore?
Snug in the pocket of a woman
on her way to methadone treatment?
Buried beneath the ground
of a vineyard in Provence?
If we could puzzle the pieces together,
could we restore St. Vincent or St. Catherine?

I give thanks I am not holy enough
for bones and teeth to shatter,
spread through the world as spores,
as disease, as light, as language,
passed from mother to maiden,
believer to pagan, hand to hand.

Meditations on a Restaurant Hamburger

Howard Wang

Think
of the platonic vacancy
of the beast, whose unexamined life
provided in part for my meal.
Mark the absence of questions
and the plurality of grass.
I have read somewhere
that there is no significance
in constant chewing
and dedicated digestion
without purpose.
Nevertheless
I have enjoyed
the bovine tenderness
of this soul,
the wisdom of his flesh
that has now passed to me.
Our dialogue is intimate
because
is it not this animal
with its clumsy, enormous breath
who now lends me the strength
of everyday life?
So let us say
without pretense
that there is a bond between us,
the cow and me.
Why then
should I not mourn this creature?
Why should I not celebrate
its limbs and its liver

that others have forsaken
for the manes of horses
and the hearts of men?
Yes, I shall revel
in the cow's brilliant and remarkable blood,
its passionate
erudite bellows
that have been ignored
for the dishonest crooning of birds!
I shall gloat about
its lack of beauty,
the grace
in its wet, sloppy nose,
and the stoicism
with which it approached
the slaughter.

Not Everyone Needs to Be a Writer

(Notes to a Seventh-Grade Class)

Graham Thomas Shelby

Not everyone wants to be a writer
And that's alright.
It's alright if you want to be
A fashion designer
A diamond miner
The owner of a '50s diner
Captain of a jet airliner
Or a San Francisco 49er
Why, some folks would rather be cooks
Or crooks
Than write books

But whatever work works for you
Whether you sell sails to sailors
Or tell tales to tailors
It's okay
To stay
In your room
Some days
And bounce your fingers
Off computer keys
And tell your secrets to the screen
Like the day
You caught
That high pop-fly
Or that cute boy's eye
Or whatever's
Sliding around your mind
Don't fight it
Just write it

And so what
If there's some fluctuation
In your spelling or punctuation?
And on occasion
When you're not so thrilled
With your creation
Don't act defeated
You don't have to delete it
You don't have to destroy it
You don't have to be great at this
To enjoy it

Not everyone needs to be a writer
But everyone needs a friend
The kind who loves to listen
Who never forgets what you've said
The spiral-bound, college-ruled kind of friend
Who'll let you write
All over them

Not everyone wants to be a writer
And that's okay
But to anyone, I say
Some days
When things are goin' wrong
What you need
Is to go 'n write

Caregiving

Linda Caldwell

Winter breathes
down my collar.

Nothing's left
to warm me:

not a remembered red leaf
nor migrating bird.

Constellations
of summer pass,

and Orion stretches
across the sky without my notice.

You see I know these things
without looking.

You always think
every poem is about you.

You take the bright blue weather.
You steal my joy.

About the Poets and Poems

Tammy Ramsey

Tammy Ramsey teaches English and journalism at Bluegrass Community and Technical College. She holds master's degrees from the University of Kentucky and Spalding University. Her poems have recently appeared in The Louisville Review and Arable.

Genesis for *Living Among Us*

Most of us are lucky enough to have that one friend who tells it like it is, the friend we can consistently count on for good, solid, no-nonsense advice and perspective. My wisely cynical friend Pat has served this role for me for decades.

One sunny afternoon, Pat and I were discussing books we'd been reading, when he surprised me by suggesting it was entirely possible that aliens were living among us. He had been reading Leap of Faith, a biography of the astronaut Gordon Cooper. Cooper's status, even to the usually skeptical Pat, lent credibility to his claims of UFO visits and government cover-ups. In turn, Pat's record of clear-sightedness wouldn't let me dismiss his confidence in Cooper's claims. Such "dominoes of credibility," as Pat calls them, prompt us to reconsider our tightly held beliefs, to entertain another person's point of view.

Living Among Us was written as an exploration of encounters I have had with people who believe in aliens. "One believer falls on top of another," Pat says, explaining his domino theory, and each crash puts a chink in disbelief, be that about aliens or some other mind-boggling phenomenon.

The day-to-day is astounding enough—a child's unabashed laughter; the beauty of changing seasons; the power of one person, for better or worse, to affect the life of another—but as the dominoes of credibility lean in, the evidence builds that the world is even more rich and magical than we had imagined. Why is that so hard for us to believe?

Bianca Spriggs

Bianca Lynne Spriggs is currently an English Instructor at Bowling Green Technical College. She received her Bachelor's Degree in History at Transylvania University and a Master's Degree in English with an emphasis in Creative Writing at the University of Wisconsin-Milwaukee. She is currently pursuing a second Master's in Folklore at Western Kentucky University. An Affrilachian Poet and Cave Canem Fellow, Bianca has enjoyed growing up and living in the Bluegrass Region mostly because of the inherent qualities of rich lore and tradition that thrive among the people here.

Genesis for *Whitewash*

Basically, I worked in Versailles, KY off and on for a couple of years at a local corner store. A regular came in and told me about the courthouse that used to be in downtown where they tried and sentenced people of color. Now there was just a park with a creek running through it that used to run past the old courthouse. So, the imagery took hold regarding this notion of a black woman scrubbing her white laundry clean in front of this site where the ground that used to suck in blood is now a receptacle for cleansing.

Sherry Chandler

Sherry Chandler is the author of two chapbooks, *Dance the Black-Eyed Girl* (Finishing Line) and *My Will and Testament Is on the Desk* (FootHills). Her work has been awarded the Betty Gabehart and Joy Bale Boone prizes, and she has received professional development support through the Kentucky Arts Council.

Genesis for *Human Kindness* and *At 2 A.M.*

Several years ago I shared an office with a young man who had studied creative writing at Morehead State University. "All the poets at Morehead," he'd say with a certain disdain, "write poems called 'My Grandmother's Quilt.'" With this witticism, he defined one of the central tensions in my writing.

I have certain portraits I want to draw, some small stories I want to tell. The challenge is to find ways to do it without falling into sentimentality or, worse still, a sort of hardship kitsch. Having read and heard countless grandmother poems, I have been touched, inspired, and amused. But I have not often found poetry.

One problem with grandmother poems is that story precedes language. The end of the poem is a punch line or a moral, and there is none of that element of discovery which led Frost to say, "No surprise for the writer, no surprise for the reader."

Working in meter is one way to put the discovery back into short narratives like *Human Kindness* and *At 2 A.M.*. Free verse, in all but the most skilled hands, has a tendency to relax into prose, especially when the poem is working toward a preconceived ending. I find that meter brings music back into the line, lifts it off the page and puts it in the mouth. The poems included here are irregular in meter—too much regularity is doggerel—but with an underlying iambic foot that, I hope, drives the poem down the page.

Meter does not come easy to me. I once heard Andrew Hudgins say you could learn to write an iambic pentameter line in an afternoon. It is not so with me, but I have found the very struggle valuable. It keeps me from writing on cruise control. It makes me surprise myself.

Karen George

Karen George's work has appeared in *The Cortland Review*, *The Barcelona Review*, *Drexel Online Journal*, and *Wind Magazine*. She has received a Kentucky Arts Council Grant and two Creative Writing Awards from Thomas More College. She is currently working on a novel and enrolled in Spalding University's MFA in Writing Program.

Genesis for *Botany Lesson, A First Date*

I conceived the poem *Botany Lesson, A First Date* in Madison, Indiana, during the fall of the year, while attending OKI (Ohio Kentucky Indiana) Writers Roundtable in Carrollton, Kentucky, another historic town along the Ohio River. I was picnicking with a friend beneath a large, aged sycamore. We watched river traffic, listened to birds, with leaves swirling around us, and sun and wind altering everything in their paths. The sun and wind also altered everything. To me, there is nothing more divine than to witness a tree transfigured with wind, or view the underside of leaves transparent with sun. It was one of those magical occasions I felt compelled to crystallize in words—to recapture the mood, and recreate the essence and intensity of the experience.

This lush setting begged for something to happen within it. So I decided to tweak the poem by delving into the genesis of a new relationship, with all the apprehension, awkwardness, anticipation, and blind belief such a situation engenders, set against the backdrop of a beautiful fall day along a river.

I also wanted to play with the relationship between the human and the natural world, to show people mirrored and/or contrasted by the elements of Nature surrounding them.

Tom Hunley

Tom Hunley is an assistant professor of English at Western Kentucky University, director of Steel Toe Books (www.steeltoebooks.com), and author of *The Tongue* (Wind Publications 2004), *Still, There's a Glimmer* (WordTech Editions 2004), *My Life as a Minor Character* (Pecan Grove Press 2005), and *Teaching Poetry Writing: A Five Canon Approach* (Multilingual Matters LTD. 2007).

Genesis for *Sports Chat with the Nine Muses after Albert Goldbarth* and *My Father's Necktie*

In his collection Heaven and Earth: A Cosmology, Albert Goldbarth has a poem called "The Sciences Sing a Lullaby," in which the speakers are Physics, Geology, Astronomy, Zoology, Psychology, Biology, and History, and all of these unlikely personages discuss sleep in ways that are unusual, coming from anyone else, but perfectly in character for them. For example, "Astronomy says: the sun will rise tomorrow," and "Biology says: the body-clocks are stopped all over town." I liked the idea of tackling some form of everyday discourse using voices that we normally wouldn't expect to hear in that particular discussion. So I decided to think about what the nine muses might say if they found themselves on ESPN Radio, and I ended up with *Sports Chat with the Nine Muses*. *My Father's Necktie* is one of many poems that I have written about my relationship with my father. The earlier poems are bitter and sorrowful, but the latter poems reflect some degree of healing, I think. Becoming a father myself has helped me to better understand my father. I have a lot advantages that he didn't have, and I still find the task in front of me quite daunting.

Joanie DiMartino

Joanie DiMartino has work published or forthcoming in *Alimentum, Calyx, Wicked Alice Poetry Journal*, and *Modern Haiku*. Her poems have appeared in Sideshow, a collaborative exhibit displaying poetry and art at several venues in Lexington, Kentucky. A past winner of the Betty Gabehart Prize for poetry from the Women Writers Conference, she is a founding member of the women's poetry group Mosaic.

Genesis for *Milch*

I am a historian as well as a poet. Historical topics often find their way into my poems. *Milch* was written in response to a non-fiction history book I was reading on the history of witch trials, where the author pointed out the high amount of accusations that were related to food in some way, especially milk and dairy production. Historians are still studying the reasons women would accuse other women of hexing and witchcraft, and it is interesting to note that within the domestic realm of responsibilities for colonial-era women, culinary arts appear magical. The blending of several natural items, under the influence of an elemental force, usually heat, creates the sustenance needed to feed a family. I became fascinated with the impact of fear on food production: if the cheese didn't set properly, or if the baby refused to nurse, there was a very real threat of mortality. Without a scientific explanation for the occasional failure of the cooking process, colonial women within their own sphere looked to supernatural reasons. Also, as women's bodies provide the food for newborns and infants, the concerns and anxieties surrounding cow and goat's milk extended to breast milk. I preferred the archaic spelling, 'milch,' to set the tone and invoke the world these women inhabited, and it is pronounced the same as the current spelling, 'milk.' The poem originally contained sections with a modern first-person narrator, but in subsequent revisions I realized the poem was strongest when the focus was on the goodwives alone.

Leatha Kendrick

Leatha Kendrick has written two volumes of poetry, *Science in Your Own Back Yard* (2003) and *Heart Cake* (2000), and the script for a documentary film: *A Lasting Thing for the World—The Photography of Doris Ulmann* (2002). She writes, edits, and teaches writing workshops in and around Kentucky.

Genesis for *Animal Husbandry*

I wrote *Animal Husbandry* soon after I had adopted a dog from the Humane Society. I was realizing again why I had hesitated to get another dog after our last one had died. Our children were grown; I loved the mobility of my new freedom from caring for a household; and (as my husband, Will, reasonably pointed out) there was no reason to tie ourselves down again. Yet I spent hours thinking about getting a dog, researching breeds, believing that somewhere out there I could find "the perfect dog" for us. Ultimately, I found that dog when I wasn't looking for him—barking his head off in a cage at a pet store where the Humane Society had set up an adoption outpost.

I grew up on a farm, and though that made it important to me as an adult to live with some land around me, to grow a garden, to be in contact with the woods and with animals, wild and domestic, my upbringing also taught me the relentlessness of a commitment to raising and carrying for living things. While our children were young, we had a succession of cat "dynasties" (so named by the girls) and a dog or two at all times, but no livestock. I didn't want any. Our eventual years of keeping goats and a few head of cattle taught us both a good deal about ourselves. I saw, with shame, the limits of my commitment to farming as a way of life. How easy to "outsource" the hard work of tending the land, the crops, the animals. I saw my selfishness, and this poem gave me a chance to finally confess to it, while also honoring the small part in me that knows I must be committed to the non-human world, because I depend on it far more than it depends on me. That, indeed, we—all of us—avoid this commitment at our own peril.

Charlie Hughes

Charlie Hughes grew up on a Kentucky farm. He is employed as an analytical chemist and is the owner of Wind Publications. His poetry and short fiction have been published in numerous literary magazines. He is the author of *Shifting for Myself*, a collection of poems.

Genesis for *Not for Nothing* and *Bread Basket*

Growing up in a rural environment, one has ample time to either suffer solitude or learn to enjoy it. Luckily, I was able to do the latter. My writing often comes from periods of solitude and contemplation. Any writing I do, especially poems, is a way for me to learn something from or about myself. I always feel I have a successful poem when it tells me, as Frost said, something I didn't know I knew. Most of my poems are narrative—they tell a story, often of a time past, or having a rural setting. I take much delight in the manipulation of words in an attempt to express a story or thought in an unusual or evocative manner. I use the phrase "manipulation of words" because I consider a piece of writing as something that is built, in the same way that one builds a house by assembling its parts. The poet may use identical bricks to build vastly different houses, or poems.

I also look at writing as a way to re-experience a happening—to enjoy it again, or to better understand it, and maybe even to transform it into what it should have been in the first place. It's difficult not to take some delight in that.

Erin Keane

Erin Keane is the author of *The One-Hit Wonders*, a chapbook of poems inspired by rock & roll. A recent Kimmel Harding Nelson fellow, she received an MFA in poetry from Spalding University. Keane lives in Louisville, Kentucky, where she directs the InKY Reading Series.

Genesis for *The Tattooed Lady's First, Etymology of a Flood, Priscilla Johnson Still Has Hands Like Leaves, That Old Green Light*, and *The Lion Tamer's Résumé*

Last Spring, seeking a break from my book project, I compiled a set of very short readings that could serve as daily writing prompts for Lent. To begin, I reached for one of my talisman books, Lu Chi's *Wen Fu*. This ancient Chinese text on the art of writing brims with solid advice, itself a poem that requires contemplation and attention. "Recognizing order / is like opening / a dam in a river" blew me away with its contradiction and led me to begin *Etymology of a Flood*.

As a writer, I crave order—I tag and file memories, experiences and desires. As a scholar, I've been trained to consider word origins as a method of discernment. While pondering the idea of Lent, I looked for *carnival* in my Latin-English dictionary but found *Carna*: "the goddess of hinges, and so of family life." From there, I started wondering why the dictionary—a source of order unlike any other—would connect the family and the hinge with such assurance. What else might the Latin-English dictionary reveal about origins and order? How does a flood—the certain, violent result of a dam breeched—reconcile with order? And what of family tragedies, the patterns they begin and perpetuate? The poem became a meditation on the act of writing, of taming the chaos of memory, of mining and cataloging family mythology.

That Old Green Light springs from the same Lenten daily writing project, inspired by the Issa haiku "Moon, plum blossoms, / this, that, / and the day goes." I wanted to flesh out the story behind the feelings of ennui and indolent anticipation, of desire and paralysis, and chose the backdrop of a house party to explore the disconnect between the character and her surroundings. That same disconnect runs through *Priscilla Johnson Still Has Hands Like Leaves*, an ekphrasis based on the Alice Neel portrait of her son's young friend and my favorite piece in Louisville's Speed Art Museum's permanent collection. Priscilla's timeless attire, her contrary expression and pose intrigued me, and I imagined this girl as a middle-aged woman, still seeking some satisfaction, even as she continues to feel at odds with the world.

I've always been drawn to the outsiders. *The Tattooed Lady's First* and *The Lion Tamer's Resumé* are from a collection of persona poems about one summer on the road with a small-time circus. The performers' voices echo back and forth as the poems talk to one another, examining the tension between public and private, the need for authentic human connection and the desire to lead self-determined lives. These two are poems of origin for those characters, as they seek to name the experiences that drive their decisions throughout the story. Storytelling and character development are main enterprises of mine, and the primary poetic lenses through which I view the world. In a way, these poems are emblematic of the majority of my work, which is concerned with arranging and aligning, with patterns of behavior and thought.

Libby Falk Jones

Libby Falk Jones is professor of English at Berea College, where she teaches courses in creative, academic, and professional writing. Her poems and essays have been published in regional and national journals and anthologies. She is currently at work on a full-length memoir and two books of poems.

Genesis for *Sex Under Glass* and *First Spring Back in Kentucky*

My poems start with surprise. From the flood of experience and language, a word or image seizes me, urges me to find words to probe it.

For *Sex Under Glass*, the image was the developed film from my annual mammogram, which—for the first time in my many years of mammograms—the technician brought out and hung above a light table. I saw and suddenly understood my body in a new, intimate way. The image stayed with me, becoming the climax of a story universal to women, a story of the shadow side of our sexuality, of pain laced with fear.

Surprise also triggered *First Spring Back in Kentucky*, written the year I returned to Kentucky after spending the previous spring in Michigan. I was surprised not only by Kentucky's natural beauty but by my forgetfulness of it. How easily we take for granted what the world offers us! Probing this idea led me to a memory of the river birch that stood by the front door of my parents' home in Baton Rouge, Louisiana. My mother loved that tree's spring flowering. In March 1980, she delayed what would be her last trip to the hospital—did she know?—in hopes of seeing the river birch spring forth one last time. Since her death, that tree flowers in my mind's eye, marking my mother's passion for life, underscoring my sorrow at her loss, and urging me to embrace beauty while I can.

Sam L. Martin

Sam L. Martin lives in the woods at the end of a road in Menifee County where he is a close friend to a family of gray foxes. He won a 2005 Denny C. Plattner Award for outstanding non-fiction. His 5th-great grandfather Joshua Penix was an original settler at Fort Boonesborough.

Genesis for *After Handwashing* and *Liberated*

After Handwashing is the easier poem to understand, and I hope it speaks for the man engaged in physical labor. At the end of the day, he dreams of trading touches, perhaps back-scrubbing, with a particular woman. Nothing else needs to be said.

Liberated has as its genesis a Pandora's box, so to speak. It grows out of years of personal experiences and observations.

My cousin, whom we will call Jean, at age 20 was completely in love with a fellow who was tricked into marrying another woman but remained married to her for the rest of his life. Jean closed and locked the door, then threw away the key. Now, she assumed that all men were unreliable, so she followed a lightly-felt lesbian lifestyle and seemed to be satisfied. After all, she was a "liberated woman" who could spend all of her high salary on herself. But then came menopause at 52 and a nervous breakdown. She whispered to me, "But now I can't have a baby," as though she were sharing a secret, her failed life. She remained a very high-ranking officer in the armed services until she retired. I wonder what she thinks about at night before she falls asleep.

So, the seeds that sprouted into this poem all had to do with making serious mistakes about our basic human nature, mistakes that can't be corrected.

Andrea O'Brien

Andrea O'Brien's poetry has appeared in various publications, including *The Cream City Review, Dogwood*, and *Wisconsin Academy Review,* as well as the anthology *Mothers and Daughters: A Poetry Celebration*. She lives in central Kentucky with her husband.

Genesis for *Relics*

A number of elements merged to create the poem *Relics*. These elements—my Catholic upbringing, the early death of my mother, and my conflicting feelings about the body—are motifs that thread through many of my poems.

The Catholic faith provided me with, among other things, a rich vocabulary and collection of images which I continually return to in my writing. One goal of poetry is, of course, to transform the words and images we have been given, to make them our own, to create something wholly new yet rooted in tradition. In my case, I am particularly intrigued by saints, these men and women we have mythologized. Being at the same time both of this world and otherworldly, saints represent the lives we wish to emulate. However, in our longing for perceived perfection and permanence, we sometimes forget their transformations often were acquired at the cost of suffering.

My mother's example—her life, her faith, her long history of cancer—shaped my understanding of Catholicism. Typically, some part of the body or personal belonging of the saint is preserved in true relics—small, often unrecognizable pieces that the faithful venerate. The genesis for this poem was the collection of actual relics that belonged to my mother. The intangible, transcendent relics of her life served to deepen the poem and quite possibly every poem I write. Behind every word and every thought is the unspoken comparison between the woman who touched those relics and the woman my memory moves inevitably closer to perfection with each passing year. Behind every action and every accomplishment is the comparison between the person I am and the person I imagine she would want me to become, the saint she believed was inside me.

Perhaps because I watched the deterioration of my mother's body at an early age, I am interested in the role of the body and its connection to the spirit. The body—no matter how frail, how sick, how weary—is the only manifestation of the spirit in this life, a truth so apparent that we go to great lengths to preserve and respect the body even after death. Still, I struggle with the way this contradicts the natural world; other species do not hold ceremonies, perform burials, or memorialize the remains and belongings of their dead. I hope "Relics" engages readers, as it did me, to explore their beliefs about the body and spirit—about what matters in this life and what survives when we are gone.

Howard Wang

Hao Wang was born sometime in the '80s and raised over following years in places such as China, Kentucky, and Oregon. Currently, he is a junior at the University of Pennsylvania but is spending his year abroad in Paris, France. He is an Affrilachian Poet. His work has appeared in *Wind* and is forthcoming in an anthology entitled *America! What's My Name?*

Genesis for *Meditations on a Restaurant Hamburger*

I am a thinker. Not the sort you would expect to see at the coffee shop, pouting over his vanilla latté. No, I am the guy that you might pass in the street, hair and jacket asunder, eyes in a late afternoon glaze, somebody who you might look over and think, *hmmm, I wonder what he is thinking about*, which is, in my case, a particularly dangerous question. An open inquiry like that would require some goggles, some dependable galoshes, and a flashlight. Luckily, I am equipped with all these necessary tools when I let loose my imagination into the dark forests of the page and proceed to chase after it.

It is this raucous and tangled trail of my imagination to which I owe *Meditations on a Restaurant Hamburger*. Well—on second thought, I owe the poem above to all the good people of Max & Erma's, a cozy gourmet hamburger chain in Lexington, Kentucky. Without the perfectly melted cheddar and the glistening harmony of bacon and buttery-crisped bread and the juicy bulk of the medium-rare patty, I would be a sadder, more incomplete man. To both gastronomical and literary extents, the hamburger served its purpose well.

But for every experience sharply etched into the annals of my brief history, I have a point of departure from which the imagination and the irrational mind embark. When I came home, I wondered, how did this culinary delight arrive in my life? How do I feel about being a carnivore? Are vegetarians also people? I twisted and turned amidst the small incongruities of my memory and my senses, and the poem consists of the revelations and philosophies I found.

Still, this wasn't the hardest part. What was the most difficult was the tongue-in-cheek smirk I sought to give this piece because for all the ridiculousness inherent in its title, it is not that ridiculous. I had less trouble alluding to the sociopolitical and metaphysical tensions or conjuring the speaker's poetic bravado. The plight and suffering of farmed animals is neither insignificant nor new. The hardest thing in writing this poem—what endeared it to me the most—was making people laugh. So I sat and constructed this beast, picked among the organs and stitches of diction and grammar, so that as it sat down and unraveled its enigmatic story, humor and sadness would be entwined in the verse. I wanted to reflect the oddness of the poem's own birth and also the overplayed insistence of the speaker—and thank goodness the English language is funny and bizarre and serious and sad all the same.

Graham Thomas Shelby

Graham Thomas Shelby grew up in a Lexington family with roots in Southeastern

Kentucky, where he spent every Thanksgiving and Christmas. A graduate of the University of Kentucky, his work has appeared in *A Kentucky Christmas* and on public radio programs. In 2005, Graham received the Al Smith Award in Creative Nonfiction from the Kentucky Arts Council. He lives in Louisville with his wife and three sons.

Genesis for *Not Everyone Wants to be a Writer* (Notes to a Seventh-Grade Class)
This poem is about writing, but it was actually born on the basketball court. I've been playing pick-up basketball with friends and strangers in gyms and playgrounds ever since I was a kid. I've had moments, but generally speaking, I'm not very good. I don't shoot very well. I'm slow and I foul a lot. Even so, I still enjoy the game. And no one ever suggests that my lack of professional-level skill means that I shouldn't play at all. That's because it's understood that you don't have to be a Basketball Player in order to just play basketball.

I spent several years as a writer-in-residence in schools in Kentucky and elsewhere. Primarily, I conducted workshops for teachers and students on writing. Some school visits lasted a few hours, others lasted months.

A few years ago, I was finishing up residencies at a couple of different schools, and I wanted to leave them with one last thought to take with them. I considered a number of potential messages to guide them in their futures ("Stay in school." "Winners read!" "Plastic."), but I settled on this: You don't have to be a writer to write. In other words, you don't have to be angling for a Pulitzer Prize or the *New York Times* Bestseller list to enjoy the act of putting your thoughts on paper. So many kids feel such pressure when it comes to writing, as if it were something with a right answer and a wrong answer, like a multiple-choice question. The beauty of writing, I've always thought, is that you make your own right answer. I wanted them to think of the notebook or the computer file as a place where they could discover, explore, play, find refuge and even freedom. I wrote this poem to try and communicate that. I hope it does.

I'd like to thank the Kentucky Arts Council, without whose support none of this work would have happened. And I want to dedicate this poem to the Kentucky students and teachers whose hard work and cooperation inspired me to write it in the spring of 2003: the third and fourth-grade students and teachers from Spencer County Elementary School, and to the incomparable Vickie Wheatley and her language arts students from North Oldham Middle School. Those kids are older now, but I would still say to them, remember folks, it's okay to miss. Just keep shooting.

Linda Caldwell

Linda Caldwell is a poet and playwright from Paint Lick, Kentucky. Among her credits are the journals: *Prairie Schooner; Chaffin Journal; Appalachian Heritage; Tears in the Fence*, and the anthologies: *Poetry as Prayer*, edited by Denise McKinney and *Of Woods and Waters*, edited by Ron Ellis.

Genesis for *Caregiving*

Living with my aunt for a year and a half in Abingdon, Virginia, was the inspiration for the poem *Caregiving*. She had Alzheimer's. She never realized how long I had been with her. She was delighted I had decided to visit. Although Abingdon is a lovely town and I loved my aunt, I became homesick for my own life, place, and voice. While I was with my aunt, I was not creative. It is still difficult to write about that period of my life. I think this is one of two poems that I have written about the experience that is print-worthy. The other was *This Moment* published by *Prairie Schooner*. They were written as companion pieces.

Discussion Questions

Living Amoung Us

1. What does "Living Among Us" suggest about the relationship of truth and perception?

Whitewash

1. Hemingway noted that art is similar to an iceberg with 7/8s of it below the surface. Do you understand what is beneath the surface of this poem? Rather than describe the scene beneath the surface, Spriggs refrains from a detailed description of the horrific acts and an emotional outburst. What is gained by this use of understatement?

2. The title *Whitewash* is an example of plurisignation, a technique wherein a word has more than one meaning and the writer wishes the audience to consider these multiple meanings. Can you explain the two basic uses of *Whitewash*?

Human Kindness and *At 2 A.M.*

1. What differences do you find reading this poem aloud from reading it silently? How does Chandler use sound and meter to reinforce meaning?

2. What comment does the poem make on the relationships in a marriage? Is the view traditional, or does it reveal an aspect seldom admitted?

Botany Lesson, a First Date

1. Often the most powerful poetry springs from the everyday. How does George transform a seemingly ordinary event into a commentary on human relationships?

2. The two most popular image patterns in Western culture seem to be the correspondence between the human world and 1) the cycle of the day and 2) the cycle of the seasons. What images does George employ to pull together the human with that of nature?

Sports Chat with the Nine Muses and *My Father's Necktie*

1. Too often we associate poetry exclusively with a stodgy world of academic

references and esoteric themes, but in *Sports Chat* Hunley ties the world of classical mythology with popular culture. Did you catch his pop allusions? Did he effectively make the desired connection? Can you supply other characters from pop culture who could fit the ancient muses?

2. What effect does the absence of punctuation have on *My Father's Necktie*? Is the technique at all confusing for you?

Milch

1. How does "Milch" blend the everyday objects and actions of the colonial kitchen with the spirit world of witches and spells?

Animal Husbandry: Winter

1. Since the mid-Twentieth Century, much American poetry has been called confessional. Kendrick admits that her piece is a confessional poem surrounding her feelings of guilt for a selfishness that has caused her to pull away from her commitment to the world of nature and nonhuman creatures. What does her poem suggest this selfishness has cost her?

Not for Nothing and *Bread Basket*

1. Hughes says that a poem is often "a way to re-experience a happening—to enjoy it again." How does he "manipulate" words to express his enjoyment at the memory of his high school years?

2. Name three metaphors Hughes uses to describe the "belly." How do they reflect different aspects of his persona's perception of this body part? What do they tell us about the persona?

The Tattooed Lady's First, Etymology of a Flood, Priscilla Johnson Still Has Hands Like Leaves, That Old Green Light, and *The Lion Tamer's Résumé*

1. How does *Etymology of a Flood* link the act of writing with the human desire for order? How does Keane use her dictionary discoveries to support the point?

2. How does Keane's *The Tattooed Lady's First* transmit the fear, anxiety, yet excitement of a first experience? What do we learn about the young girl and her perception of the world?

3. *Priscilla Johnson Still Has Hands Like Leaves* uses the technique of apostrophe, whereby the persona addresses an object as if it could reply. What do the persona's comments and questions to Priscilla reveal about the persona?

4. How does *That Old Green Light* reconcile the conflicting emotions of boredom and anticipation? How does the reconciliation affect the poem's tone?

5. *The Lion Tamer's Résumé* concerns relationships. How does Keane use contrasting imagery to suggest the stress involved in the persona's life?

Sex Under Glass and *First Spring Back in Kentucky*

1. Poetry doesn't have to be pretty. How does *Sex Under Glass* use words and images that reflect the stressful ordeal of the mammogram?

2. What makes the persona leap in thought from the view of Kentucky to her mother's Louisiana home in *First Spring in Kentucky*? Does the thought make her happy or sad?

After Handwashing and *Liberated*

1. Sometimes a poem can transmit powerful emotions with a minimum of words. What emotions are evoked by *After Handwashing*? How does Martin use the image of water to evoke emotions beyond that of a straightforward statement?

2. Martin ties *Liberated* together with two rather shocking images—"the morning sun debuted as a blood blister" and "a crimson lullaby clotting in the brain." Do you feel these conceits work effectively to transmit the theme of making serious mistakes about our basic human nature, mistakes that can't be corrected? How do they accomplish this transmission?

Relics

1. O'Brien claims *Relics* springs from her fascination with the mystic relationship between body and spirit bound up in the reverence for saints of the faith. Much of her poem is composed of questions rather than statements. What effect does this technique have on your perception of O'Brien's theme? How do you feel about her thankfulness for not being "holy enough" to become a saint?

Meditations on a Restaurant Hamburger

1. Perhaps the most engaging element of the poem is its tone. How does Wang achieve

a delicate balance between the seemingly exaggerated pean to the slaughtered cow and the deeper, more serious theme beneath the poem's surface through the tone of the persona? Did you come away from the poem simply laughing, or did it make you consider some of your assumptions about our culture?

Not Everyone Needs to be a Writer

1. Shelby's poem races down the page aided by his use of rhyme. Do you think this technique would appeal especially to a young, unsure reader? How does the technique support the poem's theme that everyone has "seeds" of writing inside? What effect does Shelby's divergence from the rhyme scheme in the penultimate stanza have on the poem?

Caregiving

1. How does Caldwell evoke a mood of sadness and despair in her poem?

Recent Kentucky

Non-Fiction

with Introductory Comments by

George Brosi

In his poem, *The Brier Sermon,* the late Jim Wayne Miller (1936-1996) of Bowling Green, Kentucky, depicts a street preacher from the hill country admonishing his listeners to take their heritage seriously:

Say you were going on a trip
knowing you wouldn't ever be coming back
and all you'd ever have of that place you knew,
that place where you'd always lived
was what you could take with you.
You'd want to think what to take along
what would travel well
what you'd really need and wouldn't need.
I'm telling you, every day you're leaving
a place you won't be coming back to ever.
What are you going to leave behind?
What are you taking with you?
Don't run off and leave the best part of yourself.

The creative non-fiction in this section of *New Growth* wrestles with this question of what we should "take along" with us, what is most valuable in our heritage as Kentucky people and what we are "going to leave behind?" We all seem to be running off, as Miller would say, and too seldom do we seriously ask what the best part of ourselves really is. Often we similarly fail to come to grips with what aspects of our heritage we need to overcome.

The authors of this section do exactly that and consider this question from many different angles, both explicitly and implicitly.

Diana McQuady confronts it quite directly in "World in a Day" by showing how she was able, in middle-age, to take her father on a short trip and re-capture the fun that his day trips had brought to her as a child. John Sparks in "My New Year's Kiss" shows how, amidst all the high technology of today's hospital vocations, humans have the same impulses they had even back in Biblical days. John's fellow-workers did not allow the encumbrances of their jobs to keep them from enjoying a little old fashioned fun in their interactions with their youngest fellow employee. Glade Blythe Brosi tells of going to the woods and recapturing the spirit of his great-grandfather, a Laurel County hunter, in his modern-day hunting tall-tale entitled, "Singing Dolly." Georgia Green Stamper writes vividly in "Where Am I From?" about the old tobacco auctions in Lexington, without lamenting the diminished role that substance plays in Kentucky life, yet she chooses explicitly to cherish the architectural significance of places as useful as dime stores and theaters. Jan Sparkman depicts controlling and abusive and insensitive adults in her childhood memoir, "Growing Up Depressed." "The Man on TV" for Graham Thomas Shelby is none other than his own father, and he can't help but wonder as a young boy why this man cares so much about his Vietnam buddy yet let his own son go. What a contrast these pieces make with the mother who Judith Victoria Hensley strives to be in "Wings to Fly." "It was my decision," Judy writes, "not to bind him to me with obligation and fear. I taught him to dream big dreams and reach for the stars." This section provides some powerful writing about what to leave behind as well as what to take with us when it comes to child-rearing. Scott D. Vander Ploeg thinks of Kentuckians as we live in neighborhoods as well as the jobs that attract us. And he can't help but connect that reality to what decision-makers have embraced as well as left behind as they run off towards the future. Thinking and writing about Kentucky's heritage just naturally leads beyond home and job to church. The title, "The White Doors" refers to the doors of the country church-house where Steven R. Cope as a young boy experiences a physical manifestation of the spiritual dimension in life and his own individual separate experience of that. Both his piece and "The Baptism" by Mary Jane Adam explicitly confront no issues, but can serve as springboards for many. Bob Sloan's essay, "Enex Ground," focuses on the past that a Rowan County graveyard reveals, but in doing so implicitly yields to thoughts about how society can formally censure but privately enjoy the escapades of generations of kinfolks.

In contrast to these emerging writers, Kentucky's established writers have tended recently to move beyond memoir in their creative non-fiction. In the year that these essays were collected, 2006, Wendell Berry of Henry County, the state's most prominent contemporary essayist, published Blessed Be the Peacemakers, a book that combines quotes from the Bible with commentary about living the Christian life. Erik Reece of Lexington published Lost Mountain about the devastating effects of mountaintop removal mining in Perry County.

How ironic that the Kentuckian who nationally has done more than perhaps anyone to both define and expand creative non-fiction, Hunter S. Thompson (1937-2005) of Louisville, lived such an urban life in contrast to the predominantly rural perspective of the writers represented here.

And also how ironic that the racial diversity of Kentucky is not well reflected in these essays despite the fact that the state boasts many distinguished Black non-fiction writers, for example Bill Turner, who grew up in Lynch and lives in Lexington and co-authored *Blacks in Appalachia*.

When the editors of this volume sent out the invitation for submissions, we did not anticipate that prospective writers would think of "Creative Non-Fiction" almost exclusively as memoir. Yet we are pleased that the results have yielded such a fine collection of personal essays which together do help us to ponder the connections between the past and present and future.

My New Years Kiss

John Sparks

Like most writers, I've never been able to give up my day job (or in my case, for a great deal of my working life, night job) to pursue my preferred avocation. I've always considered this to have been a blessing in disguise, though, since my career as a night-duty laboratory technician in a small rural hospital has given mc no end of unusual characters and sometimes comic, more often tragic, and nearly always ironic, anecdotes around which to form plots. I've spent my share, and more besides, of nights on the job and "on call" as well, and during these seasons that I've been apart from my wife and daughters I've done nearly everything from sitting bored and wishing I was home to scrabbling furiously for a good six to eight hours trying to supply crossmatched blood for the victim of an ATV accident. But of all the unusual characters I've ever had to deal with on the job, few are more vivid in my memory than the agitated emergency room patient I encountered at just about midnight between December 31, 1983, and January 1, 1984, and who gave me my very first New Year's Eve kiss as a married man—which might have been all right, I suppose, but for the fact that it wasn't *her* I was married to.

I'd graduated from college with a medical technology degree at the end of June 1983, gotten my first job in a hospital on July 11, and had wed Sheila, my girlfriend, on July 22. Thus a great many changes occurred for Sheila and me within one month's time, not counting our trials with the ancient four-room coal-company house we were trying to refurbish into our first home. But she and I were in a state of newlywed happiness, even though as low man on the totem pole at work I was saddled with the shifts no one else wanted: night weekends, most holidays, and any time during the week that any holes in the staff schedule needed plugging. We'd simply shrugged our shoulders and tried to make the best of it, though another of my outstanding memories from that time involves the first meal Sheila ever prepared for me after a long, arduous night's work. We'd gotten a generous supply of home-canned and preserved vegetables from her parents as one of our housewarming gifts. I was grateful for every bit of it, but so help me, I'll never attempt to do without food all night and then eat a late-afternoon breakfast of pickled corn and pickled beans, fried pork chops, and corn bread, ever again. Much less try to return to work on it.

I'd had to cover Labor Day and then the night before Thanksgiving, which meant that for all practical purposes I might as well have worked the day shift itself. As it was, I'd had to sleep until late afternoon on Thanksgiving Day, gotten one night and day off, and then had to pull two thirteen-hour night shifts over the long holiday weekend. Of course, as the official New Guy, I was also veritably foreordained to work Christmas Day as well and then take call until the next morning. Nonetheless, the Christmas dinner that Sheila brought to the hospital for me that afternoon, and which I ate with her in the tiny laboratory kitchen between taking phone calls and promising the emergency and medical-surgical services that I'd "be there" as soon as I could get my food swallowed, was one of the most romantic—and to me, touching—meals that I have ever enjoyed. If I recall correctly, I was paid for working twenty-seven hours in a twenty-four hour period that Christmas, but when I brought up the glitch to my supervisor, he'd just grinned and told me not to worry. It was likely that I had actually done twenty-seven hours' worth of work that day, he said, and I already knew that I'd earned every penny.

All those months of successfully parrying anything that the emergency room and the med-surg. services could throw my way late at night had given me a feeling of toughness that perhaps only a twenty-two year-old man (or twenty-two year-old boy, as I see things now) could appreciate. I was in my prime, married to the girl I loved, we were already talking about starting a family, and I felt like my back and shoulders had toughened to the point that there was no burden that I couldn't bear. But perhaps understandably, I was nearly "holidayed out" by the time December 31 rolled around. Since I'd had to work on Christmas, I'd somehow gained an exemption for New Year's Day itself, but as luck would have it I drew the late shift again on New Year's Eve. Once more, that meant that I'd essentially be out of commission for most of the actual holiday, and worse, Sheila and I couldn't celebrate our first New Year together. In other words, I wouldn't even get my kiss at midnight. Still, work was work and pay was pay, and if in fact Sheila and I did start our family any time in the near future, that extra late-night money would be welcome. I went to work that night with a heart that was, if not entirely happy, at least hopeful for better years, and better shifts, ahead.

As I recall it now, things were fairly peaceful—until perhaps a quarter to midnight. Then the phone rang and I heard the peacock squawk of the emergency room ward clerk on the other end: "CBC and blood alcohol level in the ER, stat." I thought that if I should die and go to hell there'd be a tape loop of her voice playing over and over down there, but I don't think I ever told her that. Oh well, one had to expect a few alcohol-related casualties on New Year's Eve, so I picked up my collection tray and headed up the hall towards the ER door.

No sooner than I had entered the emergency ward, I heard a female voice behind a curtain in one corner, vigorously spewing graphic profanity of the very hottest sort. The doctor and a nurse stepped out from behind the curtain with disgusted looks. "Here's your patient," the physician muttered to me with a shrug of his shoulders and a casual wave toward the curtain. The unseen figure behind it continued to blister the air, but at least the doctor's departure had quietened the patient perhaps a fraction of a decibel.

"Car wreck?" I muttered back, giving the curtain an anxious look and for some reason, not feeling quite as tough as my usual twenty-two year-old machismo required.

"Claims her boyfriend smacked her in the head with a two-by-four," the nurse replied, rolling her eyes as the doctor merely shrugged again and returned to his desk in the cubicle outside the door. "She does have one horrendous pumpknot on her head, whatever happened. Probably lucky she's drunk. A lick like that to her head would've killed her if she'd been sober, but she won't even let the Doc stitch up the cut. Well, try and get the tests for us quick, okay?" she finished as she turned away.

"Whoa, hold it! She won't let Doc stitch her?" I whispered anxiously. "Then what makes you think she'll let me draw this blood without the same kind of fight that I just heard? You're…gonna stick around and hold her arm for me, right?" My facial expression must have been a study in hope.

With a grin and a pat to my shoulder, she just chuckled, "Aw, John, you'll be just fine. You're a big boy, you can handle her." Perhaps I should mention here that I probably did at least give the appearance of being as capable as this nurse had just alleged that I was. A child of the seventies on his first full-time hourly job in the early eighties, I kept both my hair and my beard a bit longer than I wear them now. I would never have been considered small or slight at any time in my entire life. Moreover, it was wintertime and I usually worked several hours away from the eyes of the lab supervisor and the hospital administrators, so I had acquired the habit of wearing blue jeans, plaid work shirts, and high-top lumberjack work boots on duty rather than white coats and scrubs. On another night I'd scared one poor fellow suffering from the D.T.'s nearly out of his skin, fearful that Paul Bunyan had just risen up out of the nest of snakes he saw wherever he looked. But right now, I felt like I'd rather tackle a grown man or even that poor guy's imagined nest of snakes than that high-voiced source of the most eloquent, vivid profanity I had ever heard, even among my friends in high school and college. The nurse walked off with a smile, and I felt my heart drain into my boots. Oh, well. This was what they paid me for, and tonight I'd earn it.

I lifted the curtain and stepped gingerly behind it, making sure to swallow and clear my throat before I informed my patient that the doctor had ordered tests and I needed to draw blood from her arm. As I finished my rote speech, I stopped short and looked at her: she was maybe five or six years older than I was, and except for her inebriation and the ugly contusion on the right side of her head, she was quite attractive. Still, I fully expected to be answered with another blistering red haze of profanity, but she merely looked at me—she had big blue eyes, if I recall correctly, though they were red-rimmed and watery with alcohol—and lay back on the ER gurney, sighing, "Okay."

All right, Sparks, you've lucked out for some reason, I remember thinking as I tightened a tourniquet around her left arm and began to search at the bend of her elbow for her antecubital vein. Now get this blood drawn quick, while she's peaceful, and pound your feet out of here before she starts thinking about her boyfriend, the two-by-four, and the doctor again. There's no way anybody can reason with a drunk. But no sooner than I had bent over her arm, found the vein, and begun the venipuncture, my scalp tightened involuntarily, and not from any nebulous unease or imagined fear either. The patient had lifted her right arm up and over and she was running her fingers through my hair. And from all that I could tell, enjoying doing it.

All of a sudden I understood, in a most personal way, why Joseph was so keen to get away from Potiphar's wife. Twenty-two years old, country-outlaw debonair and macho, able to handle any crazy circumstance that might occur in a hospital late at night? Yeah, right. Sure I was. Six or eight years of my life blew away before my eyes like chaff in the wind. I was a gawky adolescent again, an older woman was flirting with me, and I was scared utterly to the core. Any latent regrets I may have harbored about taking myself out of circulation for holy wedlock went flying out the window. I tried to pretend that nothing out of the ordinary was happening. My hands shook and I missed the vein. I tried to correct the angle of the needle without resorting to a second venipuncture, my hands and arms shaking more as her palm enjoyed the time of its life across my scalp. I thought I was already as uncomfortable as I could be. I found out just how badly mistaken I was when she began to moan: "Ohhhhh, baby, baby, don't hurt me, baby, *bayyyybee*."

I could already hear muffled giggles outside the curtain. If I started earning giggles or more moans now from the patient inside it...my face felt like it was going to explode. Good God, what did the nurses think I was doing back here? What if *Sheila* decided to slip to the hospital and surprise me with a late-night New Year's snack? Why did I ever get into this line of work? Somehow I managed to draw one or perhaps two milliliters of blood—grace under pressure, or maybe just plain old luck—and I snapped the tourniquet off, hurriedly stuffed the tubes in my shirt pocket, and applied a pressure compress to the venipuncture just as her right hand slipped down to the back of my neck and held on tight. I raised my head to meet those deep, watery, alcohol-saturated blue eyes as she lifted her torso and brought her face towards mine, her mouth open—maybe she'd remembered that it had just turned 1984; I don't know and I danged sure didn't think to ask—and I lifted my face a fraction so the smacking, boozy kiss she had aimed at my lips caught me slightly to the right on my jaw.

I've often wondered about time. Seconds go by so quickly, usually. But that one instant at the conjunction of 1983 and 1984 seemed to last an eternity as I tried to process the situation and figure what the heck Joseph could do with Potiphar's wife now, without hurting or insulting her but still saving his own multicolored lab coat and sorry testosterone-cured hide. I guess I started backward even further, but I did manage to get a band-aid on her arm and cough and warble out the words, "Don't! Are you tryin' to lose my job for me here, or what?" Her hand slipped, I grabbed my tray, and I fled the scene like a scalded cat.

I was greeted with howls of laughter from the nurses as well as the doctor and ward clerk, and maybe even some applause as well, but that latter memory may only be my mind playing tricks on me. I must have been redder than a beet. I remember hearing some quick jibes like, "Well, did she cuss you?" and "Tight place there, Big Bad John?" as I tried to collect what was left of my dignity and get back to the lab. But soon enough, we all temporarily forgot it in the haste of a busy night. I was literally terrified that I might not have gotten enough blood from her arm to do the tests, but somehow I managed. By the time the ER called me back to deal with the cases that followed—a heart attack, another delirium tremens, and a pretty little rich girl from town, decked out in her beautiful new ball gown and nursing a nick on her temple that she'd gotten from a glancing whiskey bottle thrown at a party, all of whom came in practically at the same time—the X-ray technician was having her own difficulties with the two-by-four lady and I didn't have to deal with her any more. Even so, as the med-surg. aides came to take her upstairs for an overnight observation, she did throw one more brazen glance my way as if to say, Buddy, you had your chance with a beautiful woman like me and you blew it. All that naive little Joseph could do was to look away guiltily and to inform the little rich town girl from whom he was now drawing another blood alcohol that *no*, she was *not* going to throw up on him because he'd had a rough enough night already.

The lab's day crew enjoyed the story of my adventure almost as much as the ER nurses had the night before, although it was the common consensus among the male techs that the patient's finding me attractive only proved how drunk she really was. I even told Sheila about it when I got home. She's not the jealous sort, so she had her laugh along with all the others—but when I stepped to the bathroom to wash my face before trying to catch a few hours of sleep, she told me to be sure to wash my beard thoroughly. Unless my memory fails me, she insisted on helping with that chore too, and very vigorously.

Over the years, I've seen a lot more tragedies than comedies in my line of work, and even at their funniest, the comedies tend to be dark. But for a lucky fluke, this incident could have turned out to be one of the most tragic. I never saw the two-by-four lady again, and I've often wondered whatever became of her and her boyfriend.

I hope they've both grown up, and that Sheila and I have as well. The whole incident is probably best forgotten by every one of us that was involved. But I will always remember the clove of the years 1983 and 1984 in the good old Death Valley Days America of Ronald Reagan, my New Year's kiss, and the one that I let slip away—*ever* so gladly and thankfully.

John Sparks

John Sparks, a Pikeville College graduate, is a writer, historian, healthcare professional, clergyman, husband, and father (not necessarily in that order). He has written two nonfiction works on Appalachian and Kentucky religious history, *The Roots of Appalachian Christianity: the Life and Legacy of Elder Shubal Stearns*, and *Raccoon John Smith: Frontier Kentucky's Most Famous Preacher*, both published by the University Press of Kentucky. He lives in Johnson County.

Genesis for *My New Year's Kiss*

My New Year's Kiss is one of a multitude of memories I've collected in a quarter century of working the "hoot owl shift" in rural eastern Kentucky hospitals. In order to survive in the healthcare industry, whether in the rural South or elsewhere, you have to develop an appreciation of the ironic, and it doesn't hurt to take a lesson from the turtle and try to grow a bit of a protective shell around your heart either—so long as you don't lose your soul in the process. I suppose you can say you've finally reached maturity whenever you figure out how to keep a touch of the wry in your sense of humor while not letting yourself descend to the sardonic. Some of my memories give me a smile; at least as many or more make me wipe away a tear from time to time; and all make me appreciate what it means to be a human being searching for the transcendent, in a very short sojourn on a little dust speck known as earth.

Over the years I have attempted to fictionalize and publish some of my experiences as short stories, with mixed success; others seem to go better, as John Steinbeck once suggested, when I simply spread out my paper and let the tales crawl on by themselves. I hope that this piece may be included in that latter category, but the jury's still out on how I will write, if ever I do, about the term "code brown," the guy with the throat spray bottle where I didn't think it could have been put, the mother who thought the term "sexual intercourse" defined a medical benefit chargeable to her health insurance, or... well, nonetheless, I hope that readers enjoy the piece presented here, and take it for what it is—the true story of a couple of young people caught in the act of being themselves.

The World in a Day

Diane McQuady

I'm eleven years old and riding down the road, sitting in the back seat of my parents' Buick LeSabre, the first car they bought new, the blue one with the black hardtop. Or maybe I'm seven, and the car is their old white Buick.

Let's just say it's the 1960s or early 1970s, and we're in Kentucky. Like many families, my parents take to the road, and they take my brother, sister, and me along with them. This is not the one and only overnight trip we'll take together over the course of my childhood. Instead our destination is nearby. This is one of our many "day trips."

Gasoline is cheap, people aren't as busy being busy as they'll be when I'm an adult, and the highway can take us to places past and present. We head east to My Old Kentucky Home or Abraham Lincoln's Birthplace or farther east to the Cumberland Gap. Or we go south, to Tennessee, and see Andrew Jackson's home, The Hermitage, or ride our first elevator in Nashville's tallest building, the Life & Casualty Building, to what we kids think is the top of the world. West of our home we find a monument to Jefferson Davis and Indian burial mounds at a place near where Illinois and Missouri converge with Kentucky. And north we drive across the bridge in Owensboro over the Ohio River to Indiana, to Lincoln's Boyhood Home and Santa Claus Land.

Gas may be cheap, but often there's little left over in the family budget for frivolity or adventure. Sometimes we can't even afford to go inside the attraction we visit, so we walk the grounds, maybe browse the gift shop, then head for a drive-in restaurant for dinner before heading home. My parents are practical though and seek out places that don't charge much, if anything, so this isn't of concern to us kids. And it'll become part of our family folklore to remember the places we visited but didn't go inside. As an adult I'll go into the Hermitage but My Old Kentucky Home in Bardstown will remain a mystery well into my forties.

The destination isn't the only draw. The drive itself is a major part of the fun. I hang my head out the car window, which is rolled down since there is no air conditioning in the car. (This is, of course, if I'm lucky enough to be seated by a window.) I soak in the breeze as the miles pass under the wheels, and my mind also travels along the way. It's during these early years and on these trips that I learn to go inside myself, something so necessary for a writer. As a teen I read about faraway places that sound different than the rolling countryside just outside my car window. Even today I love to be in a car, someone else at the wheel, a book in my hands or pen and paper on my lap. These day trips, these mini adventures, become part of my formation as a person and bond my family in a unique way.

It's the Monday just before Christmas 2004. I drive to my parents' house and pick them up. Daddy can't drive right now, so I'm chauffeuring him and Momma to Louisville, a drive about two hours from their home. A dozen days ago Daddy had nearly half of his liver removed, including the left lobe, at a hospital in downtown Louisville. Now he needs to have the staples, about 35 of them, taken out of his chest. The doctor's office called this morning and asked if we could come early; the doctor is trying to fill holes in his schedule.

When we arrive, we're taken back to the examination room before we even take seats in the lobby. Soon, we're on I-65 headed home, a half hour before the appointment was to begin. At last the scary ride with cancer is hitting a straight place in the road, and we can all breathe a little easier. The night before, I thought about this ride home from the doctor's office. Up to this point the drives between western Kentucky and Louisville have been fast trips, up and back, with only quick pit stops for fuel for us and the car.

This trip feels different. It needs to be different.

I stop at another service station for gasoline. As I get out of the car, I hand my dad a map of Kentucky. "Find me the best route to Glendale," I say.

"Where?"

I lean over and open the map, then point. "There, just north of E-town." The night before I'd looked at the map to get a general feel for the location.

"What's there?" my dad asks.

I smile at Daddy and then wink at Momma in the back seat. "We're going on an adventure."

About thirty minutes later we cruise into the sleepy little town. A sign welcomes us to Glendale and another lets us know the Whistle Stop is on the right just across the railroad tracks. A co-worker told me about the restaurant a few days before the drive. It's late for lunch, about 2:30 in the afternoon here and 1:30 back home. The town looks deserted as we park in front of the restaurant, located in a building at the end of a row of buildings that used to support the downtown in this railroad town. Now all the structures have been converted from hardware and drug stores to this restaurant and antique shops. An old house in view just up the road is now a bed and breakfast. Quaint sells in this time of fast highways and fast food, when people look for a connection to something old and real. Glendale is quaint.

I go up to the door of the Whistle Stop and pull the handle. It doesn't budge. I pull again, not believing that it can be locked. The sign on the building tells me why. The Whistle Stop is closed on Sunday and Monday, and today is Monday.

I see Daddy's shoulders slump. On the drive over he's talked about how he likes to be off the multi-lane highways and on these roads that once sustained and connected towns before the big roads with intermittent off ramps were built. I tell him I have a Plan B and cross my fingers that it'll work.

Back across the railroad tracks we drive. I make an immediate right into a parking lot beside a sign for The Depot. The old depot that used to shelter people on their rail-travel stopovers has been converted to a restaurant with lots of atmosphere and décor that reflects a time when the depot was busy with the business for which it was built. It's obvious that every attempt has been made to retain much of the original structure. An old bench set by two tables appears to be authentic. The tin ceiling and crown molding above us and the old wood floor under our feet are either the real thing or wonderful reproductions.

We settle into our seats at a table with two white tablecloths and look out at the window to the railroad tracks. This would have been a noisy corner in those days. Today, though, the restaurant is quiet with only two other tables seated, probably due to the late hour. We look over the menu and change our minds several times before ordering.

The food turns out to be as fantastic as the atmosphere. Momma and I go for the more upscale section of the menu and have the portabella mushroom sandwich with a side potato dish. We declare both excellent about halfway through, when we finally come up for air. Daddy has chosen the more traditional fried chicken. He, too, enjoys the food, probably more than Momma and me since it's been about two weeks since he's eaten much at all. He cleans his plate. We sit back after finishing and just be, until we finally state the obvious. The only way we'll get home is to get back in the car and drive there.

Back out on the road, we again go over those tracks, past the Whistle Stop with a promise to come back and try it again someday, then we drive out Highway 222, past homes and fields that wait for the promise of spring planting. The server at The Depot told us to make a left at the stop sign when we asked for directions to the parkway. After a while we wonder if we've somehow missed the stop sign. Just when I'm about to pull over to look at a map, we see a busy road ahead of us. It turns out to not be the parkway we expected but Highway 62, which could take us all the way to my parents' hometown of Beaver Dam if we let it and does take us to the Western Kentucky Parkway a few miles up the road. Daddy says he hasn't been on this stretch of road for years, and I realize that Highway 62 was the road he took to and from Louisville as a young man. Later, after we enter our home county, he points out places on both sides of the parkway where he'd hunted and explored as a boy, where he had his first adventures.

After dropping Momma and Daddy off at their house, I drive on to my home in Bowling Green, about forty miles south. I think about how, as my father's child, I have benefited from those adventures he had as a child as well as the ones he took us on when I was young. Those days had such a profound impact on me that I often build in time on a road trip to stop somewhere interesting that's on the way—or close to on the way. And whenever I hear someone lament over the bad economy and lack of funds for a full-fledged family vacation, I tell them about the day trips of my childhood. It doesn't take a beach and fancy hotel to make family memories. I tell them there are treasures in everyone's backyard, waiting to be discovered and explored. All they have to do is pick a day and go!

Despite the chill of this winter day, I put the window down and let the breeze carry me home. There I'll bide my time until the next "day trip" calls my name.

Diana McQuady

Diana McQuady returned to her home state of Kentucky in 1999 after living in Nashville for more than a decade. Her poetry and nonfiction work have appeared in various publications, including *Life Writing by Kentucky Feminists*, and she holds degrees from Western Kentucky University and Loyola University of New Orleans. McQuady lives in Bowling Green, where she can be found writing when she's not at a Hilltopper basketball game.

Genesis for *The World in a Day*

There's nothing like a prompt to get my writing mind going. The final product that comes from a prompt is often far from my original thoughts. This essay started with the prompt of a single-word: travel. There were many things I could have said about travel and nearly did: how I don't do it well, my freaky control issues regarding packing, the anxiety before each trip that used to rise up and fill my throat with something just short of terror, how my desire to see more of the world has pressed me to find ways to overcome some of my travel issues.

But those are all topics for another day because this time that single-word opened the floodgate of childhood memories of our many one-day trips. These memories have been activated before, when I've heard a friend or co-worker lament about not being able to take an expensive, elaborate vacation due to financial constraints. They seemed pained, often because they felt they deprived their children. I've shared the concept of an inexpensive but fun day trip with many of them. Sometimes I've seen a light in their eyes as they remembered their own similar childhood trips, long forgotten in their busyness. Sometimes it was a new concept to them, one they seemed ready to consider. And sometimes my comments were eyed with suspicion, as though the spending of gobs of money and logging of mile after mile actually made the perfect family vacation, regardless of the quality time together.

I started writing this essay just before making several not-so-fun trips from western Kentucky to Louisville, for appointments with doctors that led to more tests and consultations. As we feared, my dad was diagnosed with liver cancer, a frightening and often-deadly illness. He was hospitalized and had a serious, invasive—and ultimately successful—operation. My center was struck by a roller coaster of emotions, including fear and anger, relief and elation. I needed a way to release some of those emotions, a way to explore my adult relationship with my parents. I didn't think this last trip I made with them to Louisville needed to end with us simply going home and returning to our everyday lives as though we hadn't been through this ordeal. So, I turned it into one of our day trips and made a new memory to go with the ones from my childhood.

And then I felt compelled to include it in the essay about my childhood day trips because in a way I'd come full circle. As I wrote the essay, I could feel myself diving into the words and surfacing from the depth of my being with new understanding. I'd taken on a role different than my childhood self: driver, leader, listener, adult, parent. I came to know on a deeper level than before that simple trips can build memories and relationships and that difficult times have their own gifts. And gifts are meant to be shared, sometimes in an essay.

Where Am I From?

Georgia Green Stamper

When people ask me where I'm from these days, I hardly know how to answer them. I've only lived in Lexington for a few years, and I'm still learning how to drive in the traffic and discovering out of the way places that only the locals know about. Still, I'm fairly well settled here in a Lexington burb, and although I'm a newcomer, I've had a lifelong affection for Lexington. This southern city has been a perennial player in my life, I want to tell them.

But I grew up on a northern Kentucky tobacco farm in a community my family has claimed as its own for generations. I'd feel like Esau denying his birthright if I didn't say I was from Owen County. However, to leave out Ashland, in the far eastern tip of the state, where I lived longer than any other place on earth, doesn't seem right either.

Kentucky is where I'm from, I want to say, and leave it at that. After all, every branch of my family tree leads to the Cumberland Gap and the great westward migration that marked the years just after the American Revolution. Because my people have been breathing sweet bluegrass air for two centuries: I sop up spilt milk; I'm juberous when in doubt; I'm critical when anything looks like the last of pea time; and I often find myself between a rock and a hard place. I reckon with you all without affectation or a second thought, and in times of stress I throw my college theater director's cautions to the wind and convert the short e into a short i ("git me a pin so I can write!") At such times, I also revert to cleansing my face with a worsch rag. I also have a taste for old ham—that would be aged—salt cured in the country way that my northern friends insist tastes rotten, and I prefer our native black walnuts to pecans. I find mint juleps nauseating, but respectfully keep that opinion to myself and compensate by tearing-up when I hear "My Old Kentucky Home."

But native Kentuckians—maybe southerners in general—have an obsession with county lines and small towns and streams with archaic names. Simply to say I'm from Kentucky begs the question. The person waiting for an answer wants to know where I'm *from* as in what road have I traveled in life to get *here*. It's the first step in sizing up what sort of person I might be, because each tiny pocket of the commonwealth has a flavor and a history of its own.

And since most lifelong residents of the bluegrass state are separated by only one, maybe two degrees, they want to know if we know any of the same people. Knowing the right people in common is a character reference around here. (Knowing the wrong person too well, however, can cut a conversation short before it even gets started.)

Nevertheless, after a moment's hesitation, I answer Lexington, and let them make of that what they will. Maybe if I hold my mouth just right, they'll think I teach at the University of Kentucky or at my *alma mater*, Transylvania. On one of my good days, I think I could pass for an academic. (I doubt anyone would ever mistake me for a moneyed horse farm owner, though. I can't pull together their look of easy self-confidence and nonchalant, elegant attire. I think it's because I'm not at all athletic and am secretly afraid of large animals.)

I do have an ancient connection to Lexington. About two hundred years ago, my g-g-g-g-grandfather dropped by long enough to get himself elected a trustee of the bustling young town. A few years later, however, his son and grandson picked up and drifted north. Or as one of their disgruntled descendants later put it: "the fools left the bluegrass and came up here to Owen County looking for a damn spring."

Great-Uncle Jeff did make a pertinent economic point. Owen County's rocky hillsides don't sell for as much as Fayette County's rock walled meadows. Nevertheless, I wouldn't take a million dollars for the experience I had growing up on an Eagle Creek tobacco farm. My DNA was forged of the substance found in a Wendell Berry novel. I am *of* Owen County no matter where I wander.

But our Owen County farm also cast Lexington into a major role in the story of my early life. In our rural cocoon, life revolved around the cycles of the farm season, family, school and church. Even so, certain life events required that we venture into a city. Those occasions—bad or good—put us on the road to Lexington, about an hour away down U. S. 25. Louisville, eighty or more miles in another direction, was too far to go, we thought, and Cincinnati, though closer to us than Louisville, was a mysterious labyrinth of one-way streets across the river in a strange state. Lexington, like Goldilocks' porridge, was just right. Nearer to us, it was also smaller by half or more than either Louisville or Cincinnati, and thus was much less intimidating. We could get around Lexington by foot or car with a degree of confidence that belied our rural out-of-town-ness.

Lexington, with its huge hospitals, was our regional medical center of choice—although we would not have used words like that. We simply knew that when Dr. Cull sent you "on to Lexington" you were "bad off." The year my grandfather died of leukemia, and the year before when my mother almost died of nephritis, I spent most of my weekends at Good Samaritan Hospital, a massive structure built of Kentucky limestone appropriately located on Limestone Street. In that sterilized era, children under sixteen were not allowed to visit patients in their rooms, and I spent my time waiting for the grown-ups in Good Sam's solemn lobby. Day after day, I tried my best to conjure a smile from the thin-lipped receptionist, but my attempts at friendship never succeeded. Failing to charm the stern desk lady into letting me slip past her to the elevator, I whiled away the worried hours however I could. Mostly, I counted the black and white floor tiles in the wide, polished entrance corridor and read Nancy Drew mysteries. It was about this time that I decided not to become a doctor or a nurse and set my sights on becoming a writer. Books were better company than big city hospital receptionists, I concluded.

Happier occasions were the trips into Lexington to sell our tobacco crop. Lexington claimed to be the largest burley tobacco market in the world, and I have no reason to think the Chamber of Commerce was exaggerating. All over town, mammoth auction warehouses came right up to the edge of busy through streets like South Broadway and Fourth Street. Tobacco has been vilified now, and few mourn the demise of the auction system that was once the economic lifeblood, not only of the region's farmers but of Lexington businessmen, too. The little tobacco still grown in central and northern Kentucky is contracted to large companies before it's ever planted in the ground, and the Lexington warehouses, dinosaurs of the recent past, are vanishing. In best case scenarios, their bones are converted into condos or flea markets, but most of the time they are demolished in a scorched earth policy to make way for the newest, latest thing.

I've often wondered how many kids my age who grew up in Lexington ever stepped foot into one of those warehouses that were so important to their hometown's economy. But farm kids like me did, and the experience was something that cannot be forgotten.

The burley tobacco market (not to be confused with North Carolina's flue-cured market) opened in early December on a date carefully calculated to be the coldest of the year. The cavernous buildings were walled cheaply with sheets of tin, and meteorologists have confirmed that south of the North Pole, the wintertime warehouses were the coldest places on earth. The damp chill came up through concrete floors and attacked toes in spite of heavy oxfords and cotton socks until finally there was close to no feeling at all left in the feet. Then the ice water traveled upward through the veins until exposed noses turned into icicles and the roots of hair went numb.

Despite the deadening temperatures, excitement electrified us as the auctioneer's high-pitched, rapid-fire chant echoed off the high rafters, moving up and down the endless mile-long aisles stacked with dry, brown, neatly tied "hands" of tobacco. When he finally came to our baskets—which were not baskets at all but shoulder-high hills of small, crisp tobacco bundles stacked on a wooden pallet—we held our breath. A year's work hung in the balance of a single minute. Our hearts beat so loud we couldn't be sure of the agreed on price as the auctioneer, speaking in his quick foreign-like language moved on to sell another family's sweat and tears to the highest bidder. We moved forward quickly to see the sale price the buyer had written on the tag.

Only then could we leave the rank smelling place. The odor of dried, dusty tobacco leaves *en masse* was so intense in those warehouses that it cannot fairly be described in olfactory terms. It was something more—its presence so strident that it seemed to take on three-dimensional shape like the walls and the floor. It stormed our nostrils, seeped deep into our lungs, and then emerged through our pores to cling to our skin and to our hair. The first thing we did when we left was to breathe in the purifying, cold, outside air, as thirsty for it as we had been for ice water in August tobacco fields.

Only then could we let the euphoria well up within us as we drove downtown to where the fine stores lined up along Main Street. Then we would spend freely for one time during the year, on Christmas gifts and small luxuries for ourselves. A new electric Mixmaster for my mother, or maybe a transistor radio for me. We would eat at Walgreen's Drugstore—the "all you can eat" fried fish in a basket was always my choice—or at Purcell's Department Store's more genteel cafeteria with its fancy fruit salads and fluffy desserts.

Years later, I would learn that the Woolworth's I thought was so wonderful really was wonderful—a magnificent example of art deco architecture. Ditto for the Kentucky and Ben Ali movie theaters. I would learn that the Phoenix Hotel with its canopy that stretched from door to street, its uniformed doormen, and its thick-carpeted lobby was a pretty good version of a first class hotel. Lowenthal's fur-filled windows and Embry's vestibule heavy with the scent of an expensive perfume were as hoity-toity as shops I'd later see in much larger cities in other parts of the country.

Lexington also connected me in a tangible way to the larger world. Along with postcards and bills, the mailman delivered *The Lexington Herald* to our mailbox everyday. The arrival of the newspaper was an exciting daily event. My mother's goal was to have her chores done so that she could sit down and skim the paper as soon as it arrived in late morning, and my father always took time to read it when he came in from fields for his noontime meal. And so I learned to read by first sounding out the comics in the Lexington paper and then, as I became more proficient, I moved on to all sections of the paper. Reading *The Lexington Herald* was a large part of my education.

And the larger world, in its way, came to Lexington—and then, in its way, to me. Once, leaving the hospital when my grandfather was ill, my dad and I caught a glimpse of President Eisenhower in a motorcade traveling down Limestone Street. Years later, I would learn that the president had come to dedicate Transylvania's new library, where (in the peculiar way life has of circling back on itself) I would spend so many hours exploring "the larger world" as revealed and recorded in the library's books. I also remember my father driving me into Lexington in the fall of 1960 to stand in an open space on the UK campus to hear John F. Kennedy stump for votes. It was a warm and perfect October day, and a few years later when I heard that JFK had been shot, all I could think about was the way the Lexington sun had glanced off his hair that morning making it appear more golden in the autumn light than it looked in photographs. I had an urge to ring up the world and tell them how Kennedy had looked in Lexington—as though he may have looked different here than in other parts of the country.

For all of these reasons, and more, going off to attend college in Lexington remains one of the most thrilling events of my life. Had I been headed for New York City or Paris, France, my sense of adventure could not have been greater. Lexington did not disappoint me. With two universities, several seminaries, a population of more than a hundred thousand people—and oh, those beautiful thoroughbred horses—it provided a large venue for a country girl. It was sophisticated enough, enlightened enough, for me to shed a little of my parochial thinking and to spread my wings.

Minutes after I graduated from college, I moved to Ashland, a town of about 25,000 in the far eastern part of the state. My newly minted husband had been offered a job there, and we drove east without a clue of what awaited us. Ashland, as it turned out, is where I would spend the bulk of my adult life. That is where I taught recalcitrant high schoolers, where our three children were born and grew up, where lifelong friendships were formed. That is where I learned that the mountains were not a foreign place and began to call eastern Kentucky home.

Yet even in Ashland, Lexington remained a large part of our lives. Like so many in the smaller towns and rural areas of eastern Kentucky, we turned toward Lexington when we wanted a quick taste of urban life. We would drive the two or three hours into Lexington to watch the horses race at Keeneland in the spring, or to attend plays at the Opera House or to take our teenagers to rock concerts at Rupp Arena or to see the UK Wildcats play basketball. We liked loafing in the gigantic but genial Joseph-Beth bookstore and returning to Ashland with a season of books to read. We enjoyed eating in the restaurants that were unlike the ones back home and shopping in the big stores. We brought our schoolchildren here to participate in academic meets and speech tournaments at the University of Kentucky, and to band competitions and for the state high school basketball tournaments.

Then a few years ago, after all our children had left home for college, we found ourselves in a position to consider an early retirement. Freed from the tether of job obligations, my husband and I felt as though we had limitless choices on where we could now live. Affection for elderly family members in central Kentucky and for the Owen County land, however, seemed to pull us toward those parts of the state. Over a four-year period, as we contemplated where to light, we gave careful consideration to most of the towns in central and northern Kentucky and to the Eagle Creek farm. An accumulation of small, personal reasons eventually settled us on Lexington, and I have to say, it felt a little like a homecoming even though we'd never before called Lexington—or any city—home.

As I look around the Lexington of the 21st century, I see many people like my husband and me. Neither native to Lexington nor from out of state, we have found something that feels like home within the city. Everywhere I go in town, I bump into folks we've known from all corners of our lives and of the commonwealth. Most every county in Kentucky could form a sizable expatriate group in Fayette County, it seems to me. The people whose histories are rooted in Kentucky's small towns and farms are a large part of Lexington's vibrant community mix of city, gown, and country.

I know that there are those who decry homogenization of our Kentucky culture—or of any culture. They would say that Lexington's gain in population is the countryside's loss, and I don't pretend to argue that is not true. But each of us brings the uniqueness of where we have been to the place we are now. And Kentuckians, I think, are not easily homogenized. We tend to be strong individuals together or alone, on top of the mountaintop, in the river valley, on the farm, in town, between a rock and hard place, or at the top of our game.

So, no, I reckon I'm not from Lexington, but I do live here now. Can you all pass the ham biscuits, please?

Georgia Green Stamper

Georgia Green Stamper, a seventh generation Kentuckian, grew up on a tobacco farm in the north-central part of the state on land that has been in her family for over a century and a half. After graduating from Transylvania University, she taught high school English, speech and theater in Ashland, where she and her husband, Ernie, raised their three daughters. Stamper is a regular commentator on NPR member station WUKY in Lexington. She also writes a bi-weekly humor and memoir column, "Georgia: On My Mind," for *The Owenton News-Herald*. She and Ernie now live in Lexington.

Genesis for *Where Am I From?*

When I moved to Lexington a few years ago, I was frequently asked the perfunctory question, "Where are you from?" I was surprised when I was unable to respond with a glib, easy answer. As it has ever been for me, it was not until I put written words on the page that I began to understand why I had so much difficulty with my response. About this time, I also realized that many of my fellow Lexingtonians had life stories not terribly unlike my own. Positioned near the center of the state and home of the state's flagship university, Lexington has played a unique role in the lives of many small town and rural Kentuckians.

Growing Up Depressed

Jan Sparkman

When I think of southeastern Kentucky in the 1940s and 50s, I feel the shadow of those times invade my life. The scenes and attitudes and structure of my childhood have become so connected in my mind with what happened that the events seem to have grown out of that place and time. But, of course, they could have happened anywhere, anytime. I grew up depressed, although I didn't know what to call it back then. I only knew that my life was distorted in some way that seemed beyond my power to change.

Part of me knew that I was no different from my sisters, my neighbors, but another part perceived a disparity that colored my mind like black paint on a windowpane, blocking the light. Somehow, I developed coping skills that worked. I knew what I had to do and I did it, but I resented the necessity of such choices.

By the time of my first memory three of my brothers had succumbed to childhood diseases and all but one of my older siblings were grown and no longer lived at home. My younger brother was the beloved baby of the family. I had no specific place, though in my preschool days I gave this little thought. Nor did I know that we were poor. We never went hungry or cold. My father was respected in the community, my mother the radiance of my small world. Until I started school my life was one big sunny day spent playing. My parents knew these golden days could not last, of course—they had sent other children out into the world—but they didn't tell me.

I started to school at a one-room facility two miles from our home. It was a long walk for a six-year-old. Mrs. Ellis, the teacher, gave me my first glimpse of the strange and frightening outside world. Her teaching philosophy favored intimidation above all else. A large wooden paddle was her weapon and (I am convinced) she loved to wield it. She used that paddle in response to the smallest infraction. Freda, one big, rawboned girl, was Mrs. Ellis's special target. She and her sisters made up a large part of the student body, and they were even poorer than we were. They went barefoot well into the fall because they could not afford shoes, and the lunches they brought were shockingly skimpy. I noticed that Freda's family didn't seem to love each other the way my brother and I did. When Freda got punished at school, her sisters raced each other home to see who could be first to tell of Freda's paddling. Their father, it was said, would then beat Freda again. My heart ached, then and now, for this girl.

After I was threatened with paddling once (causing me to have nightmares and plead illness to keep from going back to school), I was as good as it was possible to be. I never broke the rules. I always did my homework. I would have turned in my best friend to avoid Mrs. Ellis's discipline, but fortunately it never came to that. Imagine adding that guilt to all the other I have carried over the years! School, that important event I had so looked forward to, lost its aura and became just something to be endured.

Sure, there were respites. The next teacher I had was kind and helpful, but I'd learned well the lessons of distrust, of holding back. I knew she was too good to be true, and the next year's move to the consolidated school and Mrs. Haswell only proved it.

One day from that era comes clearly to mind. I remember that Mrs. Haswell's ample behind hung over the edge of the small chair she drew up beside me. "Why didn't you tell me you needed to be excused?" she whispered, her lips cold against my ear.

I looked straight ahead, ignoring her and the pool of pee on the floor. My stomach was threatening to push its way out through my mouth. The room swayed. I longed for the small school I'd transferred from a month before. There everything was familiar, but here long halls twisted and turned and I could never find my way back to my classroom when I ventured into them alone. But afraid as I was of getting lost, I was doubly terrified to speak of it to the mean-eyed Mrs. Haswell.

She'd looked so motherly that first day with her soft hair and skin, her voile dress with flowers on it. It didn't take me long, though, to notice how her smile never got beyond the corners of her mouth and how icy her voice was. It changed only when she gossiped with the first grade teacher next door or fawned over a certain group of little girls who never wore the same dress twice and had lustrous hair sporting velvet ribbons.

Our classroom had both second and third graders. The third graders had shiny, blond desks with tops that opened for storing books and pencils, but we second graders sat in little chairs around oblong tables and waited for Mrs. Haswell to dole out our materials.

Saul Peak was sitting next to me that day. He inched his chair away so no one would connect him to the offensive puddle on the floor. Saul was a nice boy. He didn't laugh or point, but I knew he'd tell. How could he resist?

Mrs. Haswell asked me if I wanted to go to the restroom, clean myself up. With what, I wondered. Did she think my mother had thoughtfully provided me with extra underpants and jeans in my book bag?

I shook my head and pretended to read. Mrs. Haswell shrugged and stood up. I didn't know what I was expected to say, so I said nothing. She gave me a look of pure disgust. I will never forget it.

The rest of the afternoon I stared at my book, careful not to meet the eyes of my tablemates or glance across the room to where the older girls I so admired were no doubt laughing at me. At last the dismissal bell rang and I could leave the room, lose myself in the crush of students heading for the bus. My clothes were nearly dry by then so I never told my mother.

I was the thirteenth of fourteen children in my family, and this position gave me no (or at least questionable) status among my siblings. Besides that, I was the only child born in the blustery, unpredictable month of March, and the only one to suffer the terrible defect of bright red hair.

When I reached the point in school where appearance mattered, I found that my hair made me a target for teasing and outright hostility. My hot temper did not help. I cringed to be called "red" or "carrot top" and refused to make a joke of it. And, of course, the more upset I got, the more I was teased.

My mother's attitude was that I had to live with what God had given me, which only made me angry with God. It took years for me to understand that she was trying to elevate my self-esteem. Not that she had ever heard the term, she just thought that assuring me of God's love would make me feel better about myself.

I tried to make up for the dismal failure of my looks by being the smartest girl in class. I was an A student from the time I started school, but this did not endear me to my fellow classmates. They would have been much happier if I had been both ugly and dumb. I stopped talking to my mother about it when I saw that she had taken the subject as far as she could with her limited knowledge of school and its social hierarchy.

Mama had only a fifth grade education. She never rode a school bus to a strange community whose children were unfamiliar to her, never had to learn to interpret the confusing series of bells that formed the pattern of each day, never sat alone in a school cafeteria wondering what to do with her empty tray. Her exposure to the world of affluence in general was limited, too. I couldn't go to her and say, "Mama, I don't fit in. The other girls have nicer clothes and permanents in their hair. They live in homes with running water and inside toilets and their mothers drive cars." Besides not understanding, she would have been hurt for me and I felt I should protect her from that.

I don't know where this sense of owing her protection came from. Did I believe that she was unaware of what the real world was like, couldn't handle knowing? If so, I was wrong. My mother was orphaned at age three, hired out as a household drudge at eight, married at seventeen, bore fourteen children and gave up three to childhood illnesses, cared for a blind husband, never had time to herself. She was the strongest person I ever knew. Still, I protected her.

Once I was chosen for a part in a presentation of "Tom Thumb's Wedding." It required me to have a long, white dress. Somewhere my mother got money to buy white organdy fabric from which she made me a dress. It was quite plain, for my mother sewed from necessity and not from skill. I liked it well enough until I saw the dresses the other girls were wearing. Silky, flowing, etched with lace and ribbons. It was just as well Mama had no way to get to the school on the day of the performance. She didn't have to see how different my dress was from the others, didn't have to hear how Mrs. Haswell said, "Oh, well..." when she saw it. Also, her absence meant I didn't have to face my own shame because I secretly felt Mama would have been as out of place among the other mothers as I was among their daughters. That she not know of these feelings was somehow part and parcel of my obligation to protect her.

Sometimes it is necessary for me to drive out Old State Road. The scene has changed little in fifty years. It was a pretty day. Perfect as only a summer day with no school and a trip to town on the agenda can be. I was ten years old, companion to my blind father, promised an ice cream cone from the drugstore soda fountain as a reward for guiding him through the streets. I loved the busyness of town, the sounds of car horns and police whistles so different from anything we heard on our isolated farm, the exciting goods displayed in the stores' big, glass showcases.

The first person we saw that day was Ned, my father's friend. He patted my shoulder and offered to take me for a ride in his new car. I didn't understand, even then, why Dad said yes. He couldn't get around without me. He'd have to wait on a bench in the courthouse foyer until I returned. But he liked it there. Other men with nothing important to do came by, engaged him in conversation. Maybe that was what *he* liked about town, maybe a little girl cramped his style—or maybe he thought it would be a treat for me to ride in that new car.

I had nothing against Ned except that he was an undertaker—which made me feel creepy—it was just that I preferred to stay in town. I didn't get to go all that often. I tried to beg off, saying Daddy might need me, but Ned said he wanted to show me something special. My father said to go on, he'd be fine. So I went.

We drove out Old State, past the furniture store, the American Legion Post, across the railroad tracks, into dappled shadows cast by wooded areas on either side of the road. I wondered what special thing there was to see in this direction. Ned was talking but, enjoying the sunshine and feeling important in the luxuriant car, I was paying him no mind. Suddenly I felt his hand between my legs. I was so startled that at first I couldn't think what to do or say. Then I pushed him away and scooted to the far edge of the seat.

"I want to go back to my daddy," I said.

"In a minute," he answered. I'd never noticed before how oily his voice was, how narrow his eyes. I'd never given him any thought at all. He was just a man who came to see my father once in a while.

He made a U-turn and stopped the car in the shade of a tree. "Now, let's see how big you are," he said, reaching for me again. I scrambled for the door handle. Locked. Ned was grabbing me, holding me. His hands were everywhere.

I kept saying, "Stop, please. I want my daddy," until I ran out of breath.

Ned just laughed.

A car came by, slowed down. Ned jerked upright, put the car in gear and sped away, leaving me huddled against the door, fumbling at my clothes. I didn't know what to call what had just happened, but I knew it was bad. I knew that good girls didn't let men do things like that to them. I was crawling with shame. Ned warned me not to tell, but he didn't need to. I was already pushing the experience as far into the recesses of my brain as it would go. I had learned at school that unpleasant experiences were best not examined. Pain was only manageable if it was ignored, forbidden.

Ned delivered me back to my father and made a hasty retreat, warning me with his eyes. I wanted to tell Daddy what his "friend" had done to me, but I was sure I wouldn't be believed, that I was somehow to blame. Dad would hear nothing bad about his friends. For the first time in my life I was glad that he was blind and couldn't see my face.

I never told my mother. By the time I got home I was well on the way to convincing myself that nothing of consequence had happened there in the front seat of Ned's big, black Chrysler. I did not repress the memory as much as I deliberately chose to forget it. Using the same tactics that had worked with bad dreams in an earlier period of my life—a stern lecture to myself about what was and was not real—I managed to cope, after a fashion, but from that day on I sensed that I was weird, different, and I wondered why the sun no longer shone with quite the same brilliance as it once had.

The depression that had lurked on the fringes of my life soon took over. I have to force myself to remember the despair of those days. The way my heart pounded in my ears, the paranoia, the sleepless nights, the fear. Gradually, I got better. I went to college, got married, had my own children. But years later, at a luncheon that lasted much longer than I had expected, I found myself needing to pee. I stood it as long as I could, then rushed out of the room, embarrassing myself and the friend who had invited me there. In the restroom, I leaned against the wall, trembling. Lights were popping in my head, and my lunch rose up to choke me. It was 1946 again and I was seven years old at Milbush School in the middle of one of the worst days of my life. I was afraid to look in the mirror, sure that I'd see that little girl instead of the wife and mother I'd become. I wanted to sit on the floor and cry.

I think I did. The years-long period that began with that moment is a trifle hazy in my mind. I remember doctors, pills, hospitalization, guilt, despair, and—finally—a doctor who understood that what I needed, among other things, was to go back to second grade and wipe that smirk off Mrs. Haswell's face.

The counseling that was to help me understand my illness and to finally recover from it did not begin early enough, but it did happen. And it was the hardest work I've ever done. In spite of all I learned about the worth of believing in—of stretching—myself, I still fear to chronicle the sad effects of depression on my life. Why open up old wounds? Who really cares? What is the value of such work in the long run? I only know that I need to give meaning to that lonely journey, to articulate the pain and embrace the peace that was so long in coming.

Jan Sparkman

Jan Sparkman has been writing for more than twenty-five years and is the author of one novel, three books of nonfiction, and a collection of short stories, as well as many magazine articles and newspaper columns. She has a BA in writing and literature from Burlington College and serves on the boards of the Janice Holt Giles Society and the Laurel County Historical Society. She has been the facilitator for the London Writers Group in her hometown since it began in 2000.

Genesis for *Growing Up Depressed*

Depression cannot be experienced and forgotten like an appendectomy. Its residue has a way of clinging to the fringes of one's life long after recovery. In the midst of depression the world changes colors and even when vibrancy returns, the hues and shades of that period are always lurking. This is not a bad thing. Painful as it is to remember, to forget would be to forfeit the emotional gains, the lessons learned at great expense. The secret is to put these memories in their proper place. That is what I have tried to do in this essay. It was written not only to exorcise old ghosts, but to reaffirm the necessity of doing so.

Depression is a disease. No matter the circumstances that brought it on (and these vary from person to person), depression can be cured. The feeling that nothing will ever be right again can be replaced with enthusiasm for the future. Thank God, the societal stigma of depression has nearly been removed as people become more educated about the factors that influence its onset. The combination of modern medicine, professional counseling, and determination now provides a viable prescription for recovery. Life is not the same after this process, it is better.

The Baptism

Mary Jane Adams

Our small church is situated on Cutshin Creek in Leslie County, Kentucky. Like many of the small mountain churches in the Eastern Kentucky Mountains, there is no baptistery. And really, there is no need of one. We like the custom of using the nearby creek for our baptismal services.

There's not a time when we go down to the bank of Cutshin Creek for a baptism that I don't remember an incident that happened years ago.

We had a visiting Southern Baptist student minister preach at our church for about a week. At the end of this "Revival Time," he scheduled a baptismal service.

Sunday arrived. Pastor Jim preached a stirring message during the morning service and then we all headed for the creek. It was a beautiful summer day. The baptismal "hole" had been deepened, and the brush and trash had been properly disposed of. A group of young people from a church up north had been working for The Cutshin Mission, doing some repairs and yard work. The creek provided a good place to relax and play after a hard day's work, besides the fact that showers were scarce.

To reach this hole of water, you must go up the church driveway, through the clinic yard, and travel down a pretty steep bank to Cutshin Creek. There is a sort of beach area down there with lots of grass and pebbles, so there is plenty of room for a large group to stand and view the baptism. The opposite side of the creek is high and steep with rhododendron, mountain laurel, and trees growing thickly on its rocky side. The sounds of birds and water flowing over and around the boulders make this a perfect spot for an old fashioned baptism.

On this particular day there was only one person being baptized. Carrie was in her teens and a beautiful blond. Someone had pinned her dress together between her legs so it wouldn't float up in the water. Her hair was pulled back and hung in one long braid down her back. She made a pretty picture as she came down the bank with her mother.

After everyone got quiet, the congregation sang "What Can Wash Away My Sins?" Pastor Jim and Carrie waded slowly into the cold water. The pastor was walking very carefully that day, as he had had an ingrown toenail removed that week. His toe was very sore and was all bandaged up for protection. It was supported by an old tennis shoe with the toe cut out. Reaching the deepest part, the pastor said the appropriate words and dipped her under.

Everything had gone real well until Carrie moved away from the preacher and began to make her way back. Suddenly, she heard a big thrashing sound behind her. The preacher had stubbed his toe on some rocks, fallen backwards, and was not able to get to his feet in the deep water. Carrie simply turned around and went back to help him. She grabbed hold of his hand and arm and pulled him to his feet. Still supporting him, she led him toward the bank.

As you can imagine, the congregation was in a fit of laughter by this time. Some of the members waded out to assist the arrival of the dripping forms, who were then wrapped in towels and blankets. Pastor Jim and Carrie were hugged, kissed, patted, and cried over. Then everyone headed back to the parking lot.

We will long remember the words of Granny Adams as we helped her up that steep bank, "Well, youngins, he might have baptized her, but she shore saved him!"

Mary Jane Adams

Mary Jane Adams has two children, a girl and a boy, and five grandchildren and has been married to Raleigh Adams for forty years. She has taught at Hayes Lewis Elementary on Cutshin Creek in Leslie County for twenty years and served as chairperson of Kentuckians For The Commonwealth in the late 1980s during the campaign to abolish the broad form deed.

Genesis for *The Baptism*

Several years ago, I was taking a class from Dr. Whitaker at Eastern Kentucky University for my M.A. Ed. As an example of how you could get children to write, he read us the book *When I Was Young in the Mountains* by Cynthia Rylant, a West Virginia writer. When he had finished, he asked us to write our own story about the mountains. I wrote a shorter version of *The Baptism*. When we read our stories in class, he wanted me to make it longer and describe the setting a little more. I worked on it a little, and it was published in *Appalachian Heritage*, and now I've revised it further for this publication.

Wings to Fly

Judith Victoria Hensley

Flat gray ribbon stretches before me forever northward, splitting endless cornfields as it goes and dividing me just as surely from things I hold familiar. Perhaps if I follow too far, the road and I will fall off the edge of the earth.

Wretched summer heat and merciless concrete glare sting my eyes. We are a convoy of rolling beasts. No more than nameless soldiers across the kitchen floor we go with empty arms hoping to carry something back.

Finally I see my exit and try to interpret the handwritten map like some ancient hieroglyphics. Left at the light, ten blocks north, right at the intersection, call from BP. I try to follow precisely.

"Call me from BP and I will come and get you," he had said. "You can follow me home from there."

There is no BP. I look at every corner and see WAL-MART. Surely he can find me here. Everyone knows this place.

I try to call from the telephone in the lobby and am amazed that it does not accept quarters but will speak to me in Spanish if I press a button. Suddenly I am more tired than I have ever been in my life, vanquished in a foreign land by a machine that refuses to take my carefully prepared roll of quarters. Cold, heavy, useless they lay in my hand.

The thought hits me, "I don't even know the address to take a cab!"

Like one with Alzheimer's, I stand in this strange place unable to remember the address of my destination. Even if I could push past the weariness in my head to remember where I'm going, I can't call a cab with my useless coins.

Inspiration comes like a flash of light in my darkness. Get a calling card.

With hope stirring, I go inside and ask the greeter to direct me toward the calling cards. He blinks through stacks of wrinkles and consults a map of the store. "Go to Jewelry, half way down by the grocery aisle."

The peculiarity of this combination of merchandise strikes me. Jewelry, calling cards, groceries are all in this vast cavern of merchandise, and I wonder what all there is available under one roof. I remember the commissary at Black Star Coal Camp of my youth—a microcosm of modern trade.

Through the maze of deserted lanes, I find Jewelry. Sure enough the grocery wing faces it. There are watches, rings, necklaces, earrings, chains, decorations to adorn a variety of pierced body parts, but no calling cards. Desperately I seek help from the clerk.

“Calling cards?” she asks and looks hard at me. I feel like a fly defiling the sweetness of her day.

“Oh, you mean GREETING CARDS!” Motioning to another clerk to come before I can stop her, she barks an order, “Show her to the greeting cards.”

The girl comes quickly with a smile and speaks in a first generation Indian accent as she bids me follow her up the wrong aisle.

“No,” I say, trying to be as kind to her as I need her to be. “I need to make an important telephone call, and the machine does not take coins. I need the kind of card that lets you buy minutes to make a long distance telephone call.”

I speak these words slowly and deliberately, hoping to help her understand exactly what it is I am in need of. I do not doubt her intelligence, but I am surely doubting mine—to have come this far to this city ALONE, without even an address in my pocket.

It is clear to see that she has an idea. “Come, come,” she says to me with a wave of her hand. I follow as obediently as my son’s golden retriever on her heels. She stops at the electronics department, and I explain to yet another salesperson what I am in need of. To my amazement, she repeats what I said to him as if I have spoken in another language instead of with a southern accent.

He nods. The girl retreats with a satisfied smile, her long beautiful hair bouncing behind her. I feel a kinship with this departing girl, for we are obviously both strangers here, pilgrims in a foreign land.

The young man takes me immediately to the calling cards at the end of a telephone display, and I feel both foolish and relieved. Why didn’t I think of this connection sooner? The speckled faced youth looks at me with an impatient superiority.

Never mind. My spirits are failing, but my manners are not. “Thank you so much," I say, trying not to show my southeastern Kentucky accent. The less said, the better.

Clutching the card in my hand like a lifeline, I make my way through displays, stacks, piles, racks, and a rainbow of people. "God, please help me find the front of the store..."

Finally, I take my place in one of a string of cashiers and check out lines that must be twenty-four deep.

Out the door, I face the telephone as David may have faced Goliath, determined to conquer the foe. I punch in the series of numbers (the longest I've ever dialed in my life) and am assured by a mechanical voice that I have 599 minutes remaining.

"I'm here," I say to my son when he answers.

"I'll be there in a minute," he says.

"I'm not at BP," I say before he hangs up on me.

"Where are you?"

"I'm at Wal-Mart," I announce with confidence that I had made a smart decision in lieu of the BP that I could not find.

"Mom, there is no Wal-Mart on this side of town! Do you know how many Wal-Marts there are in this place?" He pauses. "Tell me where you are and how you got there..."

I can barely remember how I got from the Electronics Department back to the telephone. A lady using the other payphone next to me is rattling away in Espanola, which I do not speak but at least recognize. I look around for anyone who looks like they might be willing to help. There is no one.

I try to remember where I turned and significant landmarks I have passed. I might as well be trying to give the navigational co-ordinates to the back side of the moon. The phone beside of me clicks as the user hangs up. In desperation I ask her if she can tell me exactly where we are, and she feeds the information to me slowly as I repeat it over the telephone.

He finally figures out that I made the initial turn correctly but missed the BP by about six miles, crossing over another interstate and going at least half an hour out of the way. He will get there as soon as possible through the evening traffic.

Standing just outside the front doors, I have never felt so lost or alone. People come and go, speaking several languages, the least of which is English. I try to look confident but invisible at the same time as I strain my eyes into the setting sun. I count the minutes and scan every moving vehicle in the parking lot for the silver truck that carries my son to the rescue.

While I wait, I think about my parents and how brave they were to leave the familiarity of the mountains, hills, and hollows to pursue a better life in a northern city. Still teenagers, they had packed up kit and caboodle into an old Chrysler to find the promised land of good paying jobs in automobile factories. They tried on Detroit and Chicago for size before they settled in Chicago Heights, Illinois. The Ford Motor Company paycheck more than replaced the Mary Alice Coal Company script, and the smaller town was easier to live with than the crush of city life.

I acknowledge the irony in the fact that I have reversed their journey, giving up city life to teach in a mountain school that had once been part of a thriving coal community. And I realize that my son has set out on his own journey, seeking his place in the world.

I see a broad shouldered youth with a steady gate moving toward me and although the setting sun behind him obscures his face, I'd know my flesh and blood anywhere in the country, any city, or any crowd on the planet. He starts to run the last few steps, but doesn't have to because I beat him to it.

The same arms that use to cling around my neck for comfort now wrap around me as if I am the child and he the adult. He kisses the top of my head and hugs me again as we walk to my car.

"I knew something had to be wrong before you called," he says. "It was getting so late."

Back into my car I go, following the silver truck. We race ahead, barely escaping the fingers of darkness that are overtaking the sky.

"You are a crazy woman," I say to myself out loud in the silence of my moving car.

How could I have been naïve enough to drive all the way to Indianapolis without an address, without the name of the apartment complex, not even knowing there was such a thing as a telephone that doesn't take quarters? Had I been so long in the secure embrace of the mountains that I had forgotten the reality of city life?

I ought to have been better prepared. Perhaps I need to rethink the evils of cell phones before I embark on another journey northward.

It dawns on me that in spite of all my motherly worries about a son leaving the whole state of Kentucky behind to start a new life in a strange place, he is better equipped than I am to deal with the challenges of this new adventure. It is his journey now, separate from my own.

We turn in to a sprawling apartment complex that overlooks a wooded area and a lake. It can't compare with the natural beauty of the mountains, but I realize he has chosen carefully a place that will remind him of the woods and water of Harlan.

How strange it seems to be following him "home".

I know that I've poured all of me into him that I possibly can and that has to be enough. It was my decision not to bind him to me with obligation and fear. I taught him how to dream big dreams and reach for the stars. I encouraged him to live his own adventure and enjoy the journey. I believed in his ability to make something good of his life.

I chose to give him wings instead of tethers. As I open the car door in the parking lot, I take a deep, deep breath, and know the time has come that I must let him fly.

Judith Victoria Hensley

Judith Victoria Hensley has taught science at Wallins Elementary in Harlan County for twenty-three years and is widely known for the role that she and her students played in saving Black Mountain from strip-mining. An alumna of the University of the Cumberlands, she has written a column in *The Harlan Daily Enterprise* for the last ten years and is the author of *Sir Thomas the Eggslayer*, a chapter book.

Genesis for *Wings to Fly*

My mother and father were a part of the great northward migration in the 1950's of those seeking work and a future outside of the coalfields of southeastern Kentucky. Both were teenagers at the time. Through the years I often heard them speak of overcoming obstacles in the strange new city life they were trying to embrace.

Not only were there social, cultural, and emotional barriers of being separated so completely from all that was familiar to them, but also a huge language barrier. The first time my dad went to the grocery store and asked for a "poke of flour" they nearly called for an interpreter. When he explained that he needed a "sack of flour that is used to make biscuits," it didn't help.

Growing up outside of Chicago, I thought I had a pretty good grip on city life, but had no clue just how much that life had changed in the many years that have passed after I returned to reclaim my Kentucky roots. I felt like a fish out of water when I pulled in to Indianapolis and realized how totally naïve I was in that setting.

It didn't take long to see the parallels between my parents' first experiences in the city, those from other countries who have come to claim a new life in a new land, my own feelings of inadequacy in an unfamiliar situation, and my son starting a whole new life on his own.

There was quite a struggle within, wanting to keep my child a part of all things familiar and safe within our life in the mountains, yet wanting him to be unencumbered by all of those things to take his own journey and discover the wings that might take him farther from home or bring him back to us.

Meeting New Neighbors

Scott D. Vander Ploeg

In March, I noticed an unfamiliar dog in my yard. Mid-sized, mixed collie and hound, matted coat, and musty-rank, it paced toward me dutifully, though also shyly, and I quickly guessed that it expected to be beaten—yet it was friendly and did not demand attention. It came to me because it had to, but neither of us really wanted the encounter. Poor animal, I thought, my reluctance to pet it matched by its slow and disconsolate gait.

It belonged to my new next-door neighbors, whom I had not yet met. They were a painfully young couple with an infant boy. They owned a nondescript GM car that mostly sat unused. On their first day in town, he left early in the morning, climbing into a white pick-up truck with Alabama plates. A half-dozen of such plates and their vehicles would clatter in and out of the next-door driveway on an irregular schedule. He would always return shortly after dark: hot, sweaty, dirty, sore—and this was his routine on every day of the week. Once every month he would get Sunday off.

Chance finally brought us together. On a Sunday, I was hacking away at the poison ivy infesting the shrub line between our properties, and contemplating Frost's line, "Good fences make good neighbors," when out came the whole family, preparing to leave for the mall. They looked desperate. I felt I ought to welcome them at least.

I moved to intercept them. They stumbled, halted. He: tall, wiry, tense, intense—shook my proffered hand and introduced himself as Bill. She: quiet, deferential to her husband, unwilling to make eye-contact—clearly uncomfortable, clearly pregnant. Bill said, "This is my wife, Mandy, my son, Caleb." They politely withstood the torture of meeting me.

"Hi and welcome to the neighborhood—I'm Scott." Silence. "Uh, are you finding your way around town okay?"

"Well…we're from a farm in Alabama. It's a real change living in a big city. We aren't used to it." The "big city" he referred to has a population of fewer than 20,000 souls, and only one McDonald's, except for the one in the Super Wal-Mart. It is a small town by most standards, and the citizens have been proud to think of it as such. I paused to imagine the size of the place that gawky Bill and Mandy came from. I had to readjust my thoughts a little: from a remote farm perspective, this town would be big and maybe confusing. Even so, it seemed absurd to class our town with Lexington and Louisville as big cities.

The well-intentioned introduction was foundering. Clearly these people were unhappy to be here, unhappy to have to meet their neighbor, unhappy. I could do nothing to lessen their discomfort. In approaching them, I had done something wrong, threatened them with a beating they would prefer to avoid. Obedient and civil, they endured the meeting because they had to, though no one seemed to want the encounter. I might have been re-enacting the first meeting with their dog.

I am impressed with the triggers that bring these people out of their familiar homes, forcing them to leave the lands where they feel connected and the families that are their anchor and support; I wonder over the job opportunities and market forces that thrust them out into the incompatible new contexts with which they are ill-equipped to contend. How unhappy they must be. Something considerable must be at work to cause this bringing together of immiscible elements.

"So what do you do, Bill?" I continued, trying to keep the conversation alive without aiming a spotlight in the poor man's face.

"I'm just here to build chicken houses. Gonna work till the winter, then move on, I guess. We're just leasing the house."

"Economic Development" has become the mantra of western Kentucky. Since the much-hyped decline of the coal industry, residents have believed the great evil to be the lack of jobs. We seem willing to sacrifice anything to the altar of more jobs. No matter the desirability of the project, if it will bring jobs we nod our heads and look hungrily toward the proposal. Why chicken houses? Because they will help the farmers keep their jobs. Even though the truth of that is debatable, because jobs are dangled as part of the deal, Kentuckians have acquiesced to it.

We should look closely at Bill and his family: Bill was not much of a neighbor, not much of a contributor to our community. He never approached me or spoke to me again. During his stay here, he mowed his leased lawn once. He made no improvements to the wood frame house, and it seemed as sad and forlorn as their dog. By the time they left, they had paid a few dollars in retail taxes, but nothing in property assessment to help our schools and public facilities. Mandy had birthed another bundle of care and cost. They collected food stamps. Fire departments would include them in their house counts. The local clinic provided reduced cost medical care. Soon after the region's residents had noticed the eruption of chicken houses in their back yards, Bill's company sent him somewhere else to work the hard way, another town where they would feel alone, unwanted, distempered. What memory do they have of this place that I call home?

The dog ambled freely in the area and was run over by a passing car. They hadn't thought to keep him out of the street. Big city.

When I hear politicians discussing future plans, and included in their pitch is the wonderful economic development that such-and-such a business will bring to our region, I recall the dog of it: he came here because he had to, but no one, apparently, wanted the encounter.

Scott D. Vander Ploeg

Scott Vander Ploeg is a specialist in Seventeenth-century English lyric literature, holding a 1994 Ph.D. from the University of Kentucky. He developed a heightened interest in his own writing from having spent nearly two decades helping college students in Madisonville with their composition and literary skills. "Mostly," he says, "I write for the sheer fun of it." At other times he writes from a sense of social responsibility, articulating for others what needs to be said. His commentaries can be heard regularly on the Murray PBS Radio affiliate, WKMS-FM.

Genesis for *Meeting New Neighbors*

Recently, I learned that today's chicken house is no longer the little ramshackle dilapidated wood slat coop that my grandmother had on her tiny farm in Missouri. The modern version is huge, and holds thousands of birds, crammed together, as manufactured genetically selected and hormonally altered food-to-be. When I moved to Hopkins County in 1988, and purchased a house and yard, a feeling of responsibility had me asking questions about my fellow citizens, my neighbors, my role in this place. Someone who keeps track of such things noted that in 1991 there were perhaps a dozen industrial-scale chicken houses in my county. By 1997 that number had grown to over 170 such facilities. Local residents belatedly found themselves in a miasma of feathered stench, their lives ruined for no fault except having bought property and tried to live out their lives. Further investigation showed that the gain for the farmers was often marginal, and that the contracts and arrangements favored the corporation that began a chicken-flesh production slaughter house just north of us. The new neighbors were a part of that machinery. One winter, the rats that had infested a collection of such houses went hungry when the operation failed and the owner quit. They sneaked across the road and attacked a family, crawling into a crib and gnawing on an infant. At the processing plant, two loyal workers were overcome by the ammonia fumes of the waste containment area, fell in, and died. I feel the mingled emotions of sympathy and resentment and had to write about it.

The Man on TV

Graham Thomas Shelby

On Memorial Day, I sprawl out in front of my grandparents' big TV, waiting for Dan Rather to introduce me to my father. Behind me, Grandma stretches out on the orange vinyl couch. Her expression so composed and calm I can sense her discomfort. She and Pappaw both know that tonight's edition of the CBS Evening News will feature their former son-in-law, though we haven't acknowledged this. I am twelve, nearly an adolescent, nearly beyond them, and they don't know how to talk to me about hard things.

Until now, Jimmy has remained an intriguing mystery, like a ghost, spoken of in whispers but never seen, except in a handful of old, fuzzy photographs. He was like our own family Bigfoot. My Loch Ness father. Except I know he is real, that he is part of our past, part of me, though it's not clear which part. I imagine the part of me that is Jimmy is somewhere hidden inside, like my lungs and bones and all the other things I know are there that I can't see.

I know that he is tall, that he loves sweets and spicy foods, and that when he laughs hard, he will roll on the floor and kick his feet, all traits we have in common. Since my mother and I left South Carolina when I was a baby, the only interaction we'd had with him came when I was five. My mother asked him to sign papers so that my new dad could adopt me. Jimmy agreed, but on one condition. He told my mother, "Just don't ever let them turn him into a damn soldier."

Then last week, he called to tell us he was going to be on TV. Mom explained to me that in Vietnam, his best friend had been killed and Jimmy had been the one to find his body. After nearly thirteen years, Jimmy had finally written a letter to the man's mother about her son. This woman then sent the letter to a newspaper, and eventually CBS News heard about it and decided to do a story about the two of them for Memorial Day.

"Do you think you'll want to watch it?" Mom asked me.

"Yeah," I said.

"You were going to go to Grandma's that week. Do you still want to go, or would you rather watch it here?"

"I'll watch it there."

She forced a smile and I could tell she wondered what I thought of all this, but I didn't know, so I couldn't say. I knew I preferred my grandparents' house in Laurel County, where I could escape to the fields and the woods anytime I wanted. Also, I've always been afraid that my dad, who I love, will be hurt if he finds out the extent to which I wonder about the man who was my first father.

During a commercial, Grandma reaches down and takes hold of my wrist, her fingers shiny with rings and lotion. "Look at those fingernails," she says, inspecting my hand. "Flat as can be. Why, you sure take after me. Flat as a skillet." She's said this before, and always with a kind of amused tenderness, as if she were discussing a treasured family heirloom. She seems torn between her instinct to protect me from corrupting influences and an understanding that this is something I need to see. I laugh to reassure her.

"You two," Pappaw says, filling his pipe from the can of tobacco, "you won't do." He lights his pipe and shifts in his recliner, framing the TV screen with his feet. Grandma has taken the lead on judgment and anxiety about the issue, thus freeing him from the responsibility. Pappaw seems to regard Jimmy as an interesting character who passed briefly through his life. The two men used to sneak off and trade swigs from a whiskey bottle Pappaw kept hidden at the top of his closet.

Still, the subject of Jimmy makes them both uneasy. Once when I was about eight, I was watching a game show and one of the contestants was named Jimmy and his last name started with a G. I ran to the kitchen to ask my grandmother what Jimmy's last name was, to see if this was him.

"Why are you asking?" she said.

I told her about the man on TV.

"I don't think he's the type who would participate in game shows," she said, wiping her hands on her apron.

"But what was his last name?"

"Godwin," she said, as if the knowledge of it was somehow disappointing, like a wart or an age spot she couldn't remove. I returned to the TV and concluded that this man wasn't the right Jimmy. He had a cheesy mustache and was from Wisconsin or Wyoming or somewhere

I knew I had no connection.

When Dan Rather returns, he introduces another veteran's story. A doctor from New Mexico built a fifty-foot memorial to the son he lost in Vietnam. "If I ever learned the identity of the soldier that killed my son," the doctor says, "and further learned that he had met a similar fate, I would put his photo beside that of my son in the chapel." The men at the memorial wear faded green jackets like Hawkeye and B.J. wear on *M*A*S*H.* They stare up at the pyramid-shaped monument, then hang their heads and shut their eyes.

Soon another commercial, Jimmy will be next. I take my dinner plate into the kitchen and without really deciding to, I make my way to the cool, stuffy room at the back of the house where Pappaw and I sleep in Ozzie-and-Harriet beds. I don't want to think about my grandparents as I watch this, as I meet, through the TV, the man who was once my father.

I sit at the foot of Pappaw's hard mattress and click on the twelve-inch black-and-white TV. I see Dan Rather's face before I hear his voice. "...two friends who fought side-by-side in Vietnam. Only one came home. Correspondent James McManus has the story of one family's search for the meaning of life, another family's search for the meaning of a death, and how both came to find peace of mind years after the agony of war."

The screen fills with men in jungles, only the picture is faded and grainy. That's how I know it's real, because it looks fake compared to a movie or a TV show. Huge guns belch smoke and fire into the trees. The soldiers look haggard and raw as they dash across a compound. A sign rests against the wall of a makeshift building.

AIN'T NO DANGER
NEVER WAS
A 239
DUC LAP

The reporter, McManus, his voice stiff and earnest, says: "Duc Lap, Vietnam, the winter of 1969. Jim Godwin remembers his best friend, Dutch Schnabely."

Soldiers carry a wounded man to a helicopter as I hear Jimmy's voice for the first time. "We had taken about five hundred rounds of incoming mortars and rockets. Dutch said, 'You know, I'm not really afraid of dying at all.' We were afraid of being forgotten. About three o'clock in the morning, we'd finished our talk and we stood up and shook hands and he said, 'Never forget.' And I never have." His voice, so deep and thick—not molasses, tar—seems to linger even after he stops talking. My voice has just started to change. Maybe I will sound like that when I get older.

The reporter says, "Green Beret Captain Donald F. Schnabely died at Duc Lap. Sergeant Jimmy Godwin came home a shattered survivor." They show a picture of Jimmy at twenty-one, skinny and arrogant. He wears his Green Beret and a dark uniform with colorful emblems. In the picture, he is standing in front of this, my grandparents' house.

When Jimmy's today face fills the screen, I study the curve of his jaws, his eyes, nose, mouth and hair, because I want the image of him to stick in my brain. I am searching for traces of myself, for evidence beyond my fingernails that I am connected to someone in that undeniable way of the body. There is some resemblance, I think, though I can't tell the difference between wanting to find something huge and obvious and actually finding something small and subtle. Maybe it's in his chin, pointy like mine, or in the shape of his face, though that's hard to tell as his cheeks melting into his neck with no hint of a jaw line. His long, red-brown hair touches his collar, with glasses and a mustache further obscuring his features.

It occurs to me that he looks like a taller, heavier version of Ed Shelby, the man I call Dad. This makes me feel cheated somehow because, for whatever reason—my mother's affection for intense, nearsighted men—my father looks more like my dad than either of them looks like me.

"The real battle was after I came back," Jimmy says. "It was real difficult. I had a lot of problems adjusting. I'd always blamed myself for his death." The reporter again: "For thirteen years, Donald Schnabely's mother searched for someone who knew how her son had lived—and died—at Duc Lap."

Dutch's mother, Mrs. Cutlip, looks about my grandmother's age and like my grandmother, she speaks in clear, careful syllables. "We did receive a paper saying that he had been killed in the mortar pit, but I wasn't sure that that's what had happened. And as the years went by and I didn't hear from anybody, I presumed that nobody did survive."

But Jimmy had survived, and he eventually went to group therapy for veterans and realized what he needed to do. "I had to write that letter," Jimmy says. "It took me three days. It really hurt. I yelled and screamed and cussed and stomped. But I'd say that, in retrospect, was the best three days of my adult life, because I not only helped me, I helped this lady who really had been searching."

My mother kept only a few pictures of Jimmy. One came from her wedding, where his face is out of focus. Another shows him sitting in a recliner, his head cocked to the side, a sly, skinny boy. The other one I know about is a baby picture. One day when I just old enough to talk, Grandma was keeping me and I reached into a drawer filled with old photographs. I pulled out a picture of Jimmy. According to grandmother, I then turned to her, showed her the picture and asked, "Is this my daddy?"

On the screen, two boys, a little younger than me, toss a football in the yard of a big house. An American flag the size of a bedspread hangs from the porch behind them. Mom told me that Jimmy had remarried. He has two boys now, but they are not his sons; he is raising his wife's children. I wonder if that's who these boys are: his other half-sons.

Since reading Jimmy's letter, Mrs. Cutlip says, "When I go to sleep at night, I don't wonder anymore. I feel peaceful. I feel that I can sort of put that at rest." They met earlier this year for the first time, and she invited Jimmy and his current family to her house for Memorial Day weekend. "Don didn't get to come home alive. Now, we're just real excited that his best friend is coming. We're going to treat him like family, and we've prepared a homecoming for him."

Jimmy then emerges from an enormous American car. He walks with long strides that are both stiff and purposeful. "Aw, James," Mrs. Cutlip says, putting her hands on his cheeks. She seems about to cry. I cringe and want her to be quiet.

"Everything is all right," he says. "It's gonna be a great weekend." He speaks to her in the reassuring way children sometimes speak to parents. I am here, he is telling her, and I'm okay.

A quartet of toe-headed little girls in white skirts holds up a sign that reads, "Welcome Jim, Eva, Adam and Aaron." I find it jarring somehow that his wife and sons have actual names. In an alternate universe, that sign reads, "Welcome Jim, Anne and Graham."

Dutch's family and friends throw a pig roast for their visitors, and later Jimmy and Mrs. Cutlip read from his letter. "'I am writing this in loving memory of your son," he says. "Dutch and I were comrades, friends, brothers.'"

Mrs. Cutlip continues. "'He told me how you raised his brother and him. He really loved and respected you. He was what you would have wanted him to be.'" His letter has done the same thing for her that this broadcast could be doing for me—supplying information about a long-severed link between a parent and a child. Only Jimmy isn't talking to me, at least not in any way I can understand.

"It's very seldom you hear something nice about a Vietnam veteran," he says. "And not that it's so nice about me, it's nice about this warrior, you know. Because the war was bad but the warriors were not."

Now, the tall man and the old woman stand together in front of a single headstone. Long grass waves in the breeze behind them. They hug. Jimmy's smile looks real and hard earned. As they let each other go, the reporter signs off and they dissolve into Dan Rather, who tells me good night.

I turn off the TV and stare at my reflection in its blank, gray face. Something had just happened. Or not happened. I couldn't tell. I had answers to some questions. What did he look like? How did he sound when he talked? Where did he live? But I was no closer to understanding the big question: Why had he let me go? Why was I seeing him now for the first time, along with millions of strangers? In some way, I was no closer to the tall man on TV than were any of other people who watched, who met him tonight as a face on the news. And in another way I was as connected to him as it was possible to be.

Suddenly, I have to be outside. In the front room, the giant console TV still sings. I run past it, past my grandparents and their silent inspection. In the field, I spread my arms out wide and jump. I kick the air in front of me. Karate chop behind me. I return to one of my favorite fantasy escapes. The one I act out when nothing good is on TV: I am the son of Superman. And my father had left the earth. This leaves me all by myself to battle the villains from the Phantom Zone. I leap and punch and kick the air until it gets too dark to see.

Graham Thomas Shelby

Graham Thomas Shelby grew up in a Lexington family with roots in Southeastern Kentucky, where he spent every Thanksgiving and Christmas. A graduate of the University of Kentucky, his work has appeared in *A Kentucky Christmas* and on public radio programs. In, 2005, Graham received the Al Smith Award in Creative Nonfiction from the Kentucky Arts Council. He lives in Louisville with his wife and three sons.

Genesis for *The Man on TV*

I used to love my grandparents' television. It was a giant console set with patterns carved in it that made it look a little like the Lost Ark. I loved it because it was much bigger and had more channels than my parents' TV. Plus, Grandma and Pappaw let me watch it as much as I wanted. As a kid, TV was my best friend. Other children often thought I was weird, and I found them to be erratic and generally untrustworthy. But TV asked nothing of me, and consequently it never let me down.

Most of the time, TV is both intimate and impersonal. It's intimate because it's in your house, but impersonal because what comes on the TV is the same in everyone's house. The same shows, the same jokes, the same characters and commercials. And we're all equidistant from the characters and the stories. At least that's what I'd always thought.

When I stayed with my grandparents, I sometimes watched cartoons in early morning, then sitcoms and game shows, then detective shows, then more cartoons in the afternoon. At 6:30 my grandparents and I gathered in front of the TV to watch Dan Rather. I liked sitting there with them, watching the news. Even when the news was grim, watching it with them was soothing somehow. When the outside world seemed dangerous, it made the den in my grandparents' house in Laurel County feel even safer.

Almost every evening there was the same: Grandma came in from the kitchen, bringing a plate of supper for me on a Batman tray. Pappaw came up from his gardens, dried mud on his pants and shoes. She might bring him a half meal of crumble-in-cornbread dropped in a glass of milk. Often, Pappaw was snoring by 6:45, but not on this particular evening in 1983. That evening was the first time that what came on TV was both distant and personal.

Singin' Dolly

Glade Blythe Brosi

Ghosts haunt these woods," she said. "In the spring you can hear them screaming, and this time of year you can feel their eyes upon you."

I tried not to laugh and averted my eyes to the well-worn boards that made up the old woman's porch. "Yes Ma'am, there are things out here that none of us will understand." Dolly shook her head, and her ears drummed against the window of my truck; the old woman smiled and wrung her hands.

"Well, I guess you can hunt here; my boys used to before they moved off. I want you to be careful, though, and leave some coons for seed." I nodded, thanked her and left. I drove away victoriously; the town was sprawling in all directions, leaving fewer and fewer places to coon hunt, and I had just scored access to a big farm. I ran my hand across my blue-tick's back and felt the tension of her stretch.

Driving home, I rolled down Dolly's window so she could stick her head out and turned up the heat. Early December air rushed into the cab, my hands felt stiff and cold. The old woman was a friend of my girlfriend's dad. I had worked out at her place before, cutting a tree out of the driveway and weed-whacking the fence line that followed it. Last summer I walked my dogs in the woods behind her house, slowly wasting a warm day with my girlfriend at my side. I remember Anita laughing at the dogs. It was a beautiful day, and we tried to identify some wildflowers, As Anita stooped to examine a clump of sweet william, I noticed coon tracks on the creek-bank.

Coon hunting does not run in my family. Perhaps I had a great uncle who raised hounds, but I have never heard anyone talk about it. I decided to become a coon hunter years ago after tagging along on a hunt with Anita's dad. His kinfolks had hunted coons for generations because it brought not just meat to the table but also some money for the hides. To me the hunt revolves around my connection with the dog and my love of the woods. The music that a hound makes cannot really be explained. I love to watch a well-trained hound tree a coon on a moonlit winter night.

The first time I brought Dolly home, I thought my dad would kill me. She barked straight through the night for what seemed like months on end; actually I think it was months on end. She's no longer a puppy, but even today I often have to yell out my bedroom window in the middle of the night, or go scare off a rabbit that has decided to graze outside her kennel. "I can't believe," my dad says, sometimes jokingly, sometimes exasperated, "that you would buy a dog that was *bred* to bark."

Three days after gaining permission I was ready to take to the woods. It was windy and cold, with just a sliver of a moon hanging in a cloudy sky. I was told not to go hunting that night: "With these winds, nothing will be stirring," Anita's father had said, "and you'll freeze for no reason." But I didn't care about the cold or the wind. I wanted to run my dog, to give her some experience, and it was a Friday, and I didn't have classes or work the next day.

Dolly whined and pawed at her kennel door. The air was wet, and I could picture my couch and television remote. But deep down I wanted Dolly to tree a coon; I wanted the bragging rights and the fur pelt as a possible Christmas gift for one of my siblings. I managed to open the rusty latch of the kennel, and Dolly sprung forward with gusto. During the daylight hours it would be impossible to tell that this slobber-mouthed, lazy dog would actually run, but night time changes Dolly in a way that can only be explained by breeding. This is what she's for; I thought as I grabbed the single shot .22 and slammed the truck door.

We followed the creek on past the barn and beyond the farthest pasture to a place where the land is boggy and the sycamores grow tall. In the darkness their branches were silhouetted against the sky, with its moving clouds and penciled-in moon. It was the kind of night that made anyone else grab for a blanket and thank God they weren't outside. It was the perfect night for coon hunting. My flashlight fought against the darkness and illuminated a small circle in front of me. The frozen air held my breath, and it made fog that circled me and blocked my vision. I stepped carefully over moss-covered logs and slate rocks.

"Skit em," I yelled at Dolly; "go get em."

Just out of sight a blue-black streak in the darkness ran past me and circled around. Dolly is almost impossible to see at night except for the green glow of her eyes. Her nose looked fastened to the ground as she ran back and forth searching for scent, easily maneuvering around any obstacle in her path. Her agility is an amazing thing to watch, and I rested, letting Dolly decide which way to go.

The cold I could stand but the wind made me uneasy. I looked around, fully expecting to see a coyote or some kind of ghost. Deep woods at night are an experience that cannot be explained. Every twig and leaf made a shadow, and I worried about traps, about poachers, or a meth-lab hidden in the woods.

Dolly's bark ended all of these fears, and I jerked my head around just in time to see her disappear across a hill. Her head was held up, and she was bawling, a long solemn bark. My heart raced, and I took off after her, excited by the thought of a coon. Everything whizzed past me as I ran; briars scratched my arms, and roots tripped me. I was in a dead run, and Dolly sounded like she was a mile away. My feet carried me on as I crossed the ridge into what surely was the Daniel Boone National Forest. Chestnut oaks grew tall in the dry soil on the top of the ridge. Walking as quickly as I could in the direction of the barking, I began to worry. It seemed strange that a coon would go up the hill and into the open woods. My experience was limited, but I figured it would run up a tree long before it would hike a mountain. With shaking, frigid hands I chambered a bullet; I could see Dolly now, she was just a hundred yards ahead. My headlamp bounced light through the tree tops as I headed toward the tree. Then Dolly was gone again and running the opposite direction back toward the farm and the creek.

"Damn it, Dolly, you slack jawed mongrel," I yelled into the night. "Get your ass back here." I was ready to whop the dog, to teach her to stay on a tree or at least find the right one. But before I could even blink she was on the opposite ridge line running hard and barking with determination.

I ran down the steep slope and charged the opposing hillside like it was a drill in football practice. When I got to the top, I turned my light down and began sneaking toward Dolly. My intent was to catch her and bring her back to the truck; I was exhausted. She was treed hard on a large hemlock that stood alone in a stand of oaks. All around the tree the ground was torn up from her running and lunging, and her mouth was full of foam, her eyes were fierce with determination. I got to her and turned my lamp on full power, scanning the tree top for whatever it was that held Dolly's fascination

When my light caught a pair of glowing eyes I had no way of preparing my heart for the surprise. There was not a coon in the tree, but a large bobcat, curled up against the trunk and baring its teeth. I shot wildly and saw the bullet hit the tree a good four feet below the cat. With shaking hands I fumbled another bullet into the gun and managed to close one eye to aim.

I don't remember the noise of the gun, or what Dolly did. What I remember was the long, slow fall of the bobcat as it came to the earth. I had hit it directly behind the ear and killed it stone dead. Dolly's barking and slobbering were all show, and she took off when the cat hit the ground. Although it posed no threat to her, it scared her and she refused to go near it. I also took my time going to the animal; this was not like a dead turkey or grouse that I rushed with the enthusiasm of the kill. I sat down in the wet leaves and sighed. It wasn't until that moment that I even thought of what I had done.

Blood trickled out of the cat's ear and down my jacket as I hoisted it over my shoulders like I had seen the guides on the Outdoor Life Network do. Dolly was at my side and breathing heavily as we walked along the creek back toward the truck. Thoughts rushed my mind like moths around a porch light. I envisioned myself pulling into town with the bobcat on the kennel in my truck, my dog sitting beside me, proudly waving her tail to the awestruck onlookers.

But something about this bobcat didn't make me want to show it off; I wanted to leave it in the woods, to put it back in the tree where I found it. I wished I could go back in time and not shoot it. Gingerly placing it in the bed of my truck I ran my hand across the yellowish brown body of the cat; I felt of its belly, its legs, and its head. I opened the mouth and looked at the teeth. Dolly jumped into the cab, and I just stood there lingering, watching the bobcat. Then I shut the tailgate and drove home.

The next morning I tele-checked the animal to the Department of Fish and Wildlife and wrote the confirmation number on the back of my license. In my possession was a dream come true, perhaps a full body mount or at least a skin and a skull. Just the license with bobcat penciled in the back are enough to frame. That morning before I skinned the bobcat, I weighed it at my girlfriend's house and showed it to her father and cousins. It weighed forty-three pounds and measured over three and a half feet long.

The old woman's ghost was probably the screams of a rutting bobcat. Dolly didn't find a coon, but instead gave me the once in a lifetime experience of a bobcat. I was lucky, and so was Dolly. As long as I hunt, I will be satisfied with never seeing another of the elusive creatures, but in my heart it means so much that they are out there, hunting in the night.

Glade Blythe Brosi

Glade Brosi is a twenty-four year old agronomy major at Eastern Kentucky University. In addition to fishing, hunting and woodworking, he also tries to write. At the Hindman Writer's Workshop last summer he found a helpful and supportive community. *Singin' Dolly* is his second published work.

Genesis for *Singin' Dolly*

Right now a red flag should be waving in the reader's mind; I am in fact the son of the editor of this section of the book. And, as a person who suffered from a school system frought with preferential treatment, let me be the first to say that I hate nepotism. So when I heard about the opportunity to write something for this book, I thought about not submitting anything. But something in my mind told me to go ahead.

Thirteen months ago I broke my right knee while working for the Kentucky Department of Fish and Wildlife on Paintsville Lake. My recovery has been slow, and I am far from the person I used to be. I now see stairs, steep slopes, and wet parking lots as obstacles that just last year I would have skipped over. My injury has slowed me down; I can no longer range for miles across the rough woods where grouse hide. Even though my steps might be fewer, I feel like this injury has made me a better hunter and outdoorsman. I look more carefully than I used to, and I always plan my steps.

Some people go to the woods to think. I go to the woods to forget. To me, hunting is something that I can share with my dead great grandpa. Hunting is ingrained in my DNA, sandwiched somewhere between my pride and my love for the wild. So when I kennel one of my dogs and head off to the Daniel Boone National Forest, I am escaping. My thoughts do not wander to next week's test or my check-book balance. Instead I try to identify different plants I don't know and imagine what animal has crossed this same path. Sometimes I like to think of my grandpa, his gear different but essentially the same. He did not have Capilene or Gore-Tex, but he had a gun and a dog. Just like cooking, canning, and mending I think there are things a person should know. A dog should romp; a horse should run, and a person should know the outdoors. I was fortunate to be raised in a family that values the knowledge of old-timey things. Although my father doesn't hunt, he can appreciate that I know where venison comes from and the delicate web that makes up our Kentucky woods.

But more than ecology, more than anything in the world, I love dogs. The first time I met my girlfriend's dad, he told me that he "loves dogs more than a cat loves cream," and I think that I am the same way. I bought Mama Crow's Singin Dolly, my little bluetick, because I wanted another dog. I love her, and I wanted to brag about her a little, and so I wrote this story. I like to think that while I am out hunting I am experiencing what my forefathers experienced. I like to think of grandpa crossing the ridge above the back forty following the call of a hound.

The White Doors

Steven R. Cope

To some of us life is simply a trip, an outing. We do this, we do that, we do the other. We go back home then to continue with our daily course and to eat or to nap as if nothing whatsoever had occurred to us. Nothing marks us; nothing leaves a scar. Memories flash in and out with little or no effect. Nothing really matters at the core, or even slightly beneath the surface. Life is lived casually at best.

And then there are the rest of us, those who feel everything so deeply it borders on punishment just to speak of it. It seems we must atone for the rest, the unfeeling ones. What they cannot feel, we must feel doubly or ten-fold. The extreme joys we experience as we move through life or on its edge—these must be paid for with longing. Have you known absolute love? Then for that, absolute loneliness is required. Have you known joy? Someone must pay. Have you encountered God? Then much darkness will be afforded you. And the deep sorrows you carry may have to be borne to the grave.

I am thinking now of a particular morning, of a particular walk up a particular road. My father, I think, walked behind me. My mother I know did, for it was at her insistence that we go. The white church up ahead was not a thousand feet away, set against an azure sky with whispers of clouds scribbled vaguely across the blue. The leafless limbs of sycamores and maples were dappled with crows and sparrows. A patch or two of snow lay here and there along the wet, paved road, banked against a gray shed or a fence, or up in the fields at the bases of hickory trees or tussled patches of briars. A rare vehicle passed, the white smoke from its tailpipe swirling.

"Slow down," my mother said, for I kept running on ahead, chasing a rock or scuffing my new shoes and letting my coat fly open and free. "Slow down!"

But I just could not slow down. It was such a glorious day. How in the world could I slow down? The sun shown brightly upon my face, upon the glistening earth, leaving a tinseled sheen over everything. The air was sparkling and pure and just chilly enough to bring water to my eyes as I ran. My heart was pounding, my legs so full of life. One simply had to kick a rock or something. I did and I did, over and over, and then warmed my hands in my furry coat pockets. In one pocket my fingers curled around the green pack of chewing gum still there from the day before, in the other the white tissues my mother had supplied me. "Don't sniff," she had told me. But I would and she knew it.

And so I skipped along, sniffing, now by the little creek that seemed to laugh beneath my feet, the tiny whitecaps among the smooth rocks gurgling and playing roundly. Now by the barn and the white breath of cattle. Now by the white country store with the single red gas pump in front smelling of town and human enterprise, and the worn oak bench for the whittlers. Now past the two front porches of the two white-washed houses, one near the road, the other several yards back and more reclusive, more pensive, with the white chickens all around it pecking sternly at the earth. A rooster crowed somewhere. A screen door slammed. A window grated open. Wings fluttered and were gone, a brief shadow passing over the eyes.

It all was so perfect. It surely was. The earth was good and I knew it and there was no pain anywhere. Like the specks of birds in the branches or on the wires strung across the road I had no thought for tomorrow. Like the dog barking off in the field I was there and nowhere else. I would not die or diminish, nor would anyone else. Or if someone did happen to die, it would be too far off in the future to concern a body now. Now was the time to move and breathe. Now was the time to be alive. And I was alive, every cell and pore of me.

I suppose then it was that I began to hear it, the music, lilting down the paved, wet road, drifting in and out of the bare treetops where the crows were perched and cawing. Such a sound I had never heard. Oh, I had heard music before. From a cousin's new record player that very Christmas had come the most magical sounds. But what I heard now was immensely different, inexpressibly different. I could hear no words, no instruments, only the most subtle and frail suggestion of a melody, but it went through me like a ghost and set me tingling. The earth was surely singing, I thought. Like me, it could not contain itself. I started to turn to see if my mother and father had heard it, had felt it as I had felt it, but I was somehow afraid that they had not, or afraid that they had.

To listen more closely, I slowed down in my walking until one of them—I don't know which—began to nudge me from behind. "What's wrong?" one or both of them might have said, but if they did, I did not answer. How could anything be wrong now? Instead of speaking, I strained even harder to listen and my little heart rejoiced. There it was again, the music. How wonderful the sound was—like the trees, the fields. Like my own heart. In the music was the soul of what I had been feeling all morning, what had been trying to get out of me since my feet had touched the wet, paved road and skipped along chasing rocks. It was full of praise like the gurgling water, but even more alive, more overflowing. It brought new tears to my eyes.

We walked on, the melody growing more distinct and lucid the nearer we came to the church. Fuller and fuller it got, until I thought my heart would burst. What joy was in it! What voices! I could hardly keep from sobbing. And then finally, from the white doors of the church, the music fairly resounded.

"You hear that?" I said, at last turning to face my mother, the lump in my throat making it all but impossible for me to speak. My mother nodded, but I could tell that she had not heard what I had heard, not exactly what I had heard. I wondered if she had heard it before—or if my father had—and if to them it was already familiar. I wondered if, when they were both just my age, they had walked together up the same wet, hard road and heard the sounds for the very first time.

Now they passed through the white doors of the church so easily it was frightening, and I waited on the porch, trembling. The music continued. It flowed out of the church and lifted high above the earth. Farmers from down the road, hand-in-hand with their families, passed by me and went on through the white doors. More farmers passed. Their children and their wives passed. And a bent old lady with a white shawl. And some perfumed and dainty town-folks. One patted me on the head; another on the back. A young girl in a frilly white dress smiled at me sweetly and beckoned for me to follow. How I wished that I could. How I wanted to. As she also passed through the doors, an old man with suspenders and a bright red bow tie came out of the church and handed me a folded green paper upon which were words. "So good to see you," he said kindly, shaking my little hand up and down. "Good to see you, too," I said, almost crying.

"Well, God be praised."

"Oh, yes."

I felt quickly in my pocket for my green pack of gum. With one hand I unwrapped a stick, popped it into my mouth, and gulped down a tiny shard of it. The lump in my throat was temporarily quelled. And when the tears welled up again I swallowed another shard. And then another. Moments passed. There came a time when I was the only soul outside the white doors.

What I could have done now seems so very simple. I could have turned and gone through the white doors. Nobody was stopping me or was going to. I could have searched out my parents, sat down meekly beside them, pulled my socks up, tied my shoes, been right there where the glorious music was, where the singers were. I could have joined in or put my head down and not looked anyone in the eye. I could have been like other children the world over.

But the thought never even occurred to me. Instead, I began running. I ran out across the road, climbed a steep, slippery embankment, hopped a wet fence, and kept right on going. I ran as far as I could run and then I walked, then I crawled, then I climbed all the way to the top of a hill and plopped down, breathless. There, I could look down on the glistening tin roof of the white church and all the bottom land that surrounded it—the two white houses with their chickens, the gas station with its whittlers' bench, upon which a lone gray whittler was now plying his trade, the asphalt road, the tops of trees.

I sat there and I listened. The music in the church had ended, but I could hear a ridge dog way off in the distance, a lowing cow, an occasional raucous cawing of the crows, a voice from time to time arising from an open window. I could hear the slightest breeze in the bare branches. The blue dome of the sky warmed above me. Patches of snow melted before my eyes, and I could hear the water seeping into the ground, or trickling off into little puddles, and minute movements in the brush as weeds and wildflowers opened up to the sun, as tiny creatures began stirring.

For hours I looked down upon the church, the earth, the people going on their way, and then all of a sudden felt like God overseeing his creation, loving it with all my heart yet somehow outside of it now, somehow superbly alone. I was not the boy I once was, right there in the thick of life. That boy no longer lived. And how he had come to die I had no clue whatsoever.

Steven R. Cope

Steven R. Cope, a native of Menifee County now living in Clark County, has been writing steadily since his first published poem, "Old Wolf," was published in *Twigs* at Pikeville College, and subsequently anthologized in *Best Poems of 1973*. It was just the kind of affirmation a young, beginning poet needed, Steve says, "to ruin him for anything practical." Wind Publications has released four collections of his poetry, a novel and a collection of fables and tales. Along with the hundreds of guitar students through the years, he has taught writing and/or literature off and on at Eastern Kentucky University, Morehead State University, and the University of Kentucky.

Genesis for *The White Doors*

The White Doors is not intended really to be an essay, not intended to be a story. I simply wanted to record briefly, without embellishment, with hardly a proofread or restructuring of a sentence (which I shall no doubt regret later), a memory that came back to me one glistening winter morning in January 2005. So much of what we become depends upon certain subtle events of our past—certain secret, quiet, but life-altering episodes that we never speak of openly because we don't know how. *The White Doors* is just an attempt to speak about one such event in my own life that, up till now, I have kept still about.

Enex Ground

Bob Sloan

The cemetery was unplanned, its existence the outcome of events unpredictable as a coin toss. If it hadn't been for a killing, the clearing would have become a cabin site or cornfield.

Toward the end of the unCivil War two young men from the Enex family were conscripted by one of the guerilla bands that infested Kentucky's Blue Ridge, even after Appomattox. Their service to the Confederacy or the Union—no one knows which side claimed the irregulars' allegiance—was brief, just a short ride deep enough into forested hills their folks never heard the shots that killed them.

Murdered for their horses and guns, the youngsters lay undiscovered for days. After seeing the work of possums and crows, ants and spiders, the kin who found them lacked heart or stomach to move the bodies too far, or allow their mothers to see. Known ever after as "the boys," they were buried where they fell.

No one's sure who decided the boys' interment made the clearing a cemetery, but sometime before 1870 the first planned grave was dug. Most likely the excavation was done by members of the Enex clan—my great-grandmother's family—to bury one of their own, but decades of snow and heat, rain and wind have erased any identification hacked into the oldest stones. We've been digging occasional graves there ever since.

All of them are family, and a few of us come together now and then to mow wild grasses seeding in from the woods, to clear dead limbs shed by a towering cedar tree. We patch broken tombstones, do other chores to show we remember people gone so long almost no one's left who heard even one of their voices. In spite of our maintenance, the cemetery doesn't much resemble family plots closer to highways and roads. It's just a clearing in thick forest, an hour's uphill walk from any house, different from other clearings only in having a couple of dozen tombstones jutting from the earth.

Not long ago the county historical society visited, a day or two after one of our clean-ups. The next issue of the local paper declared the

Enex Cemetery "abandoned." It's not, and never has been. Descendants of those buried there still maintain it, still visit the cemetery, though in fewer numbers than in earlier years.

For decades, every Decoration Day branches of our blue collar clan, home from Ohio and Indiana factory towns, trekked en masse from Cousin Milton's to the cemetery, a hard up-hill hike for children and old people. Milton provided an easier way, towing a hay wagon behind a tractor belching black smoke. The trip seemed to test the machine's limits as severely as it challenged the legs of seventy year old men.

The emergence of mountain children into adulthood is marked in small but significant events, like the presentation to a boy of his first shotgun, the first meal a girl cooks entirely unaided. Our elderly take similar short steps into their dotage: one spring their vegetable garden is a little smaller; that autumn they begin using a cane. Each year, the fact a certain child didn't ride in Milton's wagon, or an old woman climbed onto it after a minute or two of quarrelsome protest, gave notice the wheel of life had turned a few degrees.

Ahead of a dinner on the ground, elders in the crowd told stories about the kin buried there in Enex ground. They recalled how Eliza Jane, believing a tow-headed grandson to be evidence of a daughter-in-law's adultery, poked at the boy with a cane whenever he came close. "Get away from me, you damned little Underwood," she'd hiss. (The despised Underwoods, on the other side of the ridge, sported loose morals and hair blonde as an Aryan dream.)

And someone described the sad way Thomas ended his term on earth. He was only twenty when he earned his corner grave, crank starting a gas engine attached to a grist mill. He didn't get out of the way fast enough when the handle "kicked" against his belly, and his mortal injury seemed more awful for its invisibility. He was dead in three days, two of them spent in fearful delirium.

Henry and Jim, who carved most of the tombstones, were remembered by those old enough to have ridden in the brothers' mule drawn wagon, to the place they hacked slabs of workable bluestone out of a hillside. The journey and the work were recalled in detail, the memories savored.

Decades later, my father's cousin John I (the "I" standing for nothing, like the "S" in Harry S Truman), recounted larger versions of those stories, adding information not shared at Decoration Day picnics.

Thomas was blind drunk when that grist mill engine fatally struck him. Sixty years later, the older brother who warned Tom to leave the cranking to those who were sober still feels miserably responsible for the death.

Jim, the stone-cutter, never saw his fortieth birthday. A quart of poison moonshine killed him, and though the family tried to learn the seller's identity, no name ever came to light.

The grandmother whose cane fended off the attentions of the fair-haired boy who became my father was more than an amusing eccentric. Murderously senile, she over and over tried to kill her detested daughter-in-law, attacking with knives stolen from the kitchen.

John liked visiting the cemetery at least monthly, and whenever I got the chance I'd go along. I was there when he selected the bit of Enex ground we'd bring him to on an April day five or six years farther 'round the wheel of life. John meant to end his stay on earth not far from where it began. Straddling his burial plot, the old man studied the sky a moment, then declared he'd bet money he could aim a twenty two rifle into a rainbow trajectory, hit the old barn near the home place.

On sunny days it was a fine thing to sit on a convenient tombstone and listen while John recalled people he'd known personally, or repeated stories about those who died before he was born. When it was just John and me, getting comfortable never seemed disrespectful.

He'd tell how whiskey killed this one, inform me that one over there was a woman chaser, and the lady buried yonder had a baby without ever telling its daddy's name. Now and then John remembered the hard death of a sister in a 1919 flu epidemic that carried off whole families, described the awful sound of a teenaged girl's futile fight for breath, while in another room a younger brother was thought to be dying as well.

The brother survived. When he lost a leg in a car wreck after World War II, John and some cousins and nephews brought the limb to the graveyard, carried in a special box. John could show exactly where they buried it.

The old man's memory never let go of a piece of information, once it got a grip on it. Once, my sister challenged his recall. He hadn't seen her in well over a decade, during which my sister grew from gawky adolescence into a married woman with three kids. "You don't know who I am, do you John?" she teased at a family reunion.

He looked her over and said, "Well, on the fifteenth of April in nineteen and fifty three your mommy had a little girl," and went on to tell Sis how much she'd weighed at birth, what time of day she came into the world, other details of her arrival. John finished with "Your mother decided to name her little girl Joy. And here you are."

Birth dates weren't all he remembered, and in time it was those other recollections I most appreciated. In my middle twenties, like many of my cousins, I fought serious, occasionally bloody battles with alcohol and other drugs. My first trip home after finding something in the way of resolution for those miseries marked another Decoration Day. A heavy load of guilt and shame rode along when Pop and I carried John to the graves he wanted to visit.

A great high oak rises twenty or so yards from the house where one great uncle lived. Under the tree is not cemetery, but Uncle George asked to be buried there, and he was. Slouched beside that uncommon resting place, John looked me over and confided, "You know, whiskey's taken an awful toll on our family." A dreamy look, the sign John was dredging up distant memories, softened his aging eyes. "Yes sir, it's killed a slew of us."

"Like who?" I wanted to know. Reactions of my folks and others to those who'd grown up "bad to drink" suggested my generation was the first in our family's history to explore alcohol and other recreational intoxicants.

Memories settled and sorted at last, John delivered a long accounting of blood kin who lived hard, even died while figuratively swimming a rolling wild river of whiskey. That was the day I learned alcohol could be blamed for the death of my father's older brother as much as an engine's kick.

Uncle George himself, whose grave brought us to the foot of that oak tree, was a moonshiner. He died of injuries incurred while defending his still from larcenous competition. I don't recall how many names were included in John's litany, but they all had intimate relationships with liquor I'd never imagined.

Somewhere in the course of the old man's recitation I glanced at my father, whose eyes were fixed where the toe of one shoe shifted springtime dust around. When Pop looked up, I could see in his face this truth: he would have never delivered this old news. I couldn't help smiling, and turned back to John, who seemed near the end of telling how grievously alcohol beat up our family decades before my cousins and I were born.

John paused, took a long breath. "And on your mother's side…" he began, and then told me about those people.

A year or so later, he let me know my generation wasn't the first to discover illicit sex, any more than we invented an appreciation for beer and bourbon. Even in the old days "love children" were a common consequence of too much moonlight away from parental eyes. They included a wise and wonderful old man whose relationship to our family I never understood, until John explained how, in the years before he met grandma, my grandfather knew a lady up in Cincinnati.

Knew her Biblically…

Then fetched home and raised the son who was a product of that knowledge.

I learned which aunts were pregnant when they married, though they still don't know I know. John named the uncles who'd been "bad to fight," told me who among them carried personal awareness of what lay behind the iron doors of the old Rowan County Jail. John I was a wonder, a well of information freely offered, just because we were family. There didn't seem to be anything he wouldn't tell me.

Until I asked about the Driscoll House...

Cousin Fred deals in real estate and called a while back, said he'd been offered a tour of the Driscoll House in advance of its going on the market. When Fred asked if he might bring along a reasonably well behaved cousin, the lady organizing the display of the house for real estate agents said that oughtn't be a problem. So one Saturday afternoon I walked through rooms I'd heard of all my life, in which I never expected to stand.

The Driscoll House was, in the thirties, the sort of "house" where every bedroom had—still has, for that matter—a convenient sink not far from the bed. My father talks about being there as a small boy. After delivering a load of timber, with a few dollars folded into their overall pockets, Pop's older brothers and cousins sometimes stopped at the Driscoll House on their way home. He says he had no idea what was going on, but the sweet smelling women were more beautiful than anything on Holly Fork. They coaxed him down off a timber wagon with candy, while one-by-one his brothers and cousins disappeared inside for a time.

There's one tale about the house I'll probably never know in its entirety. For decades Pop occasionally reminisced about "the prettiest redheaded woman I ever saw," said she and John I had a serious thing going at one time. There was talk they might even get married, until a man running the Driscoll House stabbed her to death. More than a few who knew both claimed the redheaded woman was carrying John's baby at the end.

The man who cut her disappeared, and while some believed he went back to wherever he was from, others claimed the killer was dead before he made the county line.

A couple of years before John I died, I asked him about the redhead. Suddenly the man happy to tell secrets in which family—including himself—played embarrassing roles, the man who disclosed things my aunts and uncles believed were well-guarded secrets, a man famous for telling it all had nothing to say about that redheaded woman, or the mysterious disappearance of the man who murdered her. By and by, what John did tell, leavened with imagination, became a short story published in a literary quarterly.

About once a week Cousin Fred and I drink beer together, most often beside a pickup parked next to John I's grave. Lately we've speculated about John and that nameless redhead, wondered which kin, reference book, or brittle yellow newspaper pages might yield answers about her.

We're not sure, not yet. Nearly all John's peers are dead, and the one very old man who might be able to tell us something is deaf as a post. Asking him about anything provokes a long, detailed narration about events and people entirely unrelated to the question. Five years ago he almost surely could have told us a lot about what happened at the Driscoll House decades ago, but his memory doesn't work like it once did.

I don't know where or what the answers to our questions about that woman are, or if Fred and I will find them. We're looking, though.

That's why I don't get too caught up in genealogy. People on both sides of my family can tell me where and when a certain seventeenth century someone was born, married, and buried. But I can't find a soul to give me the name of a beautiful woman, whose red hair yet shimmers in the memory of those who met her as children, a lady gone far longer than I've been alive, but still talked about.

A lady I believe John I may have loved enough to kill for.

John was almost eighty when he took a last long breath and slipped away from us. After his well-attended funeral, a considerable crowd followed his coffin past Campbell Branch and up the hill toward the Enex ground. A hard morning rain had turned the primitive road into a muddy mess, and the hearse bogged down in the last sloppy quarter mile.

John's casket was transferred to the bed of a four-wheel drive Civil Defense pickup, and anyone driving a similar vehicle was drafted to transport the old-timers who were John's friends to his grave on Enex ground. A hundred or more stood there at the end, and it took a while to get all of us in place. Nobody minded the wait.

Appalachian spring was all around us, every breath brought the reek of renewed fertility, and the encircling forest was lively with rustling and singing from scores of birds. The birds are what no one who stood at John I's grave has forgotten. A few minutes before the minister started a brief final speech, my mother leaned close to whisper, "Watch up in the trees." And I did watch, glad to have something to look at other than a gaping raw hole in the earth.

Though it was early afternoon, entire flocks were coming to roost like it was sundown.

Every tree or bush, every limb large enough to support the negligible weight of sparrows, or the more significant presence of jays and cardinals became a perch, bending into ground-grazing arches. Strands of barbed wire fence at the limits of Enex ground sagged, then sagged lower as still more birds came to roost. A quiet country cemetery became a cacophony of sound, so much so any sort of conversation required an ever louder voice.

I do not necessarily believe in ghosts, or hold to superstitions. I'll not be disappointed if, after death, I become only so much mud. There are worse ways to spend eternity than slowly evolving into a piece of Kentucky hilltop, and with no personal sense of a world beyond this one, I'm suspicious of "spooky" tales told by others.

But I offer this single piece of truth: when Reverend Whomever opened his Bible to read a final few verses over the mortality of John I Sloan, those birds quieted as though an avian choirmaster signaled, "Enough!" John's grave side service ended in a profound hush befitting any church.

When the preacher was done, when he closed his Bible and affirmed we had gone as far with John I as anyone could go, and gently suggested we leave that great and good man to the peace and rest he'd earned, with a babel of chatter and cheep, the birds were gone, all gone, in seconds.

I can't explain, won't offer rationalization for what happened that April afternoon. I know John loved that plot of ground. In memory I still hear the rhythm of his voice explaining how all those graves came to be filled.

It would be lovely to believe the birds welcomed him to a peace and rest he assuredly deserved. In life John felt at home on Enex ground, and if there's any consciousness or awareness after death, I'm confident he's still comfortable there.

It hasn't changed much. The biggest alteration since Milton's tractor dragged a wagon load of children and old folks up the hill, a few dozen others following, breathing hard at the climb, is John's stark white V.A. tombstone.

Bob Sloan

Bob Sloan is a working writer who doesn't have, and isn't pursuing an MFA. He and his wife Julie live on thirty hillside acres east of Morehead, Kentucky, previously owned by both his grandfather and father. His commentaries have been heard on NPR's "Morning Edition," and seen on the *Herald-Leader's* editorial page, Kentucky Educational Television and in the *Christian Science Monitor*. Wind Publications has released his short story collection *Bearskin to Holly Fork* and his novel, *Home Call*. His goal as a writer is "to write honest stories that reflect the hard lot and the intelligence of the Appalachian working class and working poor."

Genesis for *Enex Ground*

Enex Ground was a fortuitous accident.

In 2000 an agent encouraged me to enter several categories in the William Faulkner Creative Writing Competition in New Orleans. After I sent the contest a short story and a novel, the agent argued I ought to enter the essay division as well. She reminded me of some postings I'd done to lists and newsgroups with a focus on Appalachian culture. "Link some of them together," the agent said. "Make an essay out of them."

Many of those off-the-cuff musings were about my namesake family's oldest cemetery in Rowan County KY, and the wonderful old man who told me about the people buried there. There are lots of reasons to come home after spending decades wandering the world like a nervous nomad, but the biggest reward for me was the relationship I formed with John I Sloan.

Hal Crowther was judging the Faulkner competition's essay division. At the time I didn't know he's in love with all things connected to Kentucky. He picked *Enex Ground* as 2000's winning entry.

My prize was a chunk of cash. a gold medal, and four days in a hotel suite that was more spacious than my house. I got to meet Crowther and his wife, the Appalachian novelist Lee Smith. Somewhere in there I spent a wine-drenched evening in the company of Pulitzer Prize winner Robert Olen Butler, whose novel *They Whisper* had fueled a decade's worth of conversations between me and an old friend.

Most importantly, Hal told me how much he wished he'd been able to spend an afternoon with John I, slouched against a tombstone at the Enex Cemetery while that old man told his tales. Butler, who'd read the piece as well, told me how fortunate I was to have known such a treasure of a man. This is the first appearance in print of *Enex Ground*, but a number of people have read it, and voiced similar sentiments.

Discussion Questions

My New Year's Kiss

1. Sparks' essay recalls an event that highlighted a humorous moment that occurred in a serious, often tragic environment. Have you ever encountered such an event? What was your reaction?

2. Looking to the past, Sparks has a chance to poke a little good-natured fun at himself as a young man. What aspects of twenty-two-year-old Sparks do you find humorous? Why?

3. Are you familiar with the story of Joseph and Potiphar's wife from the Bible? How does Sparks make the allusions particularly appropriate to his incident?

The World in a Day

1. McQuady claims that she added the account of her modern-day adventure with her mother and dad to her essay about her childhood daytrips. Do you think the addition fits the essay? Does it add to the essay's appeal? If so, how?

2. McQuady describes how her writing often starts with a "prompt," sometimes even a single word. Have you every created an essay or made up a story or poem as a result of an image that flashed across your mind or an old song you heard replayed?

3. McQuady's essay details the role reversal that has occurred in her relationship with her parents. Has getting a new perspective on a situation or person ever caused you to rethink your view on an issue or event?

Where Am I From?

1. One of the strongest aspects of Stamper's essay is the use of specific detail, whether turning a colloquial phrase or describing the stores of Lexington's past. How does her detail affect your engagement with the essay? Does it make her account come alive, or does it simply slow down your reading?

2. What do you think is the view of Kentucky—even its urban centers—by outsiders? Do you think this view is accurate? Fair?

3. If you had to answer the question "Where are you from," what would you say? What details make your home unique?

Growing Up Depressed

1. In her essay Sparkman chronicles her battle with depression and the ultimate victory over it. At the essay's conclusion, she wonders, "Who really cares?" She opines that she needed to articulate the struggle for her own well being. Do you find any value in her work, even from one who has never experience the problem?

2. Sparkman treats the absence in her childhood of those things that are so often used in today's schools to promote self-esteem in young people. Do you think she makes a convincing case for the necessity of such strategies?

3. What are some of the mechanisms that individuals use to cope with undesirable experiences? Do you think writing about them can be valuable?

The Baptism

1. Sometimes assignments for classes can be dull and perfunctory, but often they can lead us to treat aspects of our lives that call forth laughter or heartache. Can you remember a class or an assignment that caused you to recall an incident that brough a smile to your lips, perhaps a tear to your eye?

2. Granny Adams' clever turn of words brings the essay to an end. Have you ever used wordplay to comment on an incident? What figures of speech did you employ?

Wings to Fly

1. Hensley's essay describes an experience in which she encountered a strange place that unnerved her. Can you remember being put in similar circumstances? How did you cope?

2. Hensley's essay brings to mind John Updike's classic story, "Flight," in which he describes a mother's relationship with her son and her struggle to give him independence. What is involved in Hensley's decision? Why is her choice not an easy one?

3. Hensley alludes to a time in our history when many Appalachian families moved to northern cities to find jobs, but often discovered prejudice and misunderstanding. Do you think the prejudices against Appalachians still exist? Are other stereotypes of the region and its people still alive?

Meeting New Neighbors

1. Vander Ploeg's essay casts a harsh light on those forces surrounding "economic development" projects and their ultimate costs. Have you ever experienced any of the results of this sort of development in your community? Do you find the gains worth the costs?

2. Vander Ploeg uses the new neighbor's dog as a symbol for all that's wrong with the arrival of economic development to a community. What specific observations does he make through his description of the pet and its actions?

3. Can you think of any ways that the move toward economic development in rural communities can be channeled in a positive direction? Must all such projects be condemned?

The Man on TV

1. Shelby's essay treats a troubling era in American history—the Vietnam War—by linking it to the struggles of a young boy to understand desertion by his father. How does Shelby use Jim's relationship with Dutch to underscore his own confusion about his relationship with Jim?

2. What role does TV play in Shelby's memoir? Why do you think he chose this medium as a vehicle? Do you agree that TV can be both intimate and impersonal?

3. Why do you think Graham's mother never appears in the essay? What is gained by having her play the role of invisible character?

Singin' Dolly

1. Brosi's essay features a strong use of detail to create not only the backdrop of the dark woods, but also the excitement of the hunt. How does he pull the reader into the action? How does he allow us to experience the event rather than simply read about it objectively?

2. In what ways does hunting tie Brosi to his bloodline? Does his desire to brave the discomfort and possible dangers of the night hunt involve more than simply the excitement and chance to bag a coon?

3. Brosi suggests a certain ambivalence as he realizes what he has killed. Why do you think in light of this "once in a lifetime" experience he wishes he had never shot the bobcat?

The White Doors

1. How does Cope's talent as a poet reveal itself in this prose essay? What poetic techniques does he employ?

2. Cope's essay is best when read aloud. How do the sound of the words and the rhythm of the phrases contribute to the mood of wonderment depicted?

3. The event described in the essay is called an epiphany (when an individual comes to a new understanding of a person or situation). What new awareness did Cope arrive at that crisp morning? Have you ever experienced an epiphany?

Enex Ground

1. Sloan's professed goal as a writer is "to write honest stories that reflect the hard lot and the intelligence of the Appalachian working class and working poor." Do you think *Enex Ground* achieves this goal? In what ways does the story strike you as "honest"?

2. Appalachian culture is a storytelling culture. What qualities of John I's reminiscences make for good storytelling? How does he capture the listener's interest?

3. What does Sloan's description of John I's funeral bring to the essay's power to engage us? Does the perhaps supernatural event detract in any way from the essay's air of truth?

For Further Discussion

by Charles Campbell & Bryan Jackson

Earlier in this anthology, you encountered discussion questions for individual works. You probably noticed several of the questions overlapped. What we'd like to do in this section is offer some comprehensive questions that cut across works and genres. We hope these questions stimulate further activity, be it personal reflection, group discussions inside a class or outside, essay prompts, or even springboards to your own creativity in the form of a memoir, poem, or story.

Who knows? Perhaps your effort will result an entry for the next anthology and the continuation of *New Growth.*

DISCUSSION QUESTIONS

(1) Discuss how the authors in the anthology are representative of Kentucky Literature. How does the anthology shape the external perception of the Kentucky author?

(2) Discuss the perceptions, impressions, and stereotypes about Kentucky as a state. What works in the anthology most closely identify with these? What works do not? Do any of the works alter your notions about contemporary life in Kentucky?

(3) What role does nature and geography play in these individual works? What works do you feel particularly deal with how the land impinges itself on the people?

(4) The collected works in this anthology, especially the fictional portrayals, seem to go in-depth, presenting characters in pursuit or amidst conflict that requires a point of self-realization or coming to know some universal truth. In what ways are the values and belief systems of the characters presented in these works? What values and beliefs, if any, did you find especially relevant to your life?

(5) Much of the work found in this anthology can be characterized

as regional literature, or literature that is concerned with preserving a history or collective experience of the people associated with a specific territorial area. In this case, the region of primary concern is the state of Kentucky. What exactly about these works make them Kentuckian? Can you think of any distinct features or characteristics in these works that stand out?

(6) Other places in the United States give birth to writers who write about what they know and where they are from, but the writers in this collection seem almost driven to set their stories in Kentucky. Why do you think a sense of place so close to home is vital to Kentucky writers? Do you think any of the works in the collection could work in alternative settings? Explain.

(7) This anthology offers many different and distinct voices that capture the oral qualities and idiosyncratic forms of dialect often associated with rural America, Appalachian culture, and Southern literature. How do these speech patterns, unique words or phrases, or colorful metaphors add or detract from the works in this collection? Do they aid readers not familiar with the region in sharing the region's experience? Do they reinforce stereotypes that prevent the works from being taken seriously? Do they do both? Explain.

(8) Though these stories came from different parts of Kentucky, they all seem to have common threads, some stereotypical to the state: coal miners, tobacco farmers, moonshiners, bootleggers, basketball, bourbon, snake-handling fundamentalists, cockfighting, and, of course, close-knit, small-town community values. How would you describe the major themes in this anthology? Do you think the themes give those native to the region a defining sense of who they are and where they come from? What do they do for those not familiar with the region?

(9) In what ways do the people and places in the non-fiction selections differ from those in the fiction works? What might this suggest about the nature of fiction writing? Non-fiction writing? The identity of the Kentucky writer?

(10) This anthology's title, *New Growth,* suggests a genealogy, a tracing of ancestry through generational growth rings to help make connections with the present. How do the works within this volume to support the book's title? What works do this most effectively? Which do not? Why?

(11) How do the writers in *New Growth* reinforce their themes through symbols? What kinds of symbols prove most effective? What are some particularly memorable symbols?

(12) In his introduction to the non-fiction section, George Brosi calls attention to a lack of diversity among the non-fiction essays. Brosi says Kentucky's urban and non-white populations are not well-represented in the essays, and neither are creative forms other than the memoir. While this view poses questions (and not necessarily problems), is this lack of diversity evident in the fiction and poetry sections?

(13) What are some social issues or concerns addressed throughout *New Growth?* Are these issues exclusive to Kentucky or are they relevant outside the state? Do the individual works offer resolution to the problems they address?

(14) One of the highlights of this anthology is the inclusion of short essays about the inspiration or genesis of each work to go along with a brief biography for each writer. How do the genesis essays illuminate the writing process? How do the essays help illuminate the works that follow? Why do you think the editors chose to include such essays?

(15) The word *anthology* comes from the Greek for flower (anthos) and collecting (logia). Collecting flowers is simple; arranging them is a far tougher task. The compilation of this book was a long, labor-intensive process. Even so, no anthology is ever a finished work. What things, if any, could be done to enhance the works in this book? How can the anthology become more representative of Kentucky and Kentuckians?